DALGLISH

The Fifty Matches
That Made the Player

Tom Brogan

pitch

First published by Pitch Publishing, 2025

1

pitch

Pitch Publishing
9 Donnington Park,
85 Birdham Road,
Chichester, West Sussex,
PO20 7AJ
www.pitchpublishing.co.uk
info@pitchpublishing.co.uk

A CIP catalogue record is available for this book

from the British Library.

ISBN 978 1 83680 171 9

Typesetting and origination by Pitch Publishing

FSC
www.fsc.org
MIX
Paper | Supporting
responsible forestry
FSC® C013604

Printed and bound in the UK on FSC® certified paper in line
with our continuing commitment to ethical business practices,
sustainability and the environment.

Printed and bound by CPI Group (UK) Ltd, Croydon, CR0 4YY

Contents

Acknowledgements

THANKS TO the late Bobby Dinnie for inviting me into his home and speaking of Kenny's days playing with Bobby's Possil YM as a young boy, and his many trips back to the club to support them over the years. Bobby was well respected by managers ranging from Bertie Mee to Jackie McNamara for all he did in the game, and it was a privilege to spend some time speaking with him, only months before he passed away at the age of 91.

Thanks to Andy Smith for providing me with a folder full of Kenny-related articles from *Shoot!*, *Match* and other football magazines.

I'd also like to thank the late Patrick Barclay, who spoke at length with me for my first and third books for Pitch. Paddy did not need to give me any time at all; many others wouldn't have, but on both occasions, Paddy spoke with me for over an hour, first about his memories of Scotland in Spain in 1982 and then of Burnley's escape from the drop in 1987. His reports on Liverpool in the 70s and 80s for *The Guardian* have also been very helpful for this book. On speaking with him I found him insightful, entertaining and encouraging. Football writers of his calibre set the standards for those of us who follow.

I have to thank the football statisticians who put their research online, freely available for others. For this book, the lfchistory.net website has been particularly helpful. As well as the archive information, those who run the site have also spent time collating information that would be painstaking to go through, such as assists and other match statistics. The Celtic Wiki is a great starting point for all things Celtic, and Londonhearts.com is a splendid resource for Scotland matches, statistics and player details.

Thanks to Jane at Pitch for giving me another opportunity to write a book. Thanks to Duncan Olner for his always excellent cover design. Thanks to Andy Bollen for advice and encouragement. See you at the Horseshoe soon.

Introduction

I WAS aware of Kenny Dalglish before I was really aware of football. Much like Scotland's other national icon Billy Connolly was the first stand-up comedian I was aware of, Kenny was the first footballer I knew of. For my dad, Kenny was one of the new breed of Celtic heroes who would come to replace the greatest of them all – the Lisbon Lions. My dad always said that when I was a small boy of four or five my mum cut my hair just like Kenny's. My mum always insisted Kenny styled his hair like mine. I haven't included any pictures here, but there's certainly a similarity.

By the time I started reading *Shoot!* Kenny was a Liverpool player, although I have a memory of a Kenny Dalglish glove puppet in a Celtic strip in the school playground. That made Liverpool my English club; sure they won everything in the 70s and 80s, but they had Kenny, and that was what mattered.

There was just something about Kenny Dalglish I loved. It was the way he moved, the way he turned, the goals he scored and the big smile on his face whenever he stuck one in. My first Scotland game was Kenny's 100th cap. I knew that time was running out then to see him in the flesh, and although he didn't score that night he displayed all the touches, turns and flair that made him my footballing hero.

On my Mount Rushmore of idols, carved in my formative years, he sits alongside Billy Connolly, Muhammad Ali, The Beatles, Al Pacino, Robert De Niro and Ken Eadie. If you saw Dalglish play then hopefully this book will bring back some memories for you of how good he was and the awe of watching him at his best. If you didn't see Kenny play hopefully this book will be some indicator of how good a player he was and why he still resonates as one of the greatest players to have played in both the Scottish and English games.

Scotland Schoolboys 1-1 England Schoolboys

14 May 1966, Victory Shield,
Ibrox Stadium

KENNY DALGLISH was six years of age when he played his first game of organised football. He played in goal.

Kenny was born on 4 March 1951. He spent his schooldays at Miltonbank Primary School in the north of Glasgow and High Possil Senior Secondary School. At primary school there was an organised team that gave Kenny his first taste of the game outside of jackets on the ground for goalposts in the playground.

When he went on to attend Possil Secondary School, his English teacher Mr Hughes took the school team. 'He gave so much of his time to us,' Dalglish told *The Telegraph* in 2006. 'I think he got as much out of it as we did.' Although no great academic, Kenny stuck in at school, did his homework, didn't let his sporting interests get in his way, and passed most subjects.

The family moved to Glasgow's southside into a flat that overlooked Ibrox Stadium, home of Rangers, the club that Kenny's dad supported, and the team that Kenny too began to follow.

Dalglish's football career progressed well as he played for Glasgow Schoolboys and Glasgow Schools, winning the Scottish Schools Cup in May 1966, beating East Ayrshire over two legs 6-1 on aggregate.

Kenny was encouraged as a youngster by his parents, Bill and Cathy. His dad took him to watch matches and was always ready for a kickabout when he wasn't working. There were a lot of parks around that area of Glasgow, so Kenny, like most young boys in the 1950s and 60s, was able to have a kickabout with friends night and day; whether there were only two of them or 40, someone would organise a game and make the numbers work.

He joined the team at Possil YM where he was coached by a guy called Bobby Dinnie. Bobby got what he termed 'a tingling sensation' in his stomach one morning on the pitch at St Augustine's Secondary School when he saw the young Dalglish, who immediately stood out among his peers. Bobby signed Kenny after a trial match. Seven of the Possil boys were wanted by Arsenal and six of them went to Highbury. The one who didn't go to London was Kenny. Kenny's dad told Bobby that as his only son he wanted the pleasure of watching Kenny play football every week.

Among the players who went to Highbury was Eddie Kelly, who would become part of Arsenal's Double-winning team of 1971.

Based in Denmark Street, Possil YM played in red and white strips, a gift from Arsenal, who kept close tabs on the boys from all the various age groups.

Bobby was proud of his association with Kenny, although he was proud of all the boys who came through his numerous boys' clubs. They included Gerry O'Brien, who played for Clydebank, Southampton and Hibs, Johnny Hamilton, who was with Rangers and Hibs, and Rangers great Bobby Russell.

'I was amazed how he used his hips,' Bobby told me when I spoke with him about Kenny in 2024. He also recalled the young Dalglish's vision and his shooting ability. Kenny played at right-half in the 'B' team. 'He had great vision for his age, and it was evident that he was going to be an international player. Although he was surrounded by great talent, Kenny was the driving force.'

Dalglish was a great addition to the Possil team in more ways than one. 'Kenny's father had this wee van, he was a marine engineer and he went out to sort boats,' Bobby recalled. 'Now, in those days, we didn't have a lot of transport. We had to hire a van. But we couldn't afford to get them too often. So Kenny's father piled all the boys into the van. When we come out of the van, we're all covered in oil. But we were happy to get to where we were.'

Bobby also told a story of Cambuslang team Morriston YMCA's president John Scott, who always stood watching as all the Possil boys exited the van, hoping that 'Wee Dalglish' wasn't among them.

'He could look after himself on the pitch,' Bobby said of Dalglish in 1998, 'all Possil boys could look after themselves.'

Knowing he was destined to play at a higher level, Bobby recommended Kenny to Rangers. 'Big Jimmy Smith was the chief scout of the Rangers at the time,' Bobby told me. 'A famous player with Rangers.' Smith scored 419 goals in 441 appearances for the Ibrox side. 'He came to me one day. He said, "Bobby, I'm not taking Kenny up, because he's getting too hippy, and he'll never get any faster." Biggest mistake he ever made. Now, Kenny was never a fast guy. But his hips; his hips were his greatest asset. Because he could knock people sideways with his hips. That made up for a lack of speed.'

In his autobiography, *The Scout*, Dinnie recalled Dalglish's attributes even at that young age. 'Kenny had a strong build, his vision was outstanding and he could see things others probably couldn't see in the game. He was not a pacey player but he more than made up for it with all the other elements he had to his game. His positional sense was terrific. He had a great shot and scored some wonderful goals.'

'Possil YM was a successful club and a happy place,' Dalglish said in 1989. 'The club helped a lot of lads, including myself, and we all appreciated Bob's help. He did it because he loved football and loved the club, he didn't do it because he wanted an accolade.' Kenny came back to Possil over the years and Bobby kept photo albums full of his appearances at award nights and raffles.

Douglas Smith scouted for Drumchapel Amateurs in the 60s and 70s. He saw Kenny play when he was 14 and considered him the best in his age group in Scotland. Smith went to Kenny's house to ask if he fancied joining Drumchapel Amateurs. Kenny rejected the approach, saying he couldn't let his side down. Smith left the option open for Kenny to call him if he ever changed his mind.

A few months into the new season Kenny did just that. He was invited in for a trial. Smith was delighted, confident that Drumchapel would sign up Dalglish, who was playing at inside-forward. However, the under-15s coach John Wilson already had Kenny's Scotland Schoolboys colleague Tommy Craig and future Scotland team-mate Asa Hartford in the same position. He told Smith he wouldn't take Kenny on, and reluctantly Smith had to tell Kenny the team didn't want him. Within months Craig had left for Aberdeen and Hartford went to West Bromwich Albion. Kenny would soon return to haunt Drumchapel as over the next few years he scored plenty against them playing for Glasgow United.

Glasgow United were formed by Sam Beck, who scoured the city and the surrounding areas for players. He recruited one of Bobby Dinnie's coaches, Bobby Keir, who took Kenny, and a few other boys, with him when he left Possil YM for the new club. While Kenny was playing at Glasgow United from 15 to 16, everyone around the club expected Rangers to ask him for a trial. Kenny knew that Rangers were aware of him. By that time he was playing for Scottish Schoolboys and it was known he was a Rangers supporter, going to see them whenever he wasn't playing. However, Rangers didn't make any advances. Kenny carried a little disappointment with him around that time. He knew he was one of the best players in his age group and when he went to his bedroom he could look out forlornly on Rangers' training ground, the Albion.

Kenny lined up at the home of his favourite club in May 1966 in the Victory Shield match against England. He had made his debut for Scotland Schoolboys a few days earlier in Belfast as the Scots beat Northern Ireland 4-3.

The young Auld Enemy fixture was a popular match for scouts from English and Scottish clubs. Peter Lorimer, who signed for Leeds, and Jim Forrest and Willie Henderson of Rangers had played in the fixture in recent years.

The English side were much bigger physically but Scotland tore into them from the off. Mullin set up Tommy Craig, who hit a post in the first minute. Martin got on the end of a Dick Menzies cross but sent the header past the post.

The opening goal came in the 17th minute when Menzies picked up a pass from the right and fired past Steve Bowtell from 25 yards. Les Donaldson saved a header from Lyndon Hughes to stop England equalising. Hughes went on to have a good career with West Bromwich Albion and Peterborough.

Craig was proving to be the lynchpin in the Scotland team and he set up Dalglish for a drive that just went inches past the post. Despite a couple of great saves from Donaldson, England got the equaliser in the first minute of the second half when Robert Allen latched on to a mistake by Smith and shot home from close range.

The match ended as a draw and England retained the Victory Shield.

The *Glasgow Herald* picked out Craig and Donaldson as the 'personalities of the day'. In the *Daily Record* reporter Waverley wrote, 'The Scots in ball control and in understanding were superior, and made their opponents look very ordinary prospects.'

'Kenny and Tommy Craig ran the show,' goalkeeper Les Donaldson told the *Daily Post* in 1988 of his experiences with the Scotland Schoolboys team. 'The other boys, including myself, were only too happy to go along with their plans. Looking back, Kenny seemed very mature.'

Donaldson went on to manage the Scotland Schools side and kept in touch with Kenny through the years, and marvelled at how Dalglish could still name all the boys who played with him in the Scotland under-15 team.

In the *Daily Record* Waverley wrote about the English clubs who were eager to make offers to the young Scots from that team. Kenny was certainly one of those being watched by scouts.

When Kenny was 15, a Scottish scout came to the house and asked if he would go down to Liverpool for a few days, along with some other promising boys. The trial went well, and he was invited down again. This time Kenny travelled down with another youngster called George Adams. They mixed with the senior pros, such as Roger Hunt and Willie Stevenson, and watched Liverpool play against Everton for the Charity Shield at Goodison. Hunt scored the game's only goal.

On 20 August 1966, Kenny played in the Liverpool B team against Southport. The Liverpool team was Lloyd, Witham, Adams, Mitchell, G. McCrae, Johnson, Bowman, Dalglish, Wilkinson, Koo, Humphries. Southport won 1-0.

Two days later, Kenny played in a trial game with other youngsters in Liverpool. Bill Shankly and Reuben Bennett dropped Kenny off at the YMCA where he was staying. 'Kenny, we like you. We think you'll make a good player at Liverpool. We'd like to sign you,' Shankly said. 'We'll send our Scottish representative to see your mum and dad.' A sheepish Kenny said nothing more than 'Thank you.'

Kenny returned to Glasgow the following day and immediately headed to Ibrox to support Rangers as they lost 4-0 to Celtic in the Glasgow Cup Final. He thought about Shankly's offer. As much as his desire was to become a professional footballer he knew that he was too young to leave home and live so far away from his parents. Things were good at Glasgow United and what he would miss most was his fortnightly visits to Ibrox to see his beloved Rangers.

Dalglish also had a trial lined up that month at West Ham United. Islay-born Doug Eadie was at West Ham with Kenny. As young sportsmen who didn't drink, the pair of them spent time going to the cinema and watching the TV in their rooms, Kenny having a particular fondness for the US show *The Untouchables*.

Eadie signed for West Ham and played twice in the first team in the last two games of the 1966/67 season. He went on to play in Scotland for Morton and Ross County, where, in 1976, he infamously vaulted a fence to take on a fan who had been giving him abuse. Eadie also played with Christchurch United and Toronto Blizzard. When his football career ended, he became an actor, appearing in the movie *The Acid House* and the popular TV series *Taggart*. Eadie passed away in 2013.

Dalglish's Possil YM team-mate Jimmy Lindsay also went down to West Ham with him. Lindsay signed for the Hammers and played 39 times in the First Division for them, then played in the lower leagues with Watford, Colchester, Hereford and Shrewsbury. Other young Scots in the shape of George Andrew and Jimmy Mullen were also there.

While at West Ham, Kenny attended the 1-1 draw with Liverpool on 3 September 1966. The youngsters who were at West Ham were sat behind the dugout. As Shankly passed he spotted the rosy-cheeked young Kenny Dalglish and shouted out to the youngster, 'Kenny!' Kenny in Glasgow vernacular 'hit a beamer' (went red with embarrassment) and carried on walking.

At that time, Harry Redknapp was a 19-year-old winger, who had played seven first-team matches. In 2022 while speaking with *Talksport* he recalled Dalglish at Upton Park. 'He came to West Ham with another little lad [Jimmy Lindsay], for about eight or nine days to train. I used to pick him up. I had a little car, a little Austin 1100, so I would pick Kenny up in the morning, took him to training, dropped him back after training with the other kid.'

Redknapp recalled watching Kenny on the training pitch. 'We had a practice match one Saturday morning. Kenny's an under-15 player but they put him in the first team against the reserves. The ball comes in to him – and you know the angle in the box, the one that he scored 100 times – he gets the ball, drops his shoulder and "bang!", bent it right in the top corner. Everyone clapped him, [including] Bobby Moore [who was] stood there on the halfway line. I can remember talking to Ron [Greenwood] about him after that game. "Will we get him?" I asked. "No chance," he said. "We've tried. Everybody wants him, but he's going to Celtic."'

One of Dalglish's team-mates at Glasgow United was Vic Davidson, whose mother believed in her son so much she wrote a letter to Sean Fallon at Celtic, asking him to come along to watch him in an upcoming match in Rutherglen. Fallon, who had made 254 appearances for Celtic in the 1950s, was the club's assistant manager but had overall responsibility for the scouting network. Celtic received many such letters, and even though Fallon years later couldn't quite put his finger on what made that letter stand out, he felt he should respond. 'So I sent the scout Alec Boden to watch him,' Fallon recalled in *Scotland on Sunday* in 1989. 'He came back with a very good report, but he also recommended another boy in the same team. That was Kenny Dalglish.'

Alec Boden played over 100 league games for Celtic during the 1940s and 50s before becoming a scout. He had heard Kenny's name before, but he knew then that Kenny could make it in the game.

Celtic now wanted a closer look at Dalglish and Davidson.

A game was arranged between Glasgow United and a team made up of Celtic ground staff boys at the club's training ground at Barrowfield. United won 3-2, Kenny scored, and there watching was Jock Stein.

Speaking to Harry Hood's biographer Matt Corr, Dalglish said, 'Jock told our manager that he liked the number 4 but that he had heard he was going to Rangers. "Well, *he* hasn't heard that," was the reply. He asked me to come to Parkhead for training, and I jumped at the chance.'

Although Kenny supported Celtic's greatest rivals, it didn't come into his thinking when Celtic showed interest. Since Jock Stein's arrival as manager in 1965 Celtic had transformed from a club that hadn't won a trophy in eight years to an inspirational, exciting and successful team who were now making their mark on Europe.

Kenny wanted to become a professional footballer; he was going to go where his dream could become a reality.

Bill Dalglish knew the footballing education his son would receive under Jock Stein, a former Celtic captain and one of the most respected men in the British and European game. It was Sean Fallon though who would personally reach out to the Dalglish family. 4 May 1967 happened to be Fallon's fourth wedding anniversary. He was on his way down to Seamill Hydro with his wife Myra when he popped into the Dalglish family home.

'The family made me feel very welcome,' Fallon told his biographer Stephen Sullivan, 'but I got the impression that Kenny's dad wanted him to become a joiner rather than a footballer because he was worried he might not make it. I think it took a good hour-and-a-half for me to get round to talking to them about bringing the lad to Celtic and, by then, I'd completely forgotten about Myra and the kids down in the car. It was only when I was coming down the stairs, having got Kenny and his father to agree to sign, that I remembered.

And I'll tell you, I wasn't popular. Myra was going mad. She told me to forget about Seamill – that the day was ruined – and to just drive home. I don't think she spoke to me for the rest of the week.'

With the deal verbally sealed, Kenny's mother Cathy made the potentially fateful decision to show Sean around their modest flat. For most teenagers, such maternal pride would be merely embarrassing – for a boy from a Rangers-supporting household about to join Celtic, it risked catastrophe. The bedroom walls stood as a shrine to his Ibrox heroes.

Over the years, the urgency of this moment grew in Dalglish's retelling. In his 1996 autobiography, he described frantically tearing down the incriminating posters before Fallon could spot them. By 2013, the story had mellowed with time, Dalglish saying when Fallon arrived there was no panic to rip them off the walls.

Fallon told Sullivan he didn't notice any Rangers pictures. 'Kenny's allegiances didn't worry me in the least. If anything, it was quite nice to know that we had brought in this great player right from under Rangers' noses. Even then, I was pretty confident he would make it. He wasn't an obvious standout at that stage, but he had great spirit and bravery about him, and obviously loved playing the game. And, right from the start, he had that great balance and ability to shield the ball. I always felt he had the necessary potential.

'The folk at Rangers thought he was too slow. A few people felt that way about Kenny at the start. But I saw that he was fast in the head.'

'What he had was speed of thought and that would overcome speed of movement,' Fallon said in the documentary series *Football's Greatest*.

Kenny's first day of training with Celtic was in July 1967. He made his way to Argyle Street in the centre of Glasgow, and there he met, for the first time, a fellow new trainee by the name of Danny McGrain, who also had a schoolboy devotion to Rangers.

While McGrain's allegiances changed quite quickly from the blue to the green half of Glasgow it took Kenny a little while to come round. In August 1967 the pair of Celtic youngsters were at an Old Firm match in the League Cup. Celtic scored and McGrain instinctively leaped up in jubilation. A shocked Dalglish couldn't believe McGrain wanted Celtic to win the tie. Celtic won the match 3-1 and qualified for the League Cup quarter-finals.

Even though Kenny was now training at Celtic, he still went on the Rangers supporters' bus to Ibrox. Stein and Fallon apparently weren't aware, but in time Kenny would drop his ties to Rangers and focus on playing for Celtic. But in his immediate future he found there was another club he would have to find loyalty towards.

It was practice at Celtic that they would farm young boys out to clubs in the junior ranks – junior in Scotland being the semi-professional leagues – in order that they could play competitive football outside their age ranges. Danny McGrain went to Maryhill in Glasgow's west end while Kenny was sent to Cumbernauld United.

Scotland: Donaldson (Stirlingshire), Milligan (Dumfriesshire), Wilson (Edinburgh), Pethard (Glasgow), Smith (Fife), Grant (Hamilton), Martin (Midlothian), Dalglish (Glasgow), Mullin (Glasgow), Craig (Glasgow), Menzies (Fife)

Scorer: Menzies (16)

England: Bowtell (East London Schools), Mitchell (Liverpool Schools), McLelland (Carlisle Schools), Sergeant (Liverpool Schools), Clarke (Chesterfield Schools), Merrick (Bristol Schools), Lowrey (Newcastle upon Tyne Schools), Hughes (Smethwick Schools), Dangerfield (Stroud Schools), Allen (Nuneaton Schools), Wilkinson (Stoke-on-Trent Schools)

Scorer: Allen (42)

Attendance: 6,000

2

Cumbernauld United 4-0 Neilston

27 April 1968, West of Scotland
Junior League (Second Division),
St Patrick's Sportsground

IN 1968 Cumbernauld United were recently reformed: they had gone out of business initially in 1923, before forming again in 1929 as Cumbernauld Thistle, only for the outbreak of the Second World War to prompt the club to dissolve once more.

In December of 1955 the Secretary of State for Scotland designated Cumbernauld a 'New Town' to meet the urgent problem of population overspill from Glasgow. In August of 1964, a working party was set up to re-establish the club and in July 1967 Cumbernauld United Juniors FC were formally admitted to the West of Scotland Junior League (Second Division). They would temporarily play their home games at St Patrick's Sportsground, Kilsyth, as their ground, Ravenswood, awaited a pavilion to be built by the district council.

As they started the season with a squad of 14 newly signed players, match secretary Bob Woods said, 'This will give us a pool of players to work with modelled on the ideas of the old master himself, Jock Stein.'

Dalglish came to Cumbernauld just as another young talent was leaving. Having played only two games for the club, Johnny Hamilton left to join Hibernian. He would play there until 1973, when he joined Rangers.

Also joining Cumbernauld, from Glasgow United, was Jim Donald, a 17-year-old left-winger. Donald had played with Kenny at Possil YM and he would later be Kenny's best man at his wedding to Marina Harkins.

Dalglish made his debut for Cumbernauld on 12 August 1967 in a 3-0 win over Glasgow Perthshire, netting once. The *Cumbernauld News* noted of his performance, 'Dalglish, on occasions, showed he packed a hefty wallop but was generally too slow, and too far out with his volleys.'

Improvements were clearly made by the time of Kenny's second appearance in the claret and sky blue two days later, as he scored four times in a 5-1 win over Yoker Athletic at Holm Park. The bonus system at the club was ten shillings for an away win and five shillings for every three goals, so Kenny's pockets must have been jingling as his bonuses mingled with his ten shillings match fee.

Sean Fallon and Celtic coach John Higgins were there as Dalglish signed provisional forms for Celtic at half-time in Cumbernauld's game at Neilston Juniors at Brig o' Lea Park on 21 August 1967. Dalglish had headed his side in front in a game they lost 3-2.

Kenny continued to train one night a week with Celtic while playing at Cumbernauld and he also worked as an apprentice joiner, although his heart wasn't entirely in it as he realised that his future lay as a professional footballer.

Kenny scored the fifth in Cumbernauld's 5-3 victory over Irvine Victoria in the West of Scotland Cup in September. The *Cumbernauld News* wrote, 'Dalglish gave another of his demonstrations of strength and ball control when he waltzed past three opponents before rounding [goalkeeper] Law to net the clincher.' Moments later, Kenny appeared to have scored direct from a corner, but with the ruck of players in the penalty box unsighting the referee, it wasn't given.

In the middle of September, Kenny was selected for a Scottish Junior XI to play against the Fife County Junior FA XI as a trial for the Junior Scotland team. 'This boy looks to have a great career in football ahead of him,' wrote the

Cumbernauld News in a piece that captioned a photo of the young player as 'Billy Dalglish'.

As the weeks at the New Town club went on, it became expected that if Kenny wasn't scoring goals, he would be running the show. The *News* wrote of his 'usual magnificent style and masterly ball control'. If he wasn't providing the final pass, his team-mates were chasing in rebounds when opposition goalkeepers couldn't hold Dalglish's rasping shots.

Kenny did find himself criticised in the pages of the local press for holding the ball too long or for not playing to the standards the reporters quickly began to expect of him. It's notable how much the match reporters looked to Dalglish, 'the boy wonder', ostensibly still a child, to drive the team of men forward. If Kenny wasn't on form, invariably the team weren't either, although just the odd flash or two of brilliance was often enough to get the New Town team the points.

In January 1968 Kenny scored the only goal of the game as Cumbernauld beat Fife side Newburgh away in the fourth round of the Scottish Junior Cup. Cumbernauld's run in the juniors' premier competition ended with a fifth-round second-replay defeat to Johnstone Burgh. Dalglish though was missing from the game as he had picked up a knock playing against Kirkintilloch Rob Roy.

By the time Neilston visited Cumbernauld in the league, Dalglish hadn't played a competitive match in more than a month due to injury, postponements and free weekends in the fixture calendar.

In the ninth minute Kenny collected a Bain pass and sent the ball in off the post to put his side one up. Six minutes later, he got on the end of a cross from Stewart to double the lead. Bain got the third with ten minutes left, and in the last minute, Kenny knocked in his hat-trick for 4-0. Although Dalglish was clearly the main man in the side, Cumbernauld worked well as a team that season.

Danny McGrain looked on enviously, 'Kenny was lucky and went to Cumbernauld, a brand new club with a new park,' he told M2 Presswire in 2012. 'I went to Maryhill Juniors, an old club with an old park, and got kicked from pillar to post. I never really enjoyed it. We never won one game in six months. It was that bad I got voted player of the year. Kenny was at Cumbernauld, scoring goals every week and was just a natural goalscorer.'

On 13 May 1968, Celtic came to open Cumbernauld's new ground, Ravenswood. Jock Stein cut the ribbon on the new pavilion. Before the match, both teams and managers posed for a joint photo. Kenny was pictured kneeling in the front row between Lisbon Lions Bobby Murdoch and Willie Wallace.

A crowd of around 4,500 turned out to see a strong Celtic team play a 15-minute-each-way challenge match, which they won 2-0. Their young starlets then took on a second-string Cumbernauld team in another 30-minute match, Celtic winning that one 4-1. Dalglish only played in the first match.

Dalglish's final game for Cumbernauld was a 3-1 away defeat to Bailleston on Saturday, 25 May 1968. Oddly, he had played the night before against Cumbernauld as Celtic's Under-21s tuned up for a mini European Cup trip to Italy by defeating Cumbernauld 5-2 at Ravenswood.

Petershill won the league with Neilston and Arthurlie finishing second and third. Cumbernauld ended the season in fourth place, and took the final promotion spot. They won 13 of their 26 league games, drawing three and losing ten. They scored 61 goals and conceded 42. They played 21 cup ties, winning 11, drawing five and losing five. Dalglish played in 36 competitive ga mes, scoring 28 goals.[1]

---

1 The most common figure cited for goals Dalglish scored at Cumbernauld is 37. However, I've calculated his games played and goals scored through weekly match reports in the *Cumbernauld News*. In June 1968 the *News* wrote that Kenny had scored 32 times for Cumbernauld. However, this figure included four goals in friendlies.

Dalglish signed full-time for Celtic in April of 1968. Bob Woods said, 'We will be sorry to see Kenny go at the end of the season, but he is a lad who deserves success and we would not try to hold him back.'

In October of 1968, Dalglish returned briefly to Cumbernauld when he was presented with an award as the season's highest goalscorer at Cumbernauld United's grand presentation dance at the Y Centre in Kildrum.

Cumbernauld United: Robertson, Wilson, Stewart, McDonald, Stevenson, McKenna, McEwan, Bain, Rae, Dalglish, Donald.

Scorers: Dalglish (9, 15, 89), Bain (80)

Neilston: Mayberry, Wilson, Anderson, Martin, Aitken, McMahon, Cochrane, Houston, Deans, Brook, White.

3

Hamilton Academical 2-4 Celtic

25 September 1968, Scottish League Cup
quarter-final, Douglas Park

'THERE'S A ferment of activity below the surface,' Sean Fallon wrote in the *Celtic View* in April 1968 in his column focusing on his reserve side. 'We're introducing youngsters all the time. It's not generally realised that we follow a consistent policy of "blooding" youngsters, calling up lads from junior clubs where they're farmed out, to show their paces with the reserves.'

Fallon was confident that the young players would maintain their progress. They had inspiration ahead of them in the Celtic team from the likes of Bobby Lennox and Jimmy Johnstone and that knowledge that if you were good enough at Celtic the opportunities to progress to the first team were there.

Celtic's policy was not to rush their young prospects; they would bring them on slowly, but they always intended for them to become first-team players eventually. Now, after a successful season in the junior ranks with Cumbernauld, Dalglish's education would continue under Fallon in the reserve team.

In August 1968, Dalglish made his debut for them in a 4-1 win over Dundee United. Lou Macari scored for Celtic after two minutes then, with four minutes gone, Macari played Joe McBride in to score. Rooney pulled one back for United, but in the second half, Jim Clarke netted Celtic's third before McBride, who was looking to get fit again after injury, scored the fourth.

A few days later in the Reserve League Cup group section, Kenny wore number 4 as Celtic took on Partick Thistle. In order to win the group, which included Rangers, and qualify for the knockout rounds, Celtic had to win by seven goals. The team was enhanced by the presence of John Clark, Bertie Auld and Joe McBride. Thistle were thrashed 12-0 with McBride and Macari each netting four. Davie Hay recalled Auld urging them to keep looking for goals. 'He gave us pelters if he thought we weren't going flat out for the entire 90 minutes,' Hay wrote in his 2009 autobiography.

Kenny spoke to Celtic's website, after Bertie Auld's death in 2021. 'He was certainly influential in the success of the football club,' Dalglish said. 'Myself, Danny McGrain, Lou Macari, George Connelly, Davie Hay, Paul Wilson, Vic Davidson – he left a mark on people's minds – he certainly left a mark on mine. When you came into your work in the morning, he just lit the place up.'

Fallon was impressed by Kenny's performance and his willingness to listen. 'John Clark in the midline guided Kenny,' Fallon said after the match. 'Kenny is making his mark at right-half. The 17-year-old has had two really good games against Dundee United in the league and against Partick Thistle, and yet he is only one of the potentially great teenagers at Parkhead.'

Kenny was now part of a team that would come to be known as the Quality Street Gang. 'The press labelled us that. Jock didn't,' Macari wrote in his 2008 autobiography. Other youngsters who were in the team alongside them were Davie Hay, George Connelly, Vic Davidson and Paul Wilson. 'We all recognised that we had major deficiencies in our game at which we had to work hard, including Kenny Dalglish,' Macari wrote. 'It makes me laugh when people regard great players like Dalglish as naturals. Yes, a lot of it is about the gifts you were born with, but Kenny did not fulfil his potential simply because he was naturally gifted, he did so as a result of hours and hours of hard graft.'

'As a young boy there is no doubt about it, he wasn't the greatest finisher you've seen,' Macari said to the *Daily Mirror* in 1997. 'In fact he was quite poor in that department. But he's an example to any youngster in football anywhere. He simply worked his cobblers off, coming back in the afternoon and working away on his finishing. He became one of the great players – by working at it. It wasn't that he was born with unbelievable talent. But he has always had that will to win that has pushed him all the way.'

In the *Glasgow Times* in 2016, Danny McGrain reminisced about the early days at Celtic when he and Kenny were still learning their trade. In particular, he recalled the time Kenny came over to stay with him for a few days in Drumchapel. 'Every day for an hour at least we would kick a ball at each other. He would talk about what kind of pass he wanted if some defender was up his backside, and I would tell him where I wanted him if I had the ball in a certain position so I could find him. We worked on all sorts of things. We didn't have to do it, we just wanted to. We knew each other's game so well and that's why it clicked on the park. Although Kenny was an easy guy to play with because he was so brilliant.'

As the young reserve side were racking up victories, Fallon and Stein began to compare the crop to the reserve team of the late fifties, which included Billy McNeill and Pat Crerand. In the 4-0 win over Falkirk in September of the XI, only John Fallon and Charlie Gallagher were out of their teens.

At 17, Dalglish was now training alongside the Lisbon Lions at one of the most exciting clubs in the world. While Dalglish was in awe of some of the famous names, the Lions, far from being aloof, welcomed and helped the youngsters, passing on tips and instilling the values they needed to become

Celtic players. The teenagers saw the standards that they had to attain. Significantly Dalglish learned something he would practise later in his career, and that was the importance of giving your time to the young players once you were an established first-teamer. Billy McNeill would pick Kenny up for training, as would other players such as Jim Craig and Bertie Auld. Sitting in the car listening to the Celtic captain and first British player to lift the European Cup, Kenny learned how to handle success and to be humble with it. It was something that he retained throughout his career and beyond.

In the League Cup quarter-final, Celtic were drawn against Hamilton Academical. In the first leg at Parkhead, a Celtic team which included eight Lisbon Lions, once Jimmy Johnstone came on as a sub, destroyed Accies 10-0, with Bobby Lennox and Stevie Chalmers scoring five apiece.

Such a victory provided the opportunity for blooding youngsters in the second leg at Douglas Park. 'I know officialdom will criticise me for playing so many of my youngsters in this game,' Jock Stein wrote in the *Celtic View*, 'pointing out that it is my duty to field a full-strength side. It is also my duty to see that Celtic maintain their high standard and position in Scottish football.'

Kenny was rested for the reserve game against Dunfermline on 21 September, a match Celtic won 3-2. Fallon indicated that this wasn't unusual for Celtic: with so many good young players they could afford to rest one or two after they had played a number of games consecutively. The rest, though, was down to Dalglish being selected for the first-team squad in the second-leg match away to Hamilton.

'Even the most optimistic Acas supporter can't see [Celtic] being in any danger tonight,' the preview in Hamilton's match programme read.

An enforced absentee was Billy McNeill, who had picked up an injury in Monday's Scotland training camp. It ended his run of 107 consecutive competitive appearances for Celtic since the league match against St Mirren on 5 November 1966.

The match signalled the first starts for Hay and Jimmy Quinn, who had appeared from the bench the previous season. Goalkeeper Bobby Wraith and defender John Gorman were making their first-team debuts, with Kenny finding a place on the bench for a match with a 5.30pm kick-off.

Joe McBride latched on to a Lou Macari pass and fired past Billy Lamont to make it 1-0 after only five minutes. An equaliser came from Johnny Lawlor, who flicked a Halpin cross past Wraith. Celtic were back in front with two minutes remaining in the first half when Pat McMahon side-footed a Gallagher corner kick past Lamont.

With five minutes gone in the second half, John Clark, who was the captain on the night, put the Celts 3-1 up with a speculative shot from 30 yards. Then came the introduction of Kenny Dalglish, with Charlie Gallagher making way.

Soon, Joe McBride had his second goal when he spun on to a Connelly pass and shot beyond Lamont. Late on, defender Tommy Halpin latched on to a loose ball, knocked it past two Celtic defenders and fired it into the net to complete the night's scoring.

Kenny went back into the reserves to continue his education. Davie Hay would play once more in the first team in 1968/69, but Kenny wouldn't make another first-team appearance for the rest of the season. Neither would Quinn, while Wraith and Gorman had made the one and only first-team appearance of their Celtic careers.

Kenny's first goal in the hoops came on 4 November 1968 at New Kilbowie Park in a friendly versus Clydebank. He put Celtic in front with a 30-yard drive after 19 minutes, as they went on to win 4-1.

Dalglish followed that up a few days later with a goal against Jordanhill College, with Celtic winning 5-1.

'Dalglish, one of the most versatile young players on our staff, was the star of the match,' said Fallon.

On 20 November, the reserves travelled to Brockville to play Falkirk in the first leg of the Reserve League Cup semi-final. Celtic won 6-0, with Kenny scoring a hat-trick.

A week later, Kenny was in the Scotland youth team to play Norway at Cappielow Park in Greenock in a European qualifier. 'Wing-half Kenny Dalglish looks another Bobby Murdoch, that's how highly we think of him,' Stein told the press ahead of the match. 'He maybe needs a bit of speeding up, a little more strength, but given the breaks, he could have a great future.'

Also in the team were Kenny's clubmates, goalkeeper Tommy Livingstone, Paul Wilson and Vic Davidson, while other notable youngsters were Rangers' Alfie Conn and Ally Robertson of West Bromwich Albion.

Scotland won 8-1, with Aberdeen forward Jim Hamilton netting a hat-trick. His club-mate, the side's captain, Tommy Craig, scored with two penalties, while Davidson, Conn and Wilson scored the others. The *Daily Record* described Kenny's performance as 'tireless'. The win qualified Scotland for the finals in Leipzig in May 1969.

Hamilton Academical: Lamont, Halpin, Hunter, Fraser, Small, Lawlor, Gaughan, Goodwin, Thomson [Gilchrist], Wardrop, Clifford

Scorers: Lawlor (23), Halpin (70)

Celtic: Wraith, Craig, Gorman, Connelly, Hay, Clark, McMahon, McBride, Quinn, Gallagher [Dalglish], Macari

Scorers: McBride (5, 56), McMahon (43), Clark (50)

Attendance: 4,000

4

Aberdeen Reserves 0-2
Celtic Reserves

*21 April 1969, Reserve League Cup
Final first leg, Pittodrie Stadium*

IN 2012, Danny McGrain spoke to M2 Presswire about the experience of playing alongside established first-teamers in the reserves. 'We were one squad. It wasn't a first-team squad and reserve squad, so we got to know each other. We would play games together. You would be playing alongside and against the likes of wee Jimmy [Johnstone], Bobby [Murdoch], Big Billy [McNeill] and Bertie [Auld]. You can't become friends as we were too young, but you got to know them, so when you made your first-team debut it was still a daunting task but you weren't as nervous. They were still the Lisbon Lions, you still had a great respect for them, and I have a great deal to thank them for. For me, Kenny, Victor and Paul to be able to play with these guys was like being at Yale University for football. We had to take everything from it, and I think we did that.'

Dalglish wasn't the only player who was moved around a lot in the reserves to find his best position. McGrain was originally a midfielder, running around and covering a lot of ground. In his time in the reserves McGrain played everywhere apart from centre-forward, centre-half and in goal. After a few years Stein came to a realisation – McGrain was a full-back. Danny himself initially thought he wasn't suited. His idea of a full-back was someone who was a hard tackler. However, once he began playing in the position he found he was comfortable.

A regular in the Celtic reserve team, although he only played a handful of games with the first XI, was Davie Cattanach. 'He was a rough and ready defender who was very enthusiastic,' McGrain recalled in 2012. 'It was good for us to see someone who was perhaps out the picture but still had great enthusiasm for the club and still worked hard. He also takes a bit of credit for our knowledge of the game.'

Celtic defeated Dundee 4-1 in the semi-final of the Reserve League Cup, setting up a two-legged final with Aberdeen.

In the first leg the visitors had a let-off in the 20th minute when the Dons' Tommy Rae was too slow to react to a rebound when the goal was at his mercy. Celtic took the lead when Davidson floated over a free kick, George Connelly ran into the area and flicked the ball past the bewildered Ernie McGarr.

Tommy Craig had Aberdeen's goal chances in the second half. The best of his three shots was a swerving left-foot drive which curled the wrong side of the post. Charlie Gallagher went on a solo run to make the match safe.

Sean Fallon was delighted with the win, as the first-team pool for an important league match with Kilmarnock contained 17 players meaning the reserves couldn't be augmented by many of the first-teamers. The most experienced player in the young Celtic side was Charlie Gallagher, who was coming back from a long time out injured. Five days later 20-year-old George Connelly also scored in the Scottish Cup Final as Celtic beat Rangers 4-0.

The second leg of the Reserve League Cup Final was played at Celtic Park on 29 April. The only change in the team was Tommy Callaghan replacing Davie Hay. Celtic won 2-0, with Macari scoring the first and Dalglish turning a Gallagher corner into the path of Davidson, who netted the second, giving Celtic the cup with a 4-0 aggregate win. Aberdeen had their revenge by beating Celtic home and away in the Second XI Cup Final.

'As far as Celtic youngsters are concerned, their progress over the season has been excellent,' Fallon said on winning the trophy. 'Remembering that most of the players were only youngsters when we competed in the Italian Youth Tournament last summer, the progress over the last few months has been remarkable. Although we are delighted that the boys have lifted one of the second XI trophies, this is not the prime objective of the reserve team.'

The reserves didn't win the league title that season. Fallon acknowledged that they probably would have done so if they had played their strongest XI at all times. 'However, the main objective of the second team is to groom youngsters for the top team, and this would not be achieved by playing first-team pool players in preference to youngsters. Conversely, younger players have got to be nursed along to make certain they're not being asked to give too much, too soon.'

Lou Macari finished as top scorer for the reserves in 1968/69 with 19 goals. Kenny netted four.

Dalglish was part of the Scotland squad that played in East Germany in the European Championship finals. The team was run by Roy Small, one of the original coaches at Scotland's famed Largs coaching academy, who would be part of FIFA's coaching academy from 1972 to 1983.

In the first match, against Poland in Jena, Vic Davidson was sent off after going in for a loose ball with the goalkeeper, but the young Scots won 1-0 thanks to Tommy Craig's goal in the 19th minute.

The Scots' second match was in Dresden against Austria; Scotland won 2-1 with goals from Asa Hartford and Jim Hamilton. The downside was that Hartford and Tommy Craig, now Britain's youngest £100,000 player after his move to Sheffield Wednesday, were sent off.

In the next match, against Yugoslavia in Erfurt, Scotland played in a 4-3-3 system with Dalglish up front alongside Alfie Conn and Aberdeen's Tom Wilson. Another Possil YM graduate, Eddie Kelly of Arsenal, took over as captain in the suspended Craig's absence. The sides drew 1-1 with Vic Davidson netting the Scots' goal.

That qualified Scotland for the semi-finals, where they met East Germany in the Karl Marx Stadt in East Berlin. Hartford, who was back after serving a one-match ban, put Scotland in front on 17 minutes. However, goals from Zoelfil and Schwerske gave East Germany a 2-1 win.

A 1-0 defeat to Russia in the third-place play-off in Halle saw the Scots finish fourth, as Bulgaria beat East Germany in the final on a toss of the coin after a 1-1 draw.

Aberdeen: McGarr, Hermiston, Kirkland, Wilson, McMillan, Murray, G. Buchan, Little, Rae [Paul], Hamilton, Craig

Celtic: Wraith, McGrain, Gorman, Cattanach, Hay, Dalglish, Gallagher, Connolly, McMahon, Macari, Davidson. Sub: Jim Clarke

Scorers: Connolly (48), Gallagher (52)

5

Celtic 7-1 Raith Rovers

4 October 1969, First Division,
Celtic Park

AUTHOR EUGENE MacBride asked Bobby Lennox what impression the young Dalglish made on him. 'Kenny made a big, big impression on everyone in training,' Lennox replied. 'Before he got into the team, he was the type of boy that could come and train with the first team and not be overawed. Kenny … had great respect for the guys. He could train with the first team and that was his level, he was fine there, he was confident and comfortable. Before he ever played in the team, we knew Kenny could play.'

In August of 1969 the reserves beat Raith Rovers 5-0 in the Reserve League Cup. Included in the team alongside Dalglish were Ronnie Simpson, Tommy Callaghan and Jimmy Johnstone. Kenny and the other youngsters were benefitting from not just training with, but playing alongside some of the established first-team players in competitive matches.

In September, the *Celtic View* asked chief scout John Higgins who out of all the youngsters at Parkhead was most likely to become a first-team regular. He was hopeful that with time the majority – if not all – of the youngsters would establish themselves, and if they didn't he felt that was a mistake of his, not the young players. He stressed though that the important thing was not to rush young boys' progress; an early breakthrough was good but it shouldn't be forced. He himself had signed from school at 16 in January 1950, but didn't play regularly for the first team until the 1953/54 season.

In the Reserve League that month, Celtic beat Rangers 4-1. Sean Fallon said the result was down to 'teamwork, tenacity and flashes of brilliant individualism'. Particularly pleasing for Fallon was the Rangers team included experienced first-team men such as Andy Penman, Alex Ferguson, Colin Jackson and Erik Sorensen. 'Young Ken Dalglish has recently been playing a free-running style of football. Here we changed his role to play it tight in the middle with centre-half Cattanach. Dalglish adapted admirably and was one of the reasons keeper Simpson had so little to do.'

The headline in the *Daily Record*'s sports pages on Saturday, 4 October 1969 was 'Dalgleish [sic] Gets Celtic Call-Up'. Bob Patience's article focused on Kenny being the most high-profile of a number of youngsters who were playing that day in the Scottish League. They included the Aberdeen pair Joe Harper and Derek Mackay.

In *The Scotsman*, John Rafferty wrote that Celtic had been worried about Bobby Murdoch's form and the word was coming through from those watching the reserves that Kenny Dalglish would be the man to eventually replace him. The comparisons with such a complete player as Bobby Murdoch ensured there was excited speculation about Kenny's starting place in the Celtic team.

Jock Stein called for Kenny to come to his office. Stein told him he wouldn't be playing for the reserves at the weekend, instead he'd be in the first-team squad. Dalglish could only focus on the fact that he was missing the reserve game – he hadn't even considered he might be playing against Raith Rovers at Celtic Park.

On matchday Stein told Kenny that he would be playing in place of Bobby Murdoch. Bothwell-born Murdoch had been through a similar career trajectory to Kenny. He spent two seasons farmed out to junior club Cambuslang Rangers before returning to Celtic, still a teenager, to stake his claim for a first-team place. Murdoch played at inside-right until Jock Stein arrived as manager and moved him to right-half, a position he thrived in. He would become Celtic's playmaker; frequently at the heart of attacking build-ups.

As kick-off in the Raith game approached, Kenny's nerves began to build. But the man to help him settle was Murdoch himself. He came and sat beside Dalglish in the changing room. He took time to fill Kenny in on what he might expect from the game, giving him advice and instilling confidence in him.

Murdoch knew if Jock Stein was selecting him then Kenny must be up to the task. Murdoch's advice was simple: 'Take things easy and play your natural game.' Dalglish always remembered the assistance Murdoch gave him that day. He would pay it forward years later when he was in the position of being the senior man in the dressing room.

With Raith sporting white shirts with two horizontal blue stripes, Celtic were in their change kit of emerald green shirts, white shorts and green socks. The Raith Rovers team contained one of Kenny's idols from his days following Rangers in Ralph Brand, who had played for the Ibrox club between 1954 and 1965.

Wallace put a ball through the middle for the pacey Lennox to chase. He held the ball up and waited for Johnstone to arrive. 'Jinky' accepted the pass and then dribbled past three defenders and fired the ball home to put Celtic one up after 12 minutes.

It was 2-0 eight minutes later when Johnstone poked home a low John Hughes cross. Lennox and Wallace made it 4-0, then Colin Sinclair pounced on a mistake by John Clark to pull a goal back for Raith three minutes before the interval.

Lennox tapped home the fifth before Callaghan smacked the ball in from 25 yards. The last goal was the best of the game. Dalglish hit a cross-field ball for Hughes, who went on a run. He passed three Raith defenders before hitting a rasping shot.

The *Daily Record*'s sports editor Jack Adams wrote, 'Kenny Dalgleish[2] became the latest of Celtic's instant heroes. The young right-half refused to let the first team's tempo kill his obvious skill.' Adam's colleague Hugh Taylor rated Kenny as a highly promising player, and Celtic's most dangerous attacker.

Although Kenny wasn't in the team for the league match against Airdrie, he went back into the Celtic side for the next match against Ayr United in the semi-final of the League Cup at Hampden. It was a thrilling match that went to extra time after a 2-2 draw. Ayr, managed by Ally MacLeod, went 3-2 in front only for Bertie Auld to equalise late on.

Dalglish retained his place for the replay, again played at Hampden. Alex Ingram shocked the crowd by putting Ayr in front after 14 minutes. That though was merely the cue for Celtic to spark into life with Tommy Callaghan and Dalglish taking command in midfield.

Harry Hood equalised after 23 minutes, heading in a Tommy Gemmell cross. The winner came on 52 minutes. Dalglish frequently put himself about in attacks. His presence flustered Ayr's defenders when the ball bobbled near David Stewart's goal. Stan Quinn tried to clear, but failed and the ball fell to Steve Chalmers who scored easily.

Back in the reserves, there was a positional change for Kenny in the 5-1 win over Kilmarnock in the Second XI Cup first round replay in front of a crowd of 13,000. Kenny played at centre-forward and scored twice from the penalty spot. Fallon was pleased with his performance and that he was gaining positional experience. He now knew Kenny could be moved around the pitch without it affecting his game.

---

2 At this stage of his career the press were still spelling Kenny's surname as 'Dalgleish'.

There was another starting place for Kenny in November in a 2-0 defeat to Hearts. Later that month, he was called up for the Scotland Under-23s for an international at Hampden with France. He made the bench but didn't get on the pitch as Scotland won 4-0.

It was, however, back to the reserves for the rest of the season. Sean Fallon's philosophy on nurturing youngsters in that era had been proving successful. He felt reserve team football provided the opportunities for young players to develop their skills, grow in confidence and demonstrate their ability.

Fallon didn't set targets for how many teenagers would make the grade, but he considered two each season to be an exceptional job. He wanted to keep the standards high at Celtic, and that naturally meant that not everyone would measure up. Although Fallon would become fond of some of the young players, his commitment was turning out elite level players for the club, so the satisfaction at doing that was occasionally mixed with disappointment when some players had to be let go. 'Incidentally,' he said to the *Celtic View*, 'we don't think or talk about players at Parkhead as reserves. We look on all of them as Celtic players.'

In January 1970, Kenny was included in the Scotland Under-23s pool for a match with Wales. 'Since the day we took him from Glasgow Amateurs and placed him with Cumbernauld United, he's looked the part,' said Jock Stein on the squad's announcement. 'Maybe people were surprised when I played him in the League Cup semi-final this season. But that's the kind of confidence I have in this boy.'

The reserves won the Reserve League championship in April, confirming the title by beating Dundee 4-0, Harry Hood scoring a hat-trick. The Reserve League Cup was added with a 6-5 aggregate win over Dunfermline Athletic. From 34 games, Celtic won 27 of them, scoring 116 goals.

The top scorer was Vic Davidson with 43. Lou Macari was on 40 while Dalglish weighed in with 23.

'Kenny was rarely the leading scorer,' Billy McNeill noted in his 2004 autobiography, 'but the striker playing alongside him usually was. That was because he was the consummate team player.'

It was a successful season for Kenny, and it looked like a first-team breakthrough was imminent.

Celtic: Simpson, Hay, Gemmell, Dalglish, McNeill, Clark, Johnstone (Hood), Lennox, Wallace, Callaghan, Hughes

Scorers: Johnstone (12, 20), Lennox (37, 63), Wallace (40), Callaghan (65), Hughes (73)

Raith Rovers: Reid, Gray, Lindsay, D Miller, Polland, Cooper, A Miller (Bolton), Falconer, Sinclair, Brand, Gillespie

Scorer: Sinclair (42)

Attendance: 32,000

6

Kilmarnock 2-7 Celtic

4 May 1971, Frank Beattie Testimonial,
Rugby Park

CELTIC WENT on tour to America, Canada and Bermuda shortly after their 1970 European Cup Final loss to Feyenoord. Kenny and Vic Davidson were the two youngsters on the fringe of the first team included in the 16-man squad. Davie Hay, Lou Macari and George Connelly could also be classed as young, but they had all begun to establish themselves in the Celtic team during the previous two seasons.

In a game against the Bermudan champions Somerset on 31 May, Sean Fallon made the decision to put Kenny in from the start in place of Willie Wallace. The idea was to give him a full game to see how he did. Kenny had played a few matches on the tour but hadn't yet been given 90 minutes. He had played the first half against a Manchester United team containing George Best in Toronto in a match Celtic lost 2-0.

Despite going a goal down against Somerset in the seventh minute, Celtic came back to win 4-1. Dalglish scored the fourth goal from the penalty spot. Although these were exhibition games Kenny was gaining experience and little by little it was all going towards his maturity as a professional footballer.

Despite the fact his appearances in the Celtic first team had all been strong showings, as the 1970/71 season began, Kenny found himself back learning his trade in the reserves, where his form hadn't always been stellar. Fallon gave an assessment of how he was doing in October after he had netted a penalty in a 3-1 win away to St Johnstone. 'Kenny Dalglish had his best game of the season at left-half and scored a good goal. The young wing-half has had a sticky time recently, but at Muirton Park, he looked once more like fulfilling the promise of last season.'

Fallon was also full of praise after a 7-3 win over Airdrie, saying he was 'once again playing clever, constructive football'.

The 1970/71 season offered Kenny only five first-team appearances. In September, he came on as a substitute for Bobby Murdoch against Finns Kokkola in a 5-0 European Cup win, which gave Celtic a 14-0 aggregate victory. A substitute appearance against Airdrie in October was his last showing in the first team until a 4-3 win away at Partick Thistle in March, where again he appeared from the bench.

Stein gave Dalglish a start against Airdrie in the Scottish Cup semi-final replay in April 1971. Jim Brogan was Celtic's man of the match. 'Brogan was helped tremendously by that most up-and-coming youngster Kenny Dalglish,' read the *Evening Times* report of Celtic's 2-0 win.

Kenny kept his place for the next match, a 1-1 draw at home to Dundee United. At the end of April Dalglish came on for Willie Wallace in the title-winning match against Ayr United, played at Hampden as Celtic Park was undergoing renovations.

The final appearance for Kenny in the first team that season was away to Clyde in the Glasgow Cup semi-final. Stein decided to play a team made up predominantly of youngsters. Tommy Gemmell, John Clark, playing in his last ever match for Celtic, and Stevie Chalmers were the only regular first-teamers. Celtic's reserves had won the Reserve League and Reserve League Cup, so it was a surprise when Clyde, who also played a team of youngsters, won 2-1.

Celtic's Reserves clinched the Reserve League championship in fine style. On Thursday, 22 April, Rangers came to Parkhead. Celtic only needed one point, but they were determined to get both. Kenny ran riot, scoring four in a 7-1 rout. His first came from the penalty spot. Ward White netted the second, then Kenny dribbled round Rangers goalkeeper Gerry Neef to make it 3-0. An excellent team move by Celtic was finished by Davidson's overhead kick for four. Dalglish side-footed home a Davidson pass for his hat-trick.

Rangers' consolation came from Walker, before Dalglish hit his fourth on 83 minutes. Davidson then went on a solo run to make the final score 7-1. Fallon was delighted with Kenny's outstanding performance in front of goal and felt that in the last two months he had improved immensely and his time in the first team had led to a growth in confidence.

The reason that Kenny was sent to play up front that day was that Bobby Murdoch was in the team in an attempt to be match fit for the upcoming Scottish Cup Final, so had been selected in his usual right-half position.

The reserve league was won by winning 23 of 34 games and scoring 108 goals.

Rangers were back at Celtic Park the following week for the first leg of the Reserve League Cup Final. Celtic picked up where they had left off with Macari, White, Dalglish and Davidson scoring in a 4-1 win.

The second leg at Ibrox was even worse for Rangers. 'Brilliant Dalglish is Reserve Cup Hero' ran the *Daily Record*'s headline. He got the scoring started as he latched on to hesitation by Rangers' centre-half Gus McCallum – who like Kenny also grew up yards from Ibrox – took the ball from him and fired past Neef. Dalglish set up Davidson for number two. George Connelly scored an own goal after 19 minutes to bring Rangers back to 2-1.

McCallum pulled down Dalglish for a penalty, which Kenny converted. Just before half-time, Dalglish got on the end of a Macari cross to complete his hat-trick. McCallum's nightmare evening was complete when he scored an own goal for Celtic's fifth. With nine minutes left it was 6-1 when Davidson scored with a header.

In a Rangers match programme, the following season, McCallum was asked for his 'Blackest football memory'. He replied, 'The three defeats the reserve team had against Celtic at the end of last season.'

Celtic also won the Second XI Cup by beating Falkirk 6-1 on aggregate. Vic Davidson was top scorer with 40 while Dalglish was second with 23 goals.

The Celtic supporters who also went to see the reserve team really did consider themselves lucky and felt that those who only went to see the first team were missing out on a lot of great football and exciting talent coming through. Some letter-writers to the *Celtic View* thought that the reserve team could either rotate with the first team week by week or enter the Second Division in their own right.

Despite those outstanding performances against Rangers Reserves, the game that laid down Kenny's marker to be considered a regular starter was Frank Beattie's testimonial match at Rugby Park on a Friday night in May 1971.

'Boys are always a worry,' Matt Busby, with similar thinking to Stein, said to the *Daily Express* in 1965. 'The timing has to be right. You daren't rush them. You daren't run the risk of killing their spirit by having them overwhelmed.' Rugby Park was, coincidentally also the ground that Duncan Edwards staked his claim for a place in the Manchester United side when he played there in a friendly against Kilmarnock in 1953.

Frank Beattie was a one-club man, signing for Kilmarnock in October 1953. He skippered Killie to their greatest ever achievement, the 1964/65 Scottish League title. He also played on the losing side in three cup finals, the Scottish Cup of 1960 and the League Cup in 1960/61 and 1962/63. A part-timer until 1960, by day he was a coal miner, working in the pit at Plean. Jock Stein made sure to bring a strong side to honour a man who had played over 400 times for the Rugby Park club. Beattie had broken his leg playing in a match against Celtic 18 months earlier in a challenge with Jimmy Johnstone and had only just resumed playing.

Celtic had won the Scottish Cup two days previously, defeating Rangers 2-1 in a replay. They paraded the trophy before the match. Eight players from the final started the game. Dalglish was tried at centre-forward, instead of his normal wing-half position.

The referee for the night was RK Wilson, who had been in charge at Tynecastle in 1965 for the decisive league match between Hearts and Kilmarnock, when Killie won the league championship by 0.04 of a goal.

Kilmarnock's XI included guest players Gerry Queen of Crystal Palace, Rangers' Colin Stein and Willie Johnston and Dixie Ingram of Ayr United.

Dalglish's first goal came after 21 minutes with a flashing left-foot shot. Colin Stein equalised, but then on half an hour Dalglish latched on to a Lennox through ball to make it 2-1. Willie Johnston missed a penalty just before half-time.

Kenny had his hat-trick ten minutes into the second half. Ingram pulled a goal back two minutes later, then Bobby Murdoch latched on to a Tommy Callaghan pass and made the score 4-2 with 65 minutes gone.

Dalglish hit a further three goals in the 70th, 85th and 88th minutes.

Joe McBride, famously Celtic's top scorer in the 1966/67 season despite an injury preventing him from playing after Christmas Eve, spoke to Kenny a couple of months after the match. McBride, who had played with Beattie at Kilmarnock, told Kenny something about his performance that night – that he would have scored more goals if he hadn't been embarrassed. Kenny realised McBride was right. The more he had scored, the more he'd thought he wasn't honouring a veteran of the game in Frank Beattie, he was humiliating him.

In 1986, a Kilmarnock-based letter-writer to the *Dundee Weekly News* recalled Kenny's performance in the game. 'He got a standing ovation, and I'll always remember he came off the park with the reddest face I'd ever seen in a footballer.'

Tommy Gemmell had been on standby to play that night. Standby though meant going for a game of golf and a few drinks with Willie Wallace at Dullatur Golf Club in Cumbernauld. They were in the clubhouse a couple of pints in when Stein phoned. 'The clubmaster came looking for us,' Gemmell recalled in his 2012 autobiography, 'and we told him to say we were still out on the course. It was only after that game at Kilmarnock that Jock started to play Kenny up front. There was no looking back after that. If Willie Wallace had gone down for the game, Jock might not have played Kenny up front that day, but Kenny would still have made his breakthrough in style at some point.'

Dalglish was part of the Celtic party that travelled to Israel for a week-long stay at the end of May. He was in the team to face Hapoel Tel Aviv, whose side was augmented by some guest players, including Mordechai Spiegler, who had played for Israel at the 1970 World Cup and, a year later, would train with Celtic.

Kenny spoke to the *Sunday Post* as he left for a holiday to Majorca in June of 1971. His goals at the end of the season seemed to indicate his future as a striker at the club. 'Originally, I was an orthodox front-runner,' Kenny said. 'Then the boss gave me a try in the midfield. He stunned me a bit when I was moved for a spell into the back four in the reserves. He explained it was to let me see the game from as many angles as possible.' This was the reason, Dalglish explained, that he had been playing up front recently, although Kenny didn't think he was sharp enough to be a regular striker, but he was prepared to defer to his manager.

Whatever his position, Dalglish's performances had now made him a contender for a regular first-team place.

Kilmarnock: Hunter, Kennedy (Grimsby Town), Whyte, Beattie, McGrory, McDonald, Cook, Queen (Crystal Palace), Stein (Rangers), Ingram (Ayr United), Johnston (Rangers)

Scorers: Stein (26), Ingram (57)

Celtic: Williams, Craig, Quinn, Murdoch, McNeill, Connelly, Wallace, Macari, Dalglish, Callaghan, Lennox

Scorers: Dalglish (21, 30, 55, 70, 85, 88), Murdoch (65)

Attendance: 8,727

7

Celtic 2-0 Rangers

14 August 1971, Scottish League Cup,
Ibrox Stadium

DURING A training match, when Kenny was still on the fringes of the first team, Jock Stein took him aside and told him off for playing square passes. He explained to the young Dalglish that those passes could be intercepted by an opponent, with no chance for the intended recipient of the ball to recover. Kenny listened to what Stein had to say and nodded. He understood. However, he soon repeated the mistake. Now Jock had a solution. He called Kenny over to the touchline and told him to go and play as sweeper. Playing in this position would soon make him more aware of what Stein meant.

Dalglish hadn't been singled out. All the youngsters coming through at Celtic would experience Stein coming over to correct little things he had noticed were wrong with their play. If they listened and learned it would improve their game and their chances of success.

In 1971/72 Celtic were drawn in group 4 of the League Cup with Rangers, Ayr United and Morton. The games were played on a home and away basis, with the group winner going forward to the quarter-finals.

Ahead of the first Old Firm derby of the season Jock Stein wasn't giving anything away to the press about his team selection. His excuse was that a few players had picked up knocks in a friendly game with Queen's Park at Lesser Hampden a few days earlier. Celtic fans wanted to hear if Kenny Dalglish was going to start, but they had to be patient.

Alex Cameron, the *Record*'s chief sports reporter, rated Dalglish as potentially the best Scottish centre-forward since Lawrie Reilly, who, as one of Hibs' Famous Five, had scored 22 goals in 38 Scotland internationals. Stein still wasn't sure if Dalglish should be building from midfield or leading the forward line, and the player told Cameron he liked scoring goals but knew any attention he got for doing that was only as a result of his team-mates' skills and effort.

Dalglish had scored three in the Drybrough Cup semi-final against St Johnstone at Firhill on 4 August but credited Harry Hood with doing all the work for the third, providing the cross for Dalglish to head home. He had also scored four against Dumbarton in the previous round, and had hit four, two of them penalties, in a pre-season friendly away to Limerick. 'My team-mates were laying them on a plate for me and I just couldn't miss,' he told *Shoot!* – Dalglish remained modest throughout his career, despite all his achievements.

Aberdeen beat Celtic 2-1 in the inaugural Drybrough Cup Final at Pittodrie on 7 August, but Celtic had the League Cup to concentrate on and, with Celtic Park undergoing repairs, their 'home' match against Rangers was switched to Ibrox. The match was all-ticket. It was the first time the clubs had met at Ibrox since the Ibrox Disaster in January of that year, when 66 fans lost their lives. Dalglish had attended that day with a ticket given to him by Celtic for the away end, opposite where the tragedy on the stairs happened.

On 14 August, Jimmy Johnstone began the game in midfield and was in the kind of form he was famed for, dribbling, jinking and passing his way around the Rangers defence. He scored the opening goal in the 67th minute, trapping the ball from a corner and flashing it into the Rangers net. Three minutes later, John Hughes went through into the Rangers penalty box only to be pulled down by goalkeeper Peter McCloy. The referee awarded a penalty. Captain Billy McNeill approached the young Dalglish and told him to take it. Dalglish was hesitant, but McNeill insisted that if he could take penalties for the reserves, he could take one here.

'"Aye," I said, "but there are more photographers behind that goal than fans who turn up for reserve games,"' Dalglish said to Celtic Quick News. 'Billy was insistent – and I learned that day he was a very difficult customer to argue with. Celtic had guys on the pitch such as Wee Jinky Johnstone, Bobby Murdoch, Big Yogi [John Hughes] and Bobby Lennox who were veterans of this fixture, but the Celtic captain chose to entrust me with the kick. What could I do?'

'I wanted to get a goal against his name for posterity,' McNeill said to the *Glasgow Herald* in 1995, 'but I certainly had no worries about him being too nervous.'

Dalglish stopped to tie the lace on his boot, then approached the ball. He had a read on McCloy and knew he favoured moving to his right when facing a right-footed kicker. Dalglish's intention was to put it to his left. Kenny sent the keeper, known as the Girvan Lighthouse, the wrong way and made the score 2-0. Kenny's dad, despite being a Rangers man, was delighted.

Even though he had grown up as a Rangers fan, dreaming of playing for them, Dalglish had no mixed feelings about scoring against the club. He told the *Daily Record* in 2020, 'When you later play against them and score, it makes it a wee bit more special.'

Later in the month, on the night Celtic opened their new stand at Celtic Park, Kenny would put a penalty past the post in a League Cup group game against Morton. Celtic lost 1-0.

Celtic were back at Ibrox on 28 August for their away League Cup game at Rangers. The first half was goalless, but three minutes after the restart Bobby Murdoch picked up the ball from Evan Williams's throw-out. He hooked the ball around defender Ronnie McKinnon. Dalglish was straight on to it. He ran on, gathered the ball and fired it past McCloy.

'Dalglish's intelligent positioning was always menacing,' Jim Parkinson wrote in the *Glasgow Herald*, 'and he distributed the ball excellently to Lennox, Macari and Johnstone.'

Celtic rounded off the League Cup section with a 4-1 win over Ayr United, Dalglish netting the third. It put Celtic in the quarter-final, where they would defeat Clydebank 11-2 on aggregate.

Celtic: Williams, Craig, Hay, Murdoch, McNeill, Connelly, Johnstone, Lennox, Dalglish, Callaghan, Hughes

Scorers: Johnstone (67), Dalglish (70 pen)

Rangers: McCloy, Jardine, Mathieson, Greig, McKinnon, Jackson, McLean, Conn, Johnstone, Johnston, MacDonald

Attendance: 72,500

8

Celtic 3-1 Dundee

*16 October 1971, Scottish First
Division, Celtic Park*

CELTIC'S LEAGUE season began with the league flag being unfurled by Lady Kelly, wife of Sir Robert, Celtic's chairman, at home to Clyde. Bobby Murdoch got the scoring started after six minutes. Two minutes later, Kenny scored the first league goal of his career. It was a swashbuckling performance by the Celts, as they overwhelmed the men from Shawfield, winning 9-1.

'I have come up against Celtic's firing power in all their great seasons,' Clyde's 37-year-old goalkeeper Tommy McCulloch told *The Scotsman*, 'but never have they been so impressive. There must have been about 20 shots which could have resulted in goals. They're better now than I've ever known them and I've played against them nearly 50 times in 14 years.'

Coincidentally in 1938 after the league flag had been unfurled, at that time by Celtic chairman Tom White's daughter, Celtic had also won 9-1, Kilmarnock being the side on the receiving end.

Within a month there was a third match at Ibrox against Rangers, this time in the league. Celtic were 2-1 down when ten minutes into the second half, Kenny hooked a ball sent in from the left to equalise. The winner came with five minutes remaining when Jimmy Johnstone scored.

September saw Kenny make his first European start. Unfortunately it was a match that Jock Stein called the worst game Celtic had played in Europe. They travelled to Copenhagen to take on Boldklubben 1903, who although champions of Denmark, were all part-time amateurs. Celtic came away with a 2-1 defeat, Lou Macari getting the goal. Johnstone was substituted at half-time. Celtic still went through, thanks to a 3-0 second leg victory, without Kenny in the team.

The Danes' goalkeeper Birger Jensen would keep goal for Club Brugge in the 1978 European Cup Final.

Tommy Docherty had recently taken over as Scotland manager, and after a 2-1 win over Portugal, he spoke to the press about hoping to bring in some youngsters. There was a lot of young Scottish talent around at the time, including Willie Young at Aberdeen, John Connolly at St Johnstone and Jim Steele of Dundee. He planned to watch Celtic for himself to run the rule over Kenny, George Connelly and Lou Macari.

Kenny wouldn't have been distracted by Docherty floating his name for Scotland, but he made sure he couldn't be ignored when he took to the field against Dundee.

Dundee's Gordon Wallace was the first player to have a shot, forcing a good save from Williams early on. Macari had two good chances that went past before Dalglish hit a free kick over the crossbar. Macari missed a great chance from inside the six-yard box, while at the other end, John Duncan lobbed the ball over the Celtic bar.

The first goal eventually came in the 36th minute when Murdoch fired a pass over the heads of the Dundee defence. Dalglish had time to pick his spot and score. With only seconds gone in the second half, Macari, the top scorer in Scotland at the time, dispossessed Jim Steele and then marauded down the left wing. He played the ball across for Dalglish to chip it past Mike Hewitt in the Dundee goal for 2-0.

Dundee came right back at Celtic, and Williams lurched backwards to tip a 25-yard shot from Phillip over the bar.

From the resultant corner, Lambie played the ball into the box for Duncan to send a diving header into the Celtic net.

Then, with only five minutes played in the second half, Murdoch crossed for Dalglish to head in for his hat-trick. Two minutes later, Celtic had a penalty. Tommy Gemmell took the kick, but Hewitt blocked it with his knee.

Dalglish told *Shoot!* that he wanted to ignore all the headlines as he was still learning his trade. He knew that he still had a journey ahead of him until he could be truly mentioned in the same class as the Celtic greats that he played alongside, such as Jimmy Johnstone, Bobby Murdoch and Billy McNeill. He acknowledged the help the senior pros had offered him and modestly said that without it he would still be playing reserve team football.

A week later, Kenny played in his first final for Celtic. On *Grandstand* on Saturday, 23 October, Sam Leitch, presenter of *Football Preview*, the section of the show which would later become *Football Focus*, closed the segment at 1.10pm with the words, 'In Scotland, it's League Cup Final day at Hampden Park, where Celtic meet Partick Thistle, who have no chance.'

Although he scored Celtic's only goal, Kenny was not to finish on the winning side as the Jags shocked the country by winning the match 4-1. Thistle came out playing a 4-2-4 formation, and with 37 minutes gone were 4-0 up. It was a miserable feeling to end up with a losers' medal for Kenny. He was wise enough to know then that finals might not come around every year, but the defeat just made him more determined to one day look down on a winners' medal in his hand.

At the end of October 1971, Celtic entered the transfer market and signed Dixie Deans from Motherwell for £18,000. Dixie, whose real first name was John, had the nickname Dixie due to almost sharing a surname with Everton's legendary striker Dixie Dean. Deans had begun his career in the junior ranks with Neilston before becoming a notable goalscorer with Motherwell. That £18,000 would be looked on as one of the best pieces of business Jock Stein ever did as Deans would become a big hit at Parkhead and form a formidable partnership with Dalglish.

Celtic: Williams, Hay, Gemmell, Murdoch, McNeill, Connelly, Johnstone, Hood, Dalglish, Callaghan, Macari

Scorer: Dalglish (35, 46, 51)

Dundee: Hewitt, R. Wilson, Johnston, Steele, Phillip, Houston, Duncan, Selway, Wallace, J. Scott [Kinninmonth], Lambie

Scorer: Duncan (47)

Attendance: 32,000

9

Scotland 1-0 Belgium

*10 November 1971, European
Championship qualifier,
Pittodrie Stadium*

IN FEBRUARY, Belgium beat Scotland 3-0 in Liège, thanks to a Ronnie McKinnon own goal and a Paul Van Himst brace. At the time, Bobby Brown was in charge of the Scottish side.

The return game was played at Pittodrie, the fifth occasion and first time since 1937 that Aberdeen's home ground had hosted a full international.

Belgium's boss Raymond Goethals complained that Pittodrie was smaller than Hampden which would have the effect of the crowd almost being on top of the players. Goethals would have preferred 70,000 Scots in the bigger terraces of Hampden than half that number in closer proximity to his players. However, his Belgian side had played Scotland in Liège rather than the larger Heysel Stadium in Brussels. The fact that three Aberdeen players were in the starting line-up also caused concern for him.

One of those players, Steve Murray, who was making his international debut that night, would later become a team-mate of Kenny's at Celtic.

Belgium only needed a draw to be sure of qualifying for the 1972 European Championship quarter-final. Scotland had begun their campaign with a 1-0 win over Denmark in November 1970, before that 3-0 loss to the Belgians. Portugal had won 2-0 in Lisbon, while in Copenhagen in

60

June 1971, the Danes had gained revenge with a 1-0 win. Qualification from group 5, where only the winner went through, was impossible for Scotland.

Tommy Docherty took over as Scotland's boss in September 1971 in a part-time role on a two-game trial basis. Docherty, who had begun 1971 in charge of Oporto, was still working as assistant manager at Hull City. 'I know Scotland cannot qualify,' Docherty said on his appointment, 'but in the next two matches, I want to find something for the future. When I've been looking about in Scotland I've seen some cracking youngsters, and that's where our soccer future lies.'

Of Kenny, he said, 'I haven't been able to see Kenny Dalglish of Celtic, but I know he's good. I saw him as a kid, but I haven't seen him in Celtic's first team, although anyone who gets goals as he does, must be worth considering.'

Docherty's first match in charge was a 2-1 win over Portugal. John O'Hare and Archie Gemmill got the goals in a game where Docherty handed out three new caps to Arsenal goalkeeper Bob Wilson, his club-mate George Graham and Alex Cropley of Hibs.

Docherty was as far from a 'yes man' as football could get, and when he took over, he let the SFA know that he would be doing things his way. The selection committee was due to meet after the Belgium game to decide whether Docherty would become the permanent team manager.

When Docherty named his squad for that match, Dalglish was handed his first full international call-up. He wasn't the only one. Alan Rough of Partick Thistle, Aberdeen's Steve Murray and Jim Steele of Dundee were also included. 'I could have played safe and picked men like Frank McLintock, Denis Law or Charlie Cooke. But what would that prove?' Docherty told the press when he was asked why he had called up so many youngsters. He later called in Thistle's John Hansen and Aberdeen's 18-year-old Willie Young.

Dalglish was in Malta with Celtic, who were due to play Sliema Wanderers in the European Cup. He was lounging by the pool when Jock Stein walked up to tell him he was in his first Scotland squad. A delighted Dalglish hadn't expected the call-up, but he was ready for it.

Docherty was intent on taking the game to the Belgians. Scotland lined up in a 4-3-3 formation. Eddie Gray and Jimmy Johnstone would be on opposite wings, with instructions to cause problems for the Belgian full-backs.

Scotland went ahead in only five minutes. Gray shifted the play from the right to the left with a cross-field ball for Johnstone. There looked to be nothing on, but he effortlessly weaved his way around the Belgian defence to get down to the byline and send a cross for John O'Hare to head in off the post.

Van Himst, of Anderlecht, who had caused Scotland problems in Liège, was effectively shackled by Sandy Jardine, while Gray found space to operate in midfield.

Alex Cropley had picked up a knock shortly before half-time, and with three minutes played in the second half, Docherty decided to withdraw him and hand Kenny his international debut.

Dalglish brought new attacking vigour to Scotland's performance, providing linking passes for Murray and Johnstone. Dalglish had a shot on goal that flashed narrowly wide, and he put Johnstone in for a shot that landed on top of the crossbar.

With 11 minutes remaining, Johnstone made way for Partick's Hansen, who was also making his debut. 'I couldn't get off the bench quick enough,' Hansen said. His younger brother Alan would go on to become an important figure in Kenny's career.

The Aberdeen crowd played the part they were asked to play by making a lot of noise. 'Above all there was the skill and attacking panache and the cheekiness that is expected from a Scotland team,' John Rafferty wrote in *The Scotsman*. 'It was good to see, and that Belgian team, who had so humiliated Scotland in Liège were run into the ground and defeated more decisively than the score would suggest.'

Years later Dalglish would say he couldn't recall much about the match other than the memory that Johnstone entertained the crowd with an outstanding performance. He said the chance to fulfil his dream of playing for Scotland had come much sooner than he anticipated, but his nerves left him once he got into the game. He praised Docherty for making the team feel like world-beaters.

The manager looked back on Dalglish's first cap in an interview for *The Times* in 2019: 'Everyone told me he was too young to play at that level but he went on to do all right.' Docherty also insisted, when asked in 1997 by the *Daily Mirror*, it was not a risk to cap Dalglish, 'No, a golden player – as near as you get to being the most dedicated ever.'

Surprisingly, Kenny was unsure if he had won a Scotland cap or not, asking *Daily Record* journalist Ken Gallacher if his appearance counted, because he had been a substitute.

Dalglish was selected for his first Scotland start in an Amsterdam friendly against the Netherlands the following month. Docherty earned much praise from the media for starting with Dalglish, but insisted it wasn't a courageous decision – Kenny was a terrific player. Docherty's only problem was similar to Jock Stein's – working out what Dalglish's best position was. 'He plays so well in midfield – like John White with strength – and up front he has this terrible disease: he just keeps scoring goals.'

It wasn't the first time Kenny had been compared to the late John White. The Spurs winger, who was tragically killed by lightning at the age of 27 in 1964, was turned down by clubs, including Middlesbrough and Rangers, when he was young, as he was considered too slight. White went on to play for Alloa, Falkirk and Tottenham, where he won the 1961

Double and the European Cup Winners' Cup. His gift for finding space on the pitch led to his nickname, the Ghost, and but for his tragic death, he would surely have added many more to his 22 Scotland caps.

'I have always believed in giving young players a chance,' Docherty continued, 'and I'm certain that Kenny will do a job for me. Let's face it, once he gets inside that box he is deadly.'

Dalglish earned the first four of his 102 caps for Scotland under Docherty. His third came as a substitute away to Denmark in October 1972, and then he was on from the start in the November return at Hampden.

'For shielding the ball, scoring from seemingly impossible angles and creating chances for others, Kenny Dalglish had no equal,' Docherty wrote in his 2006 autobiography. 'Even at this stage of what was to be a much-garlanded career, he was superb at making space in the penalty area and laying the ball off. His finishing was clinical, and he always appeared to have so much time to do things … Kenny was a master of the footballing arts.'

Dalglish netted his first goal for Scotland in that match against Denmark. It came from a Peter Lorimer corner, which was turned back along the byline by Eddie Colquhoun for George Graham to play low across goal and Kenny to fire home.

In December 1972, Docherty left the Scotland job to join Manchester United. Dalglish reflected on the Doc's short tenure, writing in his *Soccer Annual*, 'He livened up the whole [Scottish international] scene. The press and the public became more interested, the players reacted to his demanding, urgent ways and it seemed as if international football was tailor-made for him. The Doc switched our tactics according to the opposition. One match we played man-to-man marking, another we played with two wingers and ran teams ragged. He never allowed the dust to settle.'

'I had just one fall-out with him and it tells you something about Kenny's attitude,' Docherty said in 1986. 'I left him out of an under-23 match once. He was just coming on to the international scene, and I had him on the bench as a reserve. He didn't like that. Not because he was worried from an egotistical point of view. No, it was simply that he wasn't going to be playing. He lives for playing the game. That's all he wants to do.'

Scotland: Clark (Aberdeen), Jardine (Rangers), Hay (Celtic), Bremner (c) (Leeds United), Buchan (Aberdeen), Stanton (Hibernian), Johnstone (Celtic) [J. Hansen (Partick Thistle)], Murray (Aberdeen), O'Hare (Derby County), E. Gray (Leeds United), Cropley (Hibernian) [Dalglish (Celtic)]

Scorer: O'Hare (5)

Belgium: Piot (Standard Liège), Stassart (Royal Racing White), Georges Heylens (Anderlecht), Dewalque (Standard Liège), Dolmans (Standard Liège), Van Moer (Standard Liège) [Martens (Royal Racing White)], Van Den Daele (RFC Brugeois), Van Himst (c) (Anderlecht), Semmeling (Standard Liège), Devrindt (PSV Eindhoven), Puis (RFC Brugeois) [Lambert (RFC Brugeois)]

Attendance: 36,500

10

England Under-23 2-2 Scotland Under-23

16 February 1972, under-23 international friendly, Baseball Ground

SCOTLAND MANAGER Tommy Docherty used his Doc's Talk column in the *Daily Record* to sing Dalglish's praises, advising any English club manager with £250,000 to spend – not much more than the record £220,000 which had just been paid by Arsenal for World Cup winner Alan Ball – to buy Dalglish. 'I rate young Kenny a better buy at that.'

Docherty noted one trait that stood out was Dalglish's unselfishness. Kenny, Docherty said, was a player whose movement and use of the ball was designed to benefit the team, and didn't play to earn glory for himself.

Despite selecting Kenny for the Scotland Under-23 squad for games against Wales and England, Docherty was keen to emphasise that he would be part of the main squad set-up and central to the 1974 World Cup qualifying campaign.

Kenny had been part of the under-23 squad in 1970, but was left on the bench. However, the experience of being involved was instrumental in his development. Speaking to the Official Scotland Podcast in 2024, he recalled, 'I still had spots on my face, so I was only very young coming in. John Blackley was there with Erich Schaedler from Hibs. And they almost babysat us … I was rooming with him and he really made us feel welcome.'

Dalglish made his under-23s debut in the 2-0 win over Wales at Pittodrie in January 1972. The press criticised his first-half passing, but the second half, with a tactical change from 4-2-4 to 4-3-3, was more like Dalglish's usual form, and he set up Sandy Jardine's first goal. Partick Thistle's Dennis McQuade added a second.

Derby County's home, the Baseball Ground, was ankle deep in mud as the young Scots took on their English counterparts in February. Docherty described the pitch as 'Not fit for horses.'

'You couldn't pass the ball on it, or even kick it more than a few yards,' said Liverpool manager Bill Shankly, one of several English First Division bosses who were in attendance.

Thirty-six hours of continuous rain had fallen on the pitch in the lead-up to the match. It was heavy and stamina-sapping for all concerned, although the Scottish press believed it was more advantageous for the 'more powerful' Englishmen.

Kevin Keegan, making his under-23 debut, performed on the right wing for England, which was a change from the free-roaming role he had at Liverpool. The English had the best of the early exchanges. However, Aberdeen's Martin Buchan and Celtic's George Connelly began to develop a grip on the game. Connelly shackled Malcolm Macdonald well and managed to still play as elegantly in the mud as he did for his club on better surfaces.

Scotland went in front when a short pass from Jimmy Bone set Kenny up to stroke the ball home in the 38th minute.

It only took England a minute to strike back when Mick Channon got his head on to a cross into the box.

In the second half, just as England had reverted to a defensive formation, they took the lead. Hunter and Brownlie got into some confusion, and Channon nipped in to make it 2-1 to England.

Dalglish's second goal and Scotland's equaliser came on 62 minutes after Lou Macari played him in.

'They all deserve great credit,' England's boss Alf Ramsey said. 'They refused to submit to the pitch and gave us a tremendous game. The teamwork of the Scots was good on the difficult pitch and I had to change my tactics because of this.'

Dalglish was picked out as the best attacker in the game by Hugh Taylor in the *Daily Record*. He stood out not just because of his brace, but also his passing and running on the atrocious pitch, maintaining his usual high work rate and moving the ball well.

The *Birmingham Daily Post* reporter wrote, 'For Scotland, Kenny Dalglish was outstanding. The 20-year-old Celtic striker scored both Scotland's goals and his coolness in attack accounted for most of England's unhappy moments.'

'His enthusiasm for the game is almost unbelievable,' Docherty said. 'I think he is one of those very rare breed of players who would play for nothing.'

It was a performance that made English managers sit up and take notice, although his team-mates Buchan, Connelly and Macari had a few English bosses salivating too.

England: Parkes (Queen's Park Rangers), Mills (Ipswich Town), Robson (Derby County), Hudson (Chelsea), Booth (Manchester City), Blockley (Coventry City), Keegan (Liverpool), Channon (Southampton), Macdonald (Newcastle United), Currie (Sheffield United), Thomas (Burnley)

Scorer: Channon (39, 68)

Scotland: Hunter (Kilmarnock), Brownlie (Hibernian), Donachie (Manchester City), Jardine (Rangers), Connelly (Celtic), Buchan (Aberdeen), Carr (Coventry City), Dalglish (Celtic), Macari (Celtic), Bone (Partick Thistle), Hartford (West Bromwich Albion)

Scorer: Dalglish (38, 72)

Attendance: 18,176

11

Celtic 0-0 Inter Milan (aet, Inter Milan won 5-4 on penalties)

19 April 1972, European Cup semi-final second leg, Celtic Park

THE KENNY Dalglish–Dixie Deans era at Celtic got off to a goalscoring start with Partick Thistle being defeated 5-1 at Firhill in November 1971. The first two goals came from corners by Harry Hood.

He sent in a low bending corner that went through a forest of legs and straight into the net, and for the second goal, when Hood's corner came in, Billy McNeill made like he was going for the ball. With defenders trailing the Celtic captain, who had scored so many memorable headers from corners, he ran past the ball, leaving Jimmy Johnstone free to head in.

Lou Macari set up Dalglish to smash the ball into the roof of the net for goal number three. Thistle pulled one back before an own goal made it four. With four minutes remaining, Dixie Deans scored his first goal for Celtic.

Kilmarnock were beaten 5-1 in December, with Kenny scoring twice and Deans netting once. Later that month, it was the same again as Motherwell were beaten 5-1, with Deans opening the scoring and Dalglish notching a brace.

On Christmas Day, Celtic beat Hearts 3-2 with Deans scoring the winner. It would turn out to be the final time Celtic played a match on Christmas Day. On the same day, the *Evening Times* announced Kenny as their Player of the

Year, saying Dalglish was the unanimous choice, with Sandy Jardine as the runner-up and Partick Thistle's strikers Frank Coulston, who was a PE teacher by day, and Jimmy Bone as joint third.

Dalglish was modest in accepting the award, saying that it was easy to play so well when he was surrounded by players who made it easy for him, as everyone in the Celtic team worked for each other. Blair noted that Dalglish had the temperament to achieve what by now the Scottish football world were expecting of him.

Clyde were on the receiving end of another battering on New Year's Day 1972. Deans hit two and Dalglish one in a 7-0 win at Shawfield. That win was followed up by a 2-1 victory over Rangers, Jim Brogan scoring the winner in injury time.

For a side famous for their *catenaccio* defence, Inter Milan's 1971/72 European Cup campaign saw a surprising amount of goals. Inter beat AEK Athens 6-4 on aggregate in the first round. In the second round, they met Borussia Mönchengladbach and in the first leg the Italians were defeated 7-1, as Inter striker Roberto Boninsegna was knocked out by a beer can thrown from the crowd. UEFA had the result annulled and Inter won what should have been the second leg 4-2 in the San Siro, before drawing 0-0 in the replayed match in Berne. In the quarter-final Inter met Standard Liège. An 80th-minute goal from Jair gave them a 1-0 win at home in the first leg and they lost 2-1 in Belgium, but went through to the semi on away goals.

'[Kenny] and I had already formed a pretty good double act up front,' Deans wrote in his 2011 autobiography. 'So as the semi against Inter loomed, we were in pretty good nick. The Italians though represented a major step up in class from the other sides we had met.'

Celtic had defeated Boldklubben 1903 of Denmark 4-2 on aggregate in the first round and Sliema Wanderers 5-0 at

Celtic Park and 2-1 in Malta in the second round. Celtic had much tougher opposition in the quarter-finals, where they were drawn against Hungary's Újpesti Dózsa, who had got past Valencia. In the Budapest first leg, the Celts came away with a magnificent 2-1 win. Lou Macari's goal was enough to claim a 1-1 draw in the second leg and take Celtic into their third European Cup semi-final.

They were drawn with Inter Milan, while in the other semi, holders Ajax took on Benfica. Celtic had to travel to Milan for the first leg. Inter refused to allow Celtic to train on the San Siro pitch, but Stein took that in his stride and had the players test the ground without kicking a ball, which he said was his intention all along.

It was a heroic performance from Celtic as they came away with a goalless draw – in particular, George Connelly and Lou Macari stood out. Teenager Pat McCluskey came on for only his third first-team appearance when Jim Brogan had to go off injured, and gave a flawless performance. 'There is only one word for that: magnificent!' Stein said.

Stein gained much praise from the press for the way that he brought his young players through, as the likes of Dalglish, Connelly, McGrain, Macari and McCluskey were now playing with composure and authority. Several of the Lisbon Lions had moved on, and the mood was that there was a great group of young players, coupled with some astute signings that could continue Celtic's legacy.

Dalglish himself said he 'couldn't have asked for anyone better' than Stein to bring him through, when he reflected on those early days in the *Daily Record* in 2021. 'He never let any player get carried away and, if anyone showed the slightest bit of that, Jock would knock you right down. And not in a too polite way.'

Between the first leg and the second leg, Celtic twice beat Kilmarnock 3-1, first in the league and then in the Scottish Cup semi-final. On the Saturday before the second leg, Celtic travelled to Bayview, where a 3-0 win over East Fife saw them claim their seventh title in a row. Dixie Deans with a brace and Harry Hood were the scorers.

Stein took his team down to Seamill in Ayrshire to prepare for the European match. Dalglish, Macari and Deans spent much of the time shooting in at Evan Williams as Stein looked for his strikers to be on form. He said that although he was aware the Italian side would probably look to nick a goal on the counter-attack like AC Milan did against Celtic in 1969, his focus was on Celtic scoring: 'We won't be lax in defence but we feel we can go out and look for goals as our principal aim.'

Inter's boss Gianni Invernizzi told the *Evening Times* he'd be happy to get a goal on the break and aim for a 1-1 draw, to go through to the final on away goals.

On a remarkable night in Glasgow, Rangers were also at home, playing Bayern Munich in the European Cup Winners' Cup semi-final. Their game kicked off at 7.30pm, while the match at Celtic Park got underway half an hour later.

From kick-off, Dalglish shot past the post. Jimmy Johnstone too came close a moment later. Celtic did what Stein had asked of them and were going all out for goal. With Inter content to play for the draw it allowed Jim Craig to make several overlapping runs and twice he had long-range drives saved by Inter's keeper Lido Vieri. Johnstone went out on the left, pulling Giacinto Facchetti with him.

With half an hour gone Williams in the Celtic goal hadn't had a save to make. But despite Celtic hammering the Inter goal they couldn't find a breakthrough. Inter with nine men back defending had a couple of breakaways but first Gabriele Oriali and then Sandro Mazzola put shots wide.

Just after the hour mark, Dalglish came off to be replaced by Dixie Deans for his European debut. It would be a night he'd rather forget. The 90 minutes ended goalless, 30 minutes of extra time couldn't produce a winner and it was then down to a penalty shoot-out.

Celtic had been integral to UEFA's decision to introduce penalty shoot-outs. After their tie with Benfica in the 1970 European Cup, which finished 3-3 on aggregate, the winner was decided by tossing a coin. Neither club thought it was a fair ending. As winners, Celtic suggested the rules were changed and at UEFA's meeting on the day of the 1970 European Cup Final, the decision was made to settle European ties that were still level after extra time with a penalty shoot-out. 'Penalty kicks are a part of the game,' Stein said at the time. 'There is skill involved in taking penalty kicks, and surely it is better to have skills winning than sheer luck. As a club, we welcome this.'

The first shoot-out in European competition came on 30 September 1970 when Budapest Honvéd beat Aberdeen 5-4 in the European Cup Winners' Cup first round.

Against Celtic, Inter were first to take a kick. Mazzola stepped up and put the Italians in front. Deans went first for Celtic. He aimed for the top left-hand corner, but put the ball over. Facchetti, Frustalupi and Pelissario scored for Inter while Craig, Johnstone and McCluskey were all successful for Celtic. The Brazilian Jair took Inter's fifth kick and put the ball to Williams's right. The Celtic keeper didn't move and the Scots were out.

Deans's miss was highlighted all the more due to it being one of the early high-profile penalty shoot-outs. The rules were so unfamiliar that when Inter went 5-3 ahead, and Celtic could no longer win, Bobby Murdoch still took their fifth penalty kick.

Stein said afterwards, 'There's no question about blaming Dixie. We'd been cracking penalty kicks home all week in practice. When the crunch comes, that's another matter.' Stein said Deans never missed a kick at Seamill, so his lack of European experience was of no concern. 'The reason

Deans took the first penalty is because he was the top man at penalties.'

In *The Guardian*, Paul Wilcox wrote that a penalty shoot-out wasn't a satisfactory way of deciding a finalist for a major European competition, advocating a play-off instead. Stein, who perhaps had forgotten how he welcomed the introduction of shoot-outs, was similarly minded, saying that Celtic had lost on 'a circus act'.

'It will be a lesson to our youngsters,' Stein said. 'Now they know you don't just step into the big time and everything goes for you. It will make them better next year.' It was painful for Kenny to have got so close to a European Cup Final, but Celtic would get another chance.

They shook off the disappointment to return to domestic competition. Motherwell were next at Celtic Park and the fans were vocal in their encouragement, particularly for Deans, who appreciated the reception he received.

Celtic won 5-2, with Bobby Murdoch scoring two penalties, despite the fans shouting for Deans to take both.

The Scottish Cup Final was the next big date on the Celtic calendar. Kenny didn't get on the scoresheet but Celtic ran riot, beating Hibs 6-1, with Deans scoring a hat-trick – the first in a Scottish Cup Final since Jimmy Quinn scored three in Celtic's 3-2 win over Rangers in 1904. It was also the first time a team had scored six in a Scottish Cup Final since Renton beat Cambuslang 6-1 in 1888. At the time of writing no club has done it since.

'Goalscoring was a trend at the club at the time,' Lou Macari told *The Scotsman* in 2001. 'We went in realising that Hibs were a good side, and it was a shock to us to get so many goals. No one sets out to rub things in, you just want to get on the scoresheet in the cup final.'

Dalglish and Deans were the only two players in the Celtic team who were winning their first Scottish Cup medals.

Celtic: Williams, Craig, McCluskey, Murdoch, McNeill, Connelly, Johnstone, Dalglish [Deans], Macari, Callaghan, Lennox

Inter Milan: Vieri, Bellugi, Facchetti, Oriali, Giubertoni, Burgnich, Jair, Bedin, Bertini, Mazzola, Frustalupi

Attendance: 75,124

12

Hibernian 0-3 Celtic,

28 April 1973, Scottish First Division,
Easter Road

IT HADN'T been an easy season for Celtic in 1972/73. In the European Cup Rosenborg had been beaten in the first round, then in the second Celtic were drawn against Újpesti Dózsa who they had played only six months previously in 1971/72's quarter-final.

Kenny scored a double in a 2-0 win at Celtic Park, a game where Celtic were relentless in attack. In the second leg, Celtic were 3-0 down by half-time. Despite Dalglish and McNeill coming close late on, they couldn't get the goal that would have taken them through.

At the end of December, Jock Stein suffered from a heart complaint which put him in hospital for ten days and kept him away from the club for over two weeks. A flu outbreak swept the country, which saw several Celtic players fall ill and led to the postponement of a game with Kilmarnock and the New Year's Day game with Morton. The first game of 1973 was the last-minute 2-1 defeat to Rangers.

Dalglish scored in wins over Dundee and Ayr United, the latter in a snowstorm. However, a defeat to bottom-of-the-league Airdrie allowed Rangers to close the gap, and concerns were raised over Celtic's ability to lift the title for an eighth successive time.

The *Glasgow Herald* reported that 'Kenny Dalglish, who not only looks like a choir boy but who is also one of the quietest fellows off the field, started to argue angrily with Danny McGrain about a particular pass.' The report also noted that several Celtic players 'took the defeat badly'. Jimmy Johnstone and Billy McNeill were both involved in skirmishes with Airdrie players and staff.

In February, Kenny had the chance to score Celtic's 6,000th league goal. Leading Kilmarnock 4-0 at Rugby Park, Jimmy Johnstone was pulled down, and a penalty was awarded. Dalglish, looking for a hat-trick, stepped up but cracked his kick off the crossbar. Bobby Murdoch hit the landmark goal a few days later in a 1-1 draw with Partick Thistle.

The Celts followed that up by dropping their sixth league point in seven weeks with a shock 2-2 draw away to East Fife. Kenny missed another penalty kick, following on from Harry Hood missing an earlier one, which had been retaken after Bobby Murdoch had missed. Kenny, though, was on the scoresheet in a 2-0 win over St Johnstone.

Dalglish's abilities were being recognised all across the country. 'This boy could be the find of the seventies,' wrote Tottenham and Scotland striker Alan Gilzean in *Book of Soccer No 15*, 'although I know they slap that tag on a lot of players – far too many in my opinion, and when they are far too young – Dalglish might just prove the exception. Why? Because this lad is such an alert striker and shows skills of a maturity beyond his years. Apart from his uncanny ability to outwit a defence, Dalglish has an explosive left foot and rarely misses a scoring chance. He's so sharp up front, and he can create chances by taking on defenders and beating them with his speed and skilful ball control.'

In March, Dalglish scored the first goal with a header in a 2-1 Scotland Under-23s win over Wales in Swansea in front of only a few hundred fans. In the league, he joined Bobby Lennox on the scoresheet in a 2-0 win over Aberdeen.

'Kenny Dalglish was a great all-rounder who could both create and score goals,' Lennox wrote in his

2007 autobiography. 'It was always a treat to play alongside him.'

The rescheduled game with Morton was won 1-0, but Rangers drew level on points at the top when Celtic drew 2-2 with Dundee United.

Wins against Hearts, Falkirk, Motherwell, St Johnstone, Dumbarton and Arbroath kept Celtic out in front on goal difference. Deans hit a hat-trick against Dumbarton and revealed he and Kenny had a £10 bet with each other over who would get the most goals in the season. Dalglish was on 34 with Deans behind on 30.

On the day that Celtic beat Arbroath, Rangers drew with Aberdeen at Pittodrie, which gave the Celts the breathing space required going into the last game.

On the last day of the league season, Celtic travelled to Edinburgh to take on Hibernian. Celtic needed only to draw to win their eighth league title in a row. Rangers had to beat East Fife and hope Celtic lost to wrest the title from them. The Ibrox club hadn't lost a league game since December and had only dropped two points – both draws with Aberdeen – since.

Hibs and Celtic had nervous openings, but Hibs almost went in front when Erich Schaedler's throw-in came off the back of McNeill's head and only just went over the bar.

With 21 minutes gone at Ibrox, Rangers were 1-0 up on East Fife after Quinton Young scored. But it wouldn't matter as Celtic were in the lead at Easter Road only a minute later when, after Callaghan had a shot blocked, the ball fell into the path of Dixie Deans, who fired home.

In the 71st minute, Dalglish was on hand when Hibs keeper Jim McArthur and defender Des Bremner collided. Kenny hammered the loose ball into the empty net to make it 2-0.

'Kenny always had incredible initiative,' Danny McGrain told the *Glasgow Times* in 2016. 'At 17 or 18 he had this incredible ability to get on the pass and how to get off a pass. He always seemed to have five options open to him. I copied that. My thinking was that if you gave yourself so many options and couldn't take one then you weren't much of a player.

'I knew where he would be when I got the ball and he knew where I was going to put the ball. It was never the case of me passing into space; I knew Kenny would be there.'

The title was wrapped up when Deans headed in a Davie Hay cross with ten minutes remaining.

As the final whistle neared, photographers crowded around the away dugout, keen to capture a picture of Jock Stein in triumph. However, Stein stuck to a philosophy he had adopted throughout his career: keep your dignity. There would be no punching the air or gesturing to fans or opposition from Stein. When the whistle sounded, the Celtic boss rose from his seat as simply as if his stop on the bus had arrived. He calmly walked over to shake the hand of Hibs manager Eddie Turnbull before departing down the tunnel.

Stein stood at the tunnel's entrance as his name rang around the ground, and his team walked the perimeter of the Easter Road pitch to take in the fans' acclaim. The crowd was recorded as 45,446, but it was estimated around 40,000 were Celtic fans.

In his 2006 autobiography Turnbull wrote that in his time as manager of Hibernian the player he feared the most was Kenny. 'He had it all, and you could never relax when he was on the ball.' Turnbull said that years later when he was helping out Jock Stein when the latter was Scotland manager, he discovered Dalglish had a secret fuel. 'We were in the team hotel late at night when Kenny wanted to go out,' wrote Turnbull. 'This was very surprising, because Kenny was a model professional who never gave any trouble. "It's OK," said Jock, who was always strict about players observing curfews, "he's just popping out for a fish supper." And the next day he played a blinder.'

Celtic and Rangers met again in the Scottish Cup Final, Dalglish opened the scoring, but Celtic fell to a 3-2 defeat in front of 122,714 fans.

Celtic's league dominance was unparalleled in Scotland. Of the legendary teams in Scottish football, the Hibs Famous Five side had won only two league championships in a row. The great Rangers teams of between the wars won five successive championships. Unlike them, Celtic had completed this run in an era when domestic success meant European competition, foreign travel and more midweek games. There were also the League Cup sectional matches that congested the fixture schedule.

Dalglish played 49 games during the campaign. He scored 41 times, and his strike partner Deans hit the net 33 times. The club came close to a Treble that season but lost in both domestic cup finals, to Hibs in the League Cup and Rangers in the Scottish Cup.

Kenny's reputation had now spread over the country. In *Shoot!* Rangers legend Jim Baxter, then a few years into retirement, said, 'Kenny Dalglish has got the lot. He's fast, direct, takes up good positions and has a deadly shot. I reckon the best of him is yet to come.' He wasn't wrong.

Hibernian: McArthur, Bremner, Schaedler, Stanton [Smith], Black, Spalding, Edwards, O'Rourke, Gordon, Cropley, Duncan

Celtic: Hunter, McGrain, Brogan, Murdoch, McNeill, Connelly, Johnstone, Deans, Dalglish, Hay, Callaghan

Scorers: Deans (22, 80), Dalglish (71)

Attendance: 45,446

13

Celtic 0-0 Atletico Madrid

*10 April 1974, European Cup semi-
final, first leg, Celtic Park*

IN THE 1973/74 league season, Celtic had dished out a few
thrashings. Clyde were beaten 5-0, Partick Thistle, with
Alan Rough in goal were beaten 7-0, Dixie Deans netting
six.

On 22 December Falkirk were beaten 6-0 with Deans
scoring four and Dalglish netting once. Deans, Dalglish and
Harry Hood scored a brace each when Dunfermline were
hammered 6-0 on 29 December.

Hood scored a hat-trick in the League Cup semi-final
win over Rangers, but Celtic suffered a shock defeat in the
League Cup Final when they were beaten 1-0 by Dundee.

In the European Cup, Celtic had beaten TPS Turku
of Finland 9-1 on aggregate in the first round. Vejle BK
of Denmark were the opposition in the second round.
It was something of a shock when they held Celtic to a
goalless draw at Parkhead in the first leg. Bobby Lennox
netted the only goal in the second leg to put Celtic into the
quarter-final.

Basel were the opposition in the last eight with the
first leg in Switzerland. Paul Wilson opened the scoring
but Ottmar Hitzfeld, who would later win the Champions
League as manager of both Borussia Dortmund and Bayern
Munich, scored twice as Basel won 3-2. Kenny scored Celtic's
second and in doing so he hit Celtic's 100th goal in the
European Cup.

In the second leg Dalglish and Deans scored within the first 18 minutes, but the Swiss champions made it 2-2 by half-time. Tommy Callaghan made it 3-2 to Celtic and the game went to extra time. Stevie Murray headed in Celtic's winner in the first period.

In the other quarter-final Red Star Belgrade had pounded Atletico Madrid but were beaten by two breakaway goals.

'This is the leg that's vital for us,' Stein said on the eve of the match. 'If we get a result at Parkhead we can start making plans for the final. If we don't we can forget all about the final in Brussels.

'What we fear most are stoppages. We don't want to be held up, don't want our free flow to be halted by fussy referees. We want to keep play moving so it would be stupid of us to try to be too physical.'

In his preview for the game, in the *Daily Record* Alex Cameron focused on the 44-year-old Istanbul businessman Dogan Babacan, who was the referee. Cameron called for him to be firm, but not to upset the rhythm of play. While noting he had been in charge of several internationals, Cameron suggested that Turkish football didn't have the white-hot atmosphere as would be in evidence at Parkhead – that may well have changed in subsequent decades – but Babacan should have the experience of dealing with temperamental players.

'I'm looking forward, as all our players are, to a great game of football, with no overtones of violence,' said Stein.

The Atletico manager was Juan Carlos Lorenzo, who had taken his FA coaching badge in England. Lorenzo was no stranger to controversy. He had been in charge of Argentina's 1966 World Cup team, which England's boss Alf Ramsey famously branded as 'animals'. Lorenzo also managed Lazio, whose players were involved in a brawl in the streets with Arsenal players after a banquet on the night of their Fairs Cup tie in Rome in September 1970. During the fracas, which reportedly lasted 15 minutes, Lorenzo lifted Arsenal manager Bertie Mee off the ground by his lapels. 'He would have a hard job treating me that way,' Jock Stein said when told the story.

Stein put out the same team that had beaten Dundee 1-0 in the Scottish Cup semi-final a week earlier.

Early in the first half Pat McCluskey took the ball out of defence. Crossing the halfway line, he played a long ball into Dalglish who in plenty of space cracked a right-foot shot just wide from the edge of the box.

Shortly after Harry Hood went down in an apparent off-the-ball incident, the first booking came when Ruben Ayala assaulted goalkeeper Denis Connaghan after the keeper picked up the ball. Ayala held his hands behind his back like a child being caught stealing sweets.

As Celtic cleared an attack, the ball was played to Kenny just outside his own penalty box. As he ran forward, he was taken out by a combination of Ramon Heredia and Ruben Diaz, number 3 Diaz getting the most on him. The free kick was played to Johnstone, and just as commentator Brian Moore was saying, 'The referee must get on top of that kind of challenge,' Diaz wrapped his studs around Johnstone's legs, sending the Celtic winger into the air. The Argentinian held up his right hand in an apologetic driving-wave motion. After a moment, Diaz, his hands behind his back, the apparent international gesture of innocence, was shown the yellow card.

Diaz and Celtic had history. The Argentinian international had been part of the Racing Club side that waged war with Celtic in the 1967 Intercontinental Cup Final. Diaz and Iselin Santos Ovejero had also been involved in a training ground punch-up, captured by *Daily Record* photographer Eric Craig that caused them both to be sent back to their rooms at the Normandy Hotel in Renfrew the day before the game.

Dalglish was next for the treatment when, with his back to goal 20 yards out, he was kicked from behind by Ovejero. 'There is some really brutal tackling going on out there which has no part in football,' Brian Moore said, 'no matter how great the tension is.'

As Atletico cleared their lines, right-winger Tommy Callaghan propelled the ball into the air, dropping it into the box where Hood and Dalglish chased it. Hood seemed to connect with the ball just as it reached the byline and cut it back to Kenny, who tapped it in on the goal line. Parkhead went mad, but only for a moment, as the referee ruled that the ball had gone out of play.

Dalglish took Javier Irureta to the cleaners in midfield as the number 10 attempted to slide in on him. Soon though Celtic players were getting involved in rough-house tactics as Jim Brogan went looking for Ayala and took his legs away from him, earning what appeared to be a justifiable booking, however afterwards match assessor Arthur McMullan said Brogan was warned by the referee but not cautioned.

Diaz was allowed another cynical foul on Johnstone, sneakily punching his stomach as he tripped him. It wasn't long before the game cranked up a notch. Despite knowing that he was bound to be assaulted, it didn't stop Johnstone running at defenders. He made straight for Diaz with the ball, and as he jinked past him, Diaz threw a right boot out which felled the winger. Hood body-checked the Argentine as he fell. Diaz now had made at least four challenges worthy of a caution, even in these carefree days of the 1970s, yet he remained, for the moment, on the pitch.

Jock Stein's only criticism of the referee was that 'he showed respect of the fixture as a European Cup semi-final by not ordering players off the park early in the game'.

At half-time Stein said all thoughts of winning the game had disappeared. He was only concerned about how long his players could endure the vicious tackling they were subject to.

The Celtic fans marked the start of the second half with a rendition of 'You'll Never Walk Alone'. The first chance of the half fell to Kenny, whose header was saved by Miguel Reina, whose son Pepe would, many years later, keep goal at Liverpool under Dalglish's management.

Callaghan played a short free kick to Johnstone, who once again fearlessly weaved his way into the Atletico defence. He stood up to two bites on the ankle from Diaz, then swerved past Francisco Melo but couldn't get out of the way of the lumbering challenge of Domingo Benegas, who wrapped his studs around Johnstone's shins and sent him spinning to the ground. Sure enough, Benegas whipped his hands behind his back as the referee approached him. After Johnstone received treatment, the referee booked Benegas.

'To be fair to Jimmy, he didn't shirk things one bit,' Tommy Callaghan said in 2023. 'He would get the ball, he would get booted into the air for a foul, and immediately he would be back demanding the ball again and he would run at them. He told us to keep giving him the ball, he was fearless. Most players would chuck it and want to get straight out of there but he was the opposite, he just kept going at them.'

Attacker Irureta received the harshest yellow of all for a handball in the build-up to an attack. Shortly afterwards Callaghan had a great shot from distance that Reina caught comfortably.

Just on the halfway line, Ayala lost the ball to Davie Hay, and as Hay turned with the ball to move forward, Ayala pulled him down from behind. He seemed stunned when the referee approached him and with him having being booked earlier showed him the red card. The Celtic fans roared their approval. 'It was bound to happen sooner or later that somebody was going to be sent off,' said Brian Moore in his commentary.

A minute later Celtic took their seventh free kick of the half, played short to Johnstone. Once again he went on a run and once again Diaz clattered him, kicking him on the shin. The referee had no choice but to send him off too.

Number 9 Jose Eulogio Garate was substituted for defender Quique. Atletico were now forced back into the last third of their half of the field.

Despite two red cards the Spanish side were not finished with their physical approach: as Hay was dragging the ball down the wing, several feet away at the edge of the penalty box Quique seemed to thump Johnstone, knocking him to the ground. The referee blew his whistle and awarded Celtic a free kick. He spoke to his linesman but took no further action.

As the ball tamely went back to Reina there was a new tactic employed by Atletico. Dixie Deans harried the keeper as he attempted to kick the ball out, which wasn't unusual in the days before a rule was put in place to allow the goalkeeper to release the ball. Reina and Deans brushed against one another causing Reina to collapse to the ground and writhe around in agony, his team-mates frantically calling for the physiotherapist to run on.

'Now Reina has gone down as if he's poleaxed,' said Brian Moore as he watched a replay. 'Let's see what did it. Absolutely nothing!' Reina was awarded a free kick, and had the benefit of wasting a couple of minutes. Moore was incredulous. 'Well, words fail me to describe what is going on. If this is the way Atletico Madrid want to win the European Cup, they [UEFA] really want to present it to them before the season starts, they seem to want it so badly.'

Wilson came on for Deans and Alberto Fernández replaced Irureta.

Everyone except for Denis Connaghan was in the Atletico half of the field as the match approached the last 15 minutes. Kenny hit a low shot from distance, but there wasn't enough power on it and it rolled harmlessly into Reina's arms. Number 2 Melo was booked for time-wasting.

Of the 13 players used by Atletico ten were either booked or sent off.

Hood had a great chance but he headed wide after Callaghan put in an excellent cross. Alberto was booked after a challenge on Hay at the edge of the box. From the kick Johnstone flighted a lovely ball into the box that Dalglish rose to take on a glancing header, but Reina caught well.

Quique cleared from Johnstone but after the ball was gone stuck a sneaky boot into Johnstone's leg. However, the referee spotted it, and Quique became the third Atletico player to be sent off. Afterwards, Mr Babacan said that Quique, having watched the game for over an hour from the bench, should have known how the match was being refereed, so he should not have been surprised that that kind of foul play wouldn't be tolerated.

'Rather like the Agatha Christie play, and now there are eight,' said Moore, referencing the 1943 adaptation of the mystery writer's 1940 novel *And Then There Were None*.

Reina picked up a booking for time-wasting at a goal kick. Atletico's idea of attack was simply launching balls for a throw-in as far up the pitch as they could.

Johnstone had a great opportunity with a header on the six-yard line from a Callaghan cross, but the ball went over the bar. Celtic were building another attack when the final whistle sounded. An astonished Brian Moore announced that only 15 seconds had been added to account for the Atletico players' time-wasting antics.

Handshakes began among the players as Celtic fans booed and whistled. The Atletico players, including those sent off, danced on the pitch, joyfully celebrating the goalless draw. But then, one incident sparked mayhem. Spanish defender Eusebio punched Jimmy Johnstone to the ground. The Celtic players weren't about to let that go unnoticed, and the touchline became a free-for-all as players from both sides were punched and kicked. The Glasgow police saw fit to intervene. 'A big inspector of police grabbed Ayala in the tunnel and held him in such a way that said: "Dixie... Davie... have a punch,"' Dixie Deans said to the *Daily Mail* in 2023. 'And we did. We helped ourselves.'

The Celtic crowd though didn't let their anger spill over into any kind of trouble, and the next day the club thanked the spectators for their good behaviour.

One of the fans there that night was Richard Jobson, who later became the lead singer of the punk band The Skids. 'It was the first time I felt the heartbeat of being a supporter, the sheer rage and anger,' he told *The Scotsman* in 2007. Jobson would namecheck Dalglish in the song 'TV Stars', co-written with Stuart Adamson which appeared as the B-side to The Skids' 1979 hit 'Into the Valley'.

Tommy Callaghan said it was the most brutal game he ever took part in, and nearly 40 years on it still left a sour taste in his mouth.

Diaz, who Callaghan remembered primarily for targeting Jimmy Johnstone all night, was quoted in the Spanish press as saying, 'We were attacked and assaulted by players, trainers, directors of Celtic and even the Scottish police.'

Marca's reporter wrote, 'The referee turned a blind eye to all the faults of Celtic, maybe because he had been bought.'

In *ABC*, Vicente Calderon, the club's president, was quoted as referring to the match as, 'the most disgusting spectacle I've seen in my life'. He went on to say, 'The referee obviously did all he could to eliminate us in favour of Celtic.'

'We should have been fitted with boxing gloves instead of football boots,' Stein said. Davie Hay told the *Herald* in 2023 that Stein had insisted that his players didn't retaliate. 'He was determined that nothing untoward came from our end, that we didn't let the club down.'

Referee Babacan told the *Record* in 2011 he was happy with the job he had done – he had tried to dampen the tension with some early yellow cards but the players had continued 'playing hard'. In 2023, Kenny Dalglish jokingly told the same paper that Atletico Madrid's aggressive tackling that night was focused on 'the good players' like Jimmy Johnstone instead of him. He noted that watching the match highlights remained shocking even 39 years later, describing the treatment of Celtic players as 'truly unbelievable'.

Dalglish criticised the Turkish referee for failing to control the game despite Celtic players asking for protection. He remarked that standing near Atletico's goalkeeper Reina was the safest place on the pitch that evening, though even Reina received a booking.

Six Spaniards were banned for the second leg. In addition to the three sent off, Ovejero, Alberto and Melo were banned as UEFA said they 'have repeatedly been cautioned during the course of the season'. UEFA also warned Atletico that their future participation in European football hinged on their behaviour in that match.

Jimmy Johnstone was pictured in the *Daily Record* dressed in only a towel showing off the bruises on his body. Stein said he was proud of Johnstone. 'He was provoked and yet he simply refused to retaliate.' Stein said the match was the worst experience Celtic ever had. 'I didn't think I would ever see scenes like these at Celtic Park.'

Johnstone was left out of the match with Dundee United to nurse his injuries. Celtic won the dress rehearsal for the Scottish Cup Final 2-0. East Fife and Aberdeen were also beaten in the league, leaving Celtic needing three points to make the title safe.

Then came the second leg in Madrid. The game was very different, played in a sporting manner with only one booking – Kenny Dalglish.

Goals late on from Garate on 75 minutes and Adelardo on 81 minutes gave Atletico a 2-0 win and a place in the 1974 European Cup Final.

Celtic celebrated winning nine Scottish league titles in a row after a Dalglish goal gave them a 1-1 draw with relegated Falkirk on 27 April. Technically Hibs could have caught them, but the players and the media seemed to neglect that fact. Falkirk had taken the lead at Brockville in only three minutes through Kirkie Lawson. It was Kenny, though, who hit the equaliser 17 minutes later, picking the ball up from 30 yards out, running to the edge of the box and smashing an unstoppable shot into the net. The title was mathematically wrapped up two days later with a 0-0 draw with Aberdeen.

The double was clinched on 4 May when Celtic beat Dundee United 3-0 in the Scottish Cup Final. Thoughts now turned to Kenny's first World Cup.

Celtic: Connaghan, Hay, Brogan, Murray, McNeill, McCluskey, Johnstone, Hood, Deans [Wilson], Callaghan, Dalglish

Atletico Madrid: Reina, Melo, Diaz, Benegas, Ovejero, Eusebio, Ayala, Adelardo, Garate [Quique], Irureta [Alberto], Heredia

Attendance: 70,000

14

Scotland 0-0 Brazil

18 June 1974, World Cup finals,
Waldstadion

'THE QUALITY of the players that were playing at that time was huge,' Dalglish said of Scotland's 1974 World Cup squad, in 2024. 'There was a great camaraderie.'

The full squad was: David Harvey (Leeds United), Sandy Jardine (Rangers), Danny McGrain (Celtic), Billy Bremner (c) (Leeds United), Jim Holton (Manchester United), John Blackley (Hibernian), Jimmy Johnstone (Celtic), Kenny Dalglish (Celtic), Joe Jordan (Leeds United), David Hay (Celtic), Peter Lorimer (Leeds United), Thomson Allan (Dundee), Jim Stewart (Kilmarnock), Martin Buchan (Manchester United), Peter Cormack (Liverpool), Willie Donachie (Manchester City), Donald Ford (Heart of Midlothian), Tommy Hutchison (Coventry City), Denis Law (Manchester City), Willie Morgan (Manchester United), Gordon McQueen (Leeds United), Erich Schaedler (Hibernian).

Kenny's childhood hero, Denis Law, was included, despite being at the end of his club career. Kenny told the *Liverpool Echo* in 1977 the excited young players were 'like wee boys' when Denis joined the squad.

When he was a youngster Dalglish played football most Saturdays and of course Law never played club football in Scotland, but every chance he got Kenny would go to see Law play for Scotland at Hampden. Kenny loved Denis's style, the sleeves pulled down, the way he leaped in the air, his quick reactions, his skills on the ball and the way he sniffed out goalscoring opportunities. Kenny also recognised that Denis had a personality, he enjoyed playing and fans responded to his antics on the pitch.

Kenny told the Scotland Podcast that in West Germany, all Law wanted to do was train, before lying in his bed in the afternoon. 'He roomed with a wee boy who played with Hearts called Donald Ford. We ended up calling Donald "Jeeves", because he used to run after Denis. Denis said, "Cup of tea," the wee man was straight out, down to the foyer to get Denis a cup of tea.'

Before the squad left for the finals there was a dispute over money. Bob Bain was a former comedian who had set himself up as a US-based entrepreneur hired by the SFA to broker a series of sponsorship deals. When he arrived at the players' camp in Largs, as they prepared for a warm-up match away to Belgium, Bain struggled to explain to the squad what benefits they would be receiving. After he'd been shown the door marked 'Get Tae… ' the squad were cheered up by Billy Connolly, who arrived to put on a show.

Ormond and captain Bremner wanted no more to do with Bain. He went incommunicado until the *Daily Record* tracked him down after the finals in a Glasgow hotel where he said he had nothing to hide, but had incurred huge expenses in trying to set up the deals and they had been slow to materialise.

While in West Germany, Kenny was presented with *Shoot!*'s Most Exciting Scottish League Player award. At the same time Billy Bremner was presented with the English award. The two honours perhaps indicate the strength of the Scotland squad.

Scotland's group opened with a match against Zaire. 'We were a wee bit unfortunate to play them first because nobody had seen them before,' Dalglish told the Official Scotland Podcast. 'There wasn't a great deal of information about them. But we beat them 2-0.' The Leeds United pair Peter Lorimer and Joe Jordan got the goals. In the other group game, Brazil and Yugoslavia drew 0-0. That result put Scotland into a good position going into the second match.

Ally MacLeod, then manager of Ayr United, previewed the game in the *Daily Record*, saying Brazil would be out if they lost. It should be noted that MacLeod, infamous for talking Scotland up to win the World Cup when he was in charge in 1978, also suggested they would win it under Willie Ormond in 1974.

Skipper Billy Bremner felt Brazil were there for the taking and, speaking to the *Record*, Ormond said, 'For once, the pressure's on Brazil.'

Ormond had said before the opening fixture that he felt Law was the man to go in for the kill against Zaire, but he might not be the man for the job against Brazil or Yugoslavia. So it proved as that match against Zaire would turn out to be Law's 55th and final cap.

'Kenny was a fine player,' Denis wrote in his 2003 autobiography, 'and the real beauty about him was that if he wasn't scoring goals his actual play was still valuable. He was a good reader of the game and a good passer of the ball with an outstanding all-round game, and there aren't many players who also score goals you can say that about. Dalglish was a team player and a goalscorer, and one of the best without a doubt.'

Prime Minister Harold Wilson was en route to Bonn for talks with West German leaders. His plane stopped in the middle of the runway at Frankfurt's airport, and he was picked up by a helicopter and taken to the Waldstadion, escorted by another helicopter.

Willie Morgan came in for Law up front while Martin Buchan replaced John Blackley in defence. Ormond had delayed his team selection. It was reported that the manager was pondering whether to replace Dalglish in his starting XI with Liverpool's Peter Cormack, who had played in all 42 of Liverpool's league games in 1973/74, but in the end, Ormond kept Kenny in his team.

He started the game up front alongside Joe Jordan, who won his 13th cap that night. Jordan recognised Kenny's strengths and enjoyed playing with him. 'Kenny was strong on the ball but he wasn't that quick,' Jordan wrote in his autobiography. 'His pace was in his mind. He was never flustered. When he received the ball he always knew what he was going to do with it, and his positional sense was quite phenomenal. Dalglish's supreme gift was to be able to read everything so well. It was amazing to see the number of people who dived in on him around the box and were left floundering. It was really the last thing they should have done against Kenny. They were just playing to his strength. He would pick up so easily on their intentions and the ball would be by them as they hit their stride. Their movement created half a yard for him and his composure on the ball did the rest.'

Brazil started well, although they didn't appear to be the smooth, skilful attacking Brazil that everyone had come to know and love from previous World Cups. Scotland were losing the game in midfield, and Ormond recognised that. He pulled Dalglish into the middle of the park and that tactical change allowed Scotland to gain more of a foothold, as Brazil found they couldn't get through them. With 20 minutes gone, Scotland, now growing in confidence, began to take the game to their opponents.

If they had come on to the pitch intimidated by the formidable reputation of their opponents, that respect dissipated and the players in dark blue began to believe the men in canary yellow could be beaten. Emerson Leao in the Brazilian goal saved from Hay, Lorimer and Jordan as Scotland searched for an opening goal. Brazil spoiled and their players took turns producing niggling fouls to stop the Scots' flow. The *New York Times* suggested that referee Arie

Van Gemert of the Netherlands 'blew his whistle more often than the teams kicked the ball'.

It can be overlooked that for all their skill, Brazil were very often a physical, if not dirty, side, and that was the case in this encounter. Rivelino went in late on Sandy Jardine after the ball was away and later pushed Bremner. The Scots captain was also involved in an altercation with Jairzinho. Lorimer was body-checked by Luis Pereira. The *Daily Record*'s Hugh Taylor called Brazil the dirtiest team at the World Cup, suggesting that the referee had been too lenient and Rivelino should have been sent off for striking out at Bremner.

Ormond told the press afterwards that every one of his players had cuts and bruises. Dalglish rated the experience as a lesson for the Scots players who were all playing in their first World Cup.

Scotland's best chance fell to Bremner, although he didn't know much about it. Lorimer floated a corner into the box that Jordan headed at goal. The downwards header was awkward for Leao to get to. He pushed the ball away, where it fell at the feet of Bremner, who, only a couple of yards out, could only poke the ball wide of the post.

He had had too little time to react when the ball came back off Leao, but Bremner acknowledged later if the ball had fallen to one of the players with a natural goalscorer's instincts, it could have gone in.

Harold Wilson visited the Scots' dressing room after the match and reported that he found the players in a 'jewel mood'. 'They were delighted to have held Brazil, but they feel they should have won,' he told the *New York Times*. 'I will return for the World Cup Final, if Scotland is in it.'

In the *Daily Record* Hugh Taylor rated the players as 'Scottish heroes'.

'Not many teams draw against Brazil and don't go through,' Kenny said in 2024. In the other group game Zaire had lost 9-0 to Yugoslavia.

Kenny had always raised an eyebrow at the fact that Zaire were coached by a Yugoslavian in Blagoje Vidinić. While recording an interview with History of Football in 2001, Kenny mentioned this. The interviewer then told Kenny that he had interviewed some players from the Zaire team who had told him that they had thrown the game as they hadn't been paid. The entourage of government and Zairean football federation officials had supposedly dipped into the players' kitty and bled it dry. Kenny shrugged his shoulders and said with a smile, 'If money was the problem, if they'd come to the lads they might have paid them.'

In the final group game against Yugoslavia, Kenny was substituted for Tommy Hutchison in the 65th minute. A late goal for either side saw the match end 1-1, and Scotland went out on goal difference without losing a match.

It was hard to argue that Kenny hadn't performed as many had expected him to in his first World Cup finals. He reflected on that fact in his 1982 autobiography, where he wrote that he didn't play well enough in the three games and felt he had let the manager down. Perhaps surprisingly, he admitted to being overawed by some of the older players in the squad and that at times he was hesitant to attempt moves on the pitch in case they didn't come off.

Doug Baillie was a journalist for the *Sunday Post*; a former centre-half with Rangers, Baillie was one of Kenny's favourite players when he was a youngster on the Ibrox terracing. Baillie wrote a piece on 30 June 1974 highlighting that Kenny looked jaded, tired and didn't play well. He suggested that while the role Ormond asked of him – to support the front runners – was one he had done at Celtic, the difference was that at Parkhead he had better support from his team-mates. 'With the champions everybody backs everybody else and gaps in the middle aren't allowed to develop.' Kenny, Baillie felt, was caught in the middle, without the stamina, after a long season, to get involved.

Baillie quoted an anonymous Celtic player who was also a Scotland international. 'Kenny is too honest,' the colleague said. 'Even when we are winning convincingly he never eases up to save himself.' He suggested that Kenny should adopt the approach former Celt Bertie Auld used. 'When a game was won, Bertie started thinking about the next one, taking a breather now and then.'

Kenny's Celtic team-mate Davie Hay turned out to be the standout Scots performer. Dalglish noted that Hay would fight and graft for the ball, allowing the players around him to show off. Hay would get the transfer to England that many thought Dalglish would earn that summer when he signed for Chelsea, although he wouldn't play for Scotland again after that World Cup.

No matter how Kenny rated his own participation, he was admired and rated by his manager at that tournament. 'I consider Kenny Dalglish to be one of the greatest players to kick a ball,' Ormond wrote in a contribution to Dalglish's 1982 autobiography. 'Not once did I think he let me down.' Ormond highlighted that one of Kenny's strengths was what he did when his team-mates had the ball. He could find space and make runs, always making himself available for a pass, plus Ormond noted he had a fantastic ability to read situations quickly.

'I know Mr Ormond has his critics,' Kenny said in 1977, 'but he was very fair to me and obviously helped my career by picking me as often as he did for Scotland.'

Scotland: Harvey (Leeds United), Jardine (Rangers), McGrain (Celtic), Holton (Manchester United), Buchan (Manchester United), Bremner (Leeds United), Hay (Celtic), Dalglish (Celtic), Morgan (Manchester United), Jordan (Leeds United), Lorimer (Leeds United)

Brazil: Leao (Palmeiras), Nelinho (Cruzeiro), Luis (Palmeiras), Marinho Peres (Santos), Wilson Piazza (Cruzeiro), Marinho (Botafogo), Jairzinho (Botafogo), Paulo Cesar (Flamengo),

Leivinha (Palmeiras), Rivelino (Corinthians) [Carpegiani (Internacional)], Mirandinha (Sao Paulo)

Attendance: 62,000

15

Dundee 0-6 Celtic

*14 December 1974, Scottish First
Division, Dens Park*

KENNY RETURNED to the Celtic team for the pre-season friendly against Preston North End, having been rested for the first two matches in the Drybrough Cup. Lining up for the opposition was Bobby Charlton, who was making his return as a player having focused on managing Preston the previous season. He would go on to play 47 times for Preston in 1974/75. The former Manchester United defender David Sadler was also in the Preston team.

Dalglish only played for half an hour but proved he was fit to play against Rangers at Hampden in the final of the Drybrough Cup the following day. In the *Glasgow Herald*, Jim Reynolds wrote that Kenny 'showed all his old skill and enthusiasm'. The Celtic fans gave him a great ovation when he was substituted for Jim Murphy.

Celtic took the lead through Andy Lynch after only 30 seconds, but Preston came back through another ex-Manchester United player, Francis Burns. The winner, greeted by tremendous enthusiasm from the Celtic fans, came from Charlton to give Preston a 2-1 win.

Just 24 hours later, 57,558 turned up at Hampden to see Celtic and Rangers play an early-season classic. The match was played with an experimental offside rule, where players could only be offside beyond a line drawn across the 18-yard line. In the *Glasgow Herald*, Ian Archer noted that the experiment 'cut out almost all of the recognisable midfield play that should be at the heart of every game'.

After three losing finals, Celtic finally won the competition. Stevie Murray put them in front on the half hour, only for Ally Scott to equalise eight minutes later. In extra time, Paul Wilson gave Celtic the lead again but a Pat McCluskey own goal sent the game to penalties. Kenny didn't take one as Celtic went on to win the shoot-out 4-2.

In August, Kenny played against Liverpool when the Merseysiders came to Celtic Park to play in Billy McNeill's testimonial. The match was the final game in which Bill Shankly took charge of Liverpool. He had stepped down in the close season, but having led the team out for the Charity Shield match with Leeds a few days earlier, he was given this match as his final time in charge.

Shankly, along with McNeill, was presented to the crowd before the match. He had made an appearance before the Celtic crowd the previous season, ahead of Celtic's friendly against Penarol of Uruguay. Shankly received a five-minute ovation from the 40,000 crowd and said that he would never forget the welcome the Celtic fans afforded him that day, and the fact it wasn't related to any team allegiance made it a bit more special for him. 'I was a Scot and they made me proud.'

This time there were 60,000 fans in the ground and they sang, 'Shankly, Shankly, Shankly,' as Bill met McNeill in the centre circle. 'I never dreamt when I used to come here as a schoolboy 30 years ago that I would end my career here with a finale as memorable as this,' Shankly said.

Kevin Keegan looked back on the game as a 'tremendous' occasion 21 years later in an interview with the *Daily Record*. It was his only appearance at Parkhead and he praised the atmosphere and Dalglish's performance. In fact, Keegan is possibly being kind in his memories of the match, as Dalglish was substituted at half-time, and the *Record* match report called his showing 'disappointing'. John Toshack had opened the scoring in the 18th minute and Dalglish's replacement Paul Wilson scored the equaliser five minutes into the second half.

In October, Celtic crashed out of the European Cup after a first round loss to Olympiakos, with a 1-1 draw at Celtic Park and a 2-0 defeat in Athens.

A week before the League Cup Final against Hibernian the sides played one another in the league. Celtic won 5-0. Dalglish played his part and helped Dixie Deans to hit a hat-trick.

The following week at Hampden 53,848 turned up to see a memorable final. Dalglish and Jimmy Johnstone were both in scintillating form. The first goal came after six minutes. Deans laid off a long ball to Dalglish at the edge of the Hibs penalty box, Kenny turned and went on a run. He slid a low left-footed cross across the six-yard box and Johnstone tapped the ball home. 'It was the genius of Kenny Dalglish that made the goal,' Arthur Montford said in his commentary.

It was two on 34 minutes when McCluskey sent a route-one ball straight through the middle from the back which Deans latched on to and shot past the advancing goalkeeper from the edge of the box.

Joe Harper, lurking in the six-yard area turned the ball in to get Hibs back in the match three minutes before the half-time whistle.

A few minutes into the second half and Johnstone weaved his way through the Hibs defence to dink a ball through for Wilson to make the score 3-1. But Harper came back at Celtic and scored his second just after the hour to make it 3-2. Deans then struck two goals in two minutes to put Celtic 5-2 up and complete his hat-trick.

With 74 minutes gone Dalglish slipped the ball into Murray, who shot home for 6-2 Celtic. Seven minutes were remaining when Harper scored his own hat-trick to make the score Celtic 6 Hibernian 3.

In the closing minutes Kenny got involved with Alex Edwards, when in a scrap for the ball Dalglish kicked him on the shin. The former Dunfermline man retaliated with a kick at Dalglish. Both players were booked. 'An unfortunate climax to a superb game of football,' said Montford.

When the final whistle was blown Kenny had his first League Cup winners' medal.

In the *Sunday Post*, reporter Jack Harkness rated five players with five out of five performances: Murray, Dalglish, Johnstone and Deans of Celtic and Hibs' Harper.

At the end of October Dixie Deans won his first cap for Scotland in a 3-0 win over East Germany at Hampden where Dalglish hit the third goal. His second cap came the following month in a 2-1 European qualifier defeat to Spain. It's quite remarkable to realise that despite Deans's sensational goalscoring feats for Celtic he was only awarded two caps for his country.

On 11 December Kenny played for Celtic in a match to benefit UNICEF at Parkhead, against Benfica. The sides drew 3-3 with the match being settled by a penalty shoot-out. Again Dalglish didn't take a kick as Billy McNeill's miss allowed Benfica to win 5-4.

Going into the league match against Dundee, Rangers were top of the table, ahead of Celtic on goal difference. Prior to the game Dundee had only lost 13 goals all season. In the *Sunday Post* Bill McFarlane described 'a swashbuckling Celtic performance in which Kenny Dalglish and Jimmy Johnstone were out of this world'.

Ronnie Glavin picked up an injury without touching the ball within two minutes and was replaced by Harry Hood. Celtic went in front after five minutes. Dave Johnston played a free kick back to his goalkeeper Thomson Allan. However, Dalglish was on top of him quickly, and the twice-capped Scotland goalkeeper dropped the ball. Kenny squared it to Jimmy Johnstone, who tapped it between Allan's legs.

A mistake by Bobby Wilson allowed Celtic's Paul Wilson to take the ball 30 yards down the left flank in the 19th minute. He crossed for Dalglish to gather the ball just a few yards out. As the panicked Dundee defenders gathered on the goal line, Kenny composed himself and comfortably knocked the ball home.

Ten minutes later, it was 3-0 when McGrain launched a ball into the Dundee penalty box. Allan attempted to fist it away, but under pressure from Dalglish, he couldn't make clean contact. Johnstone crashed the ball in for his second.

Six minutes into the second half, it was 4-0. Dalglish dispossessed Phillip and played a through ball for Wilson to slip past Allan.

Dalglish scored his second on 67 minutes, going on a solo run, reminiscent of George Best as he dribbled around Allan and shot past defenders once again scrambling to cover on the goal line. Four minutes later, he completed what McFarlane called 'the most deserved hat-trick ever'. He went round three defenders and deceived Allan with a dummy that also sent the cameramen behind the goal the wrong way as he nestled the ball in the net.

In the directors' box, Rod Stewart got to his feet and waved his hat in the air. 'I'm convinced Kenny hasn't even reached his best yet,' Stewart told the *Weekly News* after the match, believing that Kenny was still maturing as a player.

Stewart had opened a branch of Bruce's Record Shops in Dundee's Reform Street prior to the match, although he arrived at 2.30pm as opposed to the advertised between 12 noon and 1pm. It saw the Dundee streets blocked, as cars came to a standstill and police had to hold the crowds back. It meant he arrived at the game late, and then left early. The night before he had played with his band The Faces in Edinburgh and the night after he began an unprecedented run of four sold-out nights at Glasgow's Apollo Theatre.

Stewart had been over with the Scotland party at the World Cup in West Germany in the summer, so he had mainly seen Kenny at close quarters as a Scottish international. He predicted that Dalglish could become 'one of the all-time great Scots'. The singer acknowledged however that Kenny had had a disappointing World Cup. Stewart offered his own assessment on why his club form and his international success seemed to differ. At his club, Dalglish was the centrepiece – creating and scoring goals – while with Scotland he seemed to be 'just another cog in the wheel', Stewart said. The 29-year-old star attributed Dalglish's underwhelming World Cup performance to the immense pressure and expectations placed upon him.

Stewart recalled their first meeting backstage at the Apollo, where he had been surprised by Dalglish's shyness despite his ability on the football field. The footballer appeared at Stewart's dressing room door, seeming nervous to meet the musician, though Stewart himself was equally excited to meet Dalglish. They eventually became good friends.

Ken Gallacher wrote that the game at Dens was Kenny's best performance for Celtic. 'Dalglish ran the show like a compere.' Gallacher drew comparisons with Johan Cruyff and Billy Steel.

'That was probably the best individual display he has given us,' Stein said. 'It reminded me of him scoring six goals in Frank Beattie's testimonial. The point to remember, of course, is how unselfish he was at Dundee. He didn't simply score goals, he helped make them and was ready to help others. The team backed him and he responded.'

Iain Phillip was the Dundee man tasked with marking him. Phillip was in his second spell with Dundee having spent a year with Crystal Palace. There, he played against Denis Law, Kevin Keegan and Charlie George. Phillip explained to Gallacher what it was like playing against Kenny. 'He is fast off the mark, has amazing control and bewildering body swerves,' he said. 'One wee movement can send you out of the park while Kenny moves in on goal.' Phillip felt Dalglish was similar to Rodney Marsh of Manchester City, who also fearlessly took on defenders, although, Phillip said, Kenny had more vision than Marsh.

Dalglish was typically modest about his performance, telling the press, 'I want to string a few games like that together. That's the important thing. The team played really well, the best we have done for a long time. Dundee like to play football and I enjoy playing against them.'

'[Kenny] was the most complete player I ever played with,' Billy McNeill wrote in his 2004 autobiography, 'blessed with a God-given talent, but it would be wrong for anyone to try to suggest that he didn't have to work hard to bring it to the fore. It was his ability as an all-rounder which made him so exceptional. Kenny also had a potent weapon – his backside. He was well built round the rear and he used it to great effect to hold off opponents and shield the ball in a way I have seen few others manage.'

The win put Celtic on top of the league, with the same number of points as Rangers but with a better goal difference, but in 1975's New Year Old Firm game, Celtic suffered a 3-0 loss to Rangers, putting the Ibrox club at the top of the league on goal difference.

In February Celtic drew 2-2 with both Arbroath and Dumbarton, the league's bottom two teams. Later that month Celtic lost 2-1 to Hibs at Easter Road and their vice-like grip on the Scottish First Division title had all but been released. Rangers were now four points clear.

In the *Glasgow Herald* Ian Archer wrote a piece on the demise of Celtic's dominance, after they had established themselves as one of the world's great clubs. 'Not as lastingly famous as the unique Real Madrid, not as individually talented or explosive as Ajax of Amsterdam. But more friendly and better loved than Inter, more attractive than any English club since the last revival of Tottenham Hotspur. They trod more new paths than any Scotsman since David Livingstone left Blantyre.'

Now though, with Celtic's poor run of results, there was the dawning realisation that those great days were fading into the distance. 'A part of everyone who likes his football has disappeared from his soul as, in these last few weeks, the glory of the nine years has vanished in the confusion of the tenth,' Archer wrote.

At the end of March, Rangers were confirmed as league champions.

The club and Kenny had a chance to pick themselves up though with the Scottish Cup Final against Airdrie. The match would be Billy McNeill's final game as a Celtic player. Paul Wilson scored twice, with Pat McCluskey netting a penalty to help Celtic to a 3-1 win.

Dundee: Allan, Wilson, Johnston, Ford, Stewart, Phillip, Hoggan, Robinson, Hutchison, J. Scott, Caldwell [Gordon]

Celtic: Hunter, McGrain, McCluskey, Murray [MacDonald], McNeill, Connelly, Johnstone, Glavin [Hood], Dalglish, Callaghan, Wilson

Scorers: Johnstone (5, 30), Dalglish (19, 67, 71), Wilson (39)

Attendance: 14,901

16

Celtic 3-1 Heart of Midlothian

20 August 1975, League Cup,
Celtic Park

ON 6 August 1975, Dalglish asked Celtic for a transfer. This was a close season of upheaval and change for Celtic. Billy McNeill retired, and although he was 35, he had been such a dominant figure at the club's heart since the 1958/59 season that his retirement was expected to be a significant loss to the club.

In June, Jimmy Johnstone had been freed. Only 30, Johnstone had played more than 30 matches the previous season. Although he hadn't quite been the same influence on games as he had been a few years earlier, he was another big personality the fans were sorry to see leaving. The battling defender Jim Brogan had also been freed.

Jock Stein had been involved in a serious car crash in July. His assistant, Sean Fallon, was now dealing with the club's day-to-day affairs as Stein recovered from his injuries.

Celtic had offered Kenny a new contract, which he had turned down. With his contract expired, he was now playing on its option clause. He spoke to the *Daily Record*'s Ken Gallacher, who later co-authored his first autobiography, and acknowledged that while he had asked for a transfer, he really didn't want to leave, as he loved the club and its fans. 'I feel I have been forced into this,' he said.

Arsenal, Everton and Manchester United were the first clubs named as potential suitors. 'We are watching the situation,' Gunners manager Bertie Mee told the *Evening Standard*. 'But the fee must be realistic.'

Gallacher's piece implored Celtic to offer Kenny the deal that would make him stay, stating that they needed Kenny's leadership as he had now proved himself the best player in Britain.

Kenny felt a little guilt that he was making this move when Jock Stein was in hospital and he apologised to Sean Fallon for adding to the worry and strain he was clearly under. Dalglish suggested that he leave Fallon out of the discussions and instead dealt with club chairman Desmond White.

The club and the player were at an impasse as the 1975/76 season began with the League Cup sectional stages. Dalglish played and scored the winner against Aberdeen on the opening day. 'If ever a player was an entertainer and a matchwinner rolled into one, it's this young man,' Doug Baillie wrote in his *Sunday Post* match report. It was clear that Scottish journalists feared losing an outstanding talent from the Scottish game, as if Kenny left now the only place he was going to was England.

Sunderland, Manchester United and Leeds United had representatives at Celtic Park watching Kenny. Liverpool had a contingent in Scotland, too, but not at Parkhead. Manager Bob Paisley and chairman John Smith went to Tannadice to see Dundee United striker Andy Gray, directors were at Rugby Park to watch Kilmarnock's Gordon Smith take on Partick Thistle's Alan Rough and Alan Hansen, while scouts were at Fir Park to run the rule over Motherwell striker Willie Pettigrew.

There was a suggestion that Dalglish should play on the option clause for the entire campaign. Fallon wasn't interested in the record transfer fee the club might receive. 'I feel it is better to have money on the park than in the bank,' he said. 'What's the use of money these days anyway?'

On 19 August, Dalglish entered talks with the Celtic chairman. 'We have come to an agreement with Kenny

Dalglish,' White later announced, 'and he is staying with Celtic. Hopefully he will be here for the rest of his playing career.' Dalglish said he had had a problem with conditions in the original offer, which had now been cleared up. 'The Celtic fans have always been good to me,' he said. 'They were even better during this trouble. Their encouragement helped me on the field and convinced me I didn't want to play anywhere else.'

Dalglish later said that he remained at Parkhead out of loyalty and not because the club had significantly bumped up his pay.

In October 1975, Dalglish paid tribute to Jock Stein in his *Shoot!* column, suggesting that he must be the best manager in the world. He admired the way Stein listened to his players, and developed an understanding of them where he could handle each one as an individual, although Dalglish admitted 'his word is law'.

Unexpectedly, Stein attended the League Cup match against Hearts on 20 August, one foot still in plaster.

In front of 28,000, Dalglish celebrated signing a new two-year contract by leading the Celtic side out as captain. Bobby Lennox, who had been fulfilling the role since McNeill retired, was out with stomach trouble, but the word was that Dalglish's appointment would be permanent. 'I was delighted, because he was a great player, probably the best in the world at that time,' Lennox wrote in his 2007 autobiography, 'and a good choice for captain.' In 1980 Dalglish said that the two things that gave him the biggest thrill in his time with Celtic was the day he signed and the day he was appointed captain.

Dalglish orchestrated the game. Celtic fans in the Jungle section chanted his name throughout the match, delighted that Kenny had decided to remain with the club.

Celtic had lost 2-0 to Hearts at Tynecastle earlier in the section, but with less than two minutes gone, they were 1-0 up when Andy Lynch put Ronnie Glavin through to score. Lynch added a second just before half-time. Five minutes into the second half, Icelander Jóhannes Eðvaldsson headed in a Harry Hood corner to make it 3-0. Drew Busby pulled a goal back for Hearts.

A few days later, Celtic qualified for the League Cup quarter-final when they defeated Dumbarton 8-0 with Dalglish scoring twice.

In the last eight, they defeated Stenhousemuir 3-0 on aggregate. Celtic made it 11 League Cup finals in a row when they beat Partick Thistle 1-0 in October.

In the final against Rangers, Kenny returned to the side, having missed the previous match, a European Cup Winners' Cup tie with Boavista, due to an ankle injury. Unfortunately, Tom Forsyth marked him out of the game, although the Celtic camp was furious at what they felt was Forsyth's rough play. Alex MacDonald's second-half header gave Rangers the cup.

Celtic opened the new ten-team Premier League with a match away at Rangers as their rivals unfurled the league flag. Dalglish's goal put them 1-0 up, but Rangers would come back to win 2-1.

In November, Dalglish put in an outstanding performance at Somerset Park. Celtic were 5-0 up on Ayr United after 34 minutes. The first goal of Kenny's brace was a potential goal of the season. He picked up the ball in midfield, went past one Ayr player then played a one-two with Paul Wilson, received the return pass, took a step forward and unleashed a thunderbolt of a shot that flew into the net. Celtic went on to win 5-2.

In Europe Celtic had a great win against Boavista at Celtic Park, in a match where at UEFA's insistence the teams wore numbers on their jerseys for the first time. Kenny scored after 35 seconds and later made one for Deans as Celtic won 3-1.

Celtic would go out of Europe in March after a 2-1 aggregate loss to FSV Zwickau of East Germany. They lost in the Scottish Cup to Motherwell and lost the league again to Rangers. There would have to be improvements for the following season, the last on Kenny's contract.

Celtic: Latchford, McGrain, Lynch, McCluskey, McDonald, Eðvaldsson, Glavin, Wilson, Dalglish, McNamara, Hood

Scorers: Glavin (90 secs), Lynch (44), Eðvaldsson (50)

Hearts: Cruickshank, Kay, Clunie, Jeffries, Anderson, Murray, Brown, Busby, Hancock, Ford, Prentice

Scorer: Busby (76)

Attendance: 28,000

17

Scotland 2-1 England

*15 May 1976, Home Internationals,
Hampden Park*

WITH HIS appearance against Switzerland in April of 1976, Kenny made his 33rd consecutive appearance for Scotland, one away from George Young's record of 34 matches in a row. However, at the next game in May against Wales, Willie Pettigrew wore the number 7 shirt and Dalglish was left on the bench, preventing him from equalling the record. He said it was the only time Willie Ormond let him down.

Even when two Scotland players picked up knocks, Ormond still didn't put Dalglish on. It was something that Kenny puzzled over, as he never had an explanation from the manager. Dalglish, though, said he never held a grudge against Ormond, whom he regarded as an honest man who expected the same from his players.

Dalglish started the next match against Northern Ireland in May, and from there he built another run of consecutive appearances. He would break Young's record in December 1979 and go on to make 43 consecutive appearances, which ended with an appearance against Israel in February 1981.[3]

---

3 It's still (at the time of writing) the most consecutive games anyone has played for Scotland. Tom Boyd is the only other player to have passed George Young's mark, with 38 matches. John McGinn equalled Young with 34 consecutive games from September 2021 to September 2024 but an injury prevented his inclusion in Scotland's squad in October 2024. As of May 2025, Billy Gilmour with 15 consecutive appearances is the current player closest to Dalglish's record.

Scotland, without Dalglish, had beaten Wales 3-1 while Kenny netted the third in the 3-0 win over Northern Ireland. England had defeated Wales 1-0 and thrashed Northern Ireland 4-0. It ensured that whoever won the final game in the Home Internationals Championship would win the tournament. The match, which was Scotland's 400th and England's 500th international, was live on both BBC and ITV, with David Coleman commentating on the BBC and Brian Moore on mic duties for ITV.

The Scotland team included two players born in England: Colin Jackson of London, and Bruce Rioch of Aldershot.

Scotland had a shock when England took an early lead against the run of play in the 11th minute. Roy McFarland intercepted Archie Gemmill's pass to Dalglish in midfield, took it forward, released it left to Peter Taylor and ran through the middle, indicating he wanted a return pass, which Taylor gave him. Although Tom Forsyth got a tackle in to push the ball out of the penalty area, McFarland turned, then crossed into the box for Mick Channon, who got in front of Willie Donachie and sent a downward header past Rough and into the net.

Shortly after the goal, Phil Thompson sliced his clearance from Bruce Rioch's cross, sending the ball over Ray Clemence's crossbar. From the resultant corner, Joe Jordan headed narrowly over.

England's midfield consisted of Kevin Keegan, Gerry Francis and Ray Kennedy. They were well matched by Don Masson, Archie Gemmill and Bruce Rioch, keeping Kennedy in particular from having any influence on the game. The English also had to contend with Danny McGrain's runs from defence. In the Scots' defence, Tom Forsyth kept Keegan quiet whenever he came forward. In the *Sunday Post*, Doug Baillie described the Rangers man as playing 'like a van with a Rolls-Royce engine'.

Scotland's equaliser came in the 18th minute. Eddie Gray sent a corner into the area, and with two defenders marking

Jordan, Don Masson ghosted in unmarked behind him to head home.

Just before half-time, Clemence took the legs away from Dalglish in the box, after Kenny had made a run from the halfway line, skipping in between two English defenders. The ground screamed for a penalty and the English players seemingly accepted that call, although Clemence indicated that he thought Kenny had dived. Referee Karoly Palotai waved the cries away and blew the half-time whistle. He would say afterwards, 'I blew for half-time before the tackle. Otherwise, it would have been a penalty.'

At the start of the second half, Ray Kennedy ill-advisedly passed back to Clemence but was short, and Dalglish darted in. Clemence came out at his feet, and the two players collided, with the England goalkeeper coming off worse.

There were only four minutes of the second half gone when Scotland took the lead with one of the nation's most famous goals. Jordan went on a run, evading a McFarland tackle, skipping past Colin Todd and looking up before sending over a lovely cross. Dalglish controlled the ball, evaded Mick Mills and then unleashed a daisy cutter, which trundled along the Hampden pitch. Clemence bent down to gather the ball, except it rolled through his legs and over the line to put Scotland 2-1 up. The goal couldn't have been celebrated with any more fervour if Dalglish had hit a shot from 40 yards. 'And Clemence's day is now complete. A total disaster,' David Coleman exclaimed in his commentary.

'It was the worst moment of my career,' Clemence would later say. 'I thought I had the ball covered, but it bobbled and the next thing I knew it was through my legs and into the net. I wanted the Hampden pitch to open up and hide me.'

In his autobiography, Roy McFarland admitted he was out of position on the right touchline near the halfway line when, in his words, 'Joe Jordan went steaming past me.' He felt sympathy for his colleague. 'Although Ray had to carry the can,' he wrote, 'I have always felt partly responsible for Scotland's winner.'

'Ray Clemence will never concede another like that if he plays until he's 90,' Don Revie said after the match. 'He apologised to me at the end with tears in his eyes.'

Kenny would become team-mates with Clemence 15 months later. 'He shook my hand to introduce himself and said, "Keep those legs closed,"' Clemence recalled when speaking to the *Daily Mail* years later. In his 1982 autobiography, Dalglish states that he didn't mention the goal, despite John Toshack encouraging him to do so at training.

'As Gordon Banks will be remembered for that magnificent save from Pelé in the '70 World Cup, I will obviously be remembered when I finish for that Kenny Dalglish goal at Hampden Park,' Clemence said with a smile on his face when talking for a 1985 documentary on Kenny. 'It was straight at me. It was the sort of shot that I faced from 15-year-olds when I was at school. It was so easy. Because it was so easy, I didn't do the professional thing and put my body behind the ball. I went down to collect it with my legs open and as every Scotsman will know to their delight – and Englishmen to their horror – it went through my hands, through my legs and just about trickled over the line.'

It says a lot for Kenny that Clemence was quite happy to talk jovially about such a calamitous error on his part. While it became a famous goal for Scots, it didn't define Clemence's career as high-profile mistakes can occasionally do for goalkeepers. The Skegness-born Clemence earned 61 caps for his country and in 1981 became the first goalkeeper to captain England since Frank Swift in 1949.

Late on in the game, Tom Forsyth made one of the Scottish national team's most famous tackles. Keegan headed the ball on for Taylor, who played it through for Channon, who had got goalside of Forsyth at the edge of the penalty box. As Channon moved forward ready to shoot past Alan Rough, Forsyth stretched his left leg across him and cleared the ball away.

'I'm thoroughly looking forward to the flight home,' Archie Gemmill said when he emerged from the dressing room. 'Bruce Rioch, Don Masson and I are booked on the same plane as the England party. We'll give them stick.'

It was the first time Scotland had won the Home Internationals title since 1967. Revie said that this Scotland side was the best in ten years. After the summer break, it would be back to Celtic Park for Kenny in what would turn out to be his final season in the hoops.

Scotland: Rough (Partick Thistle), McGrain (Celtic), Donachie (Manchester City), Forsyth (Rangers), Jackson (Rangers), Rioch (Derby County), Masson (Queens Park Rangers), Gemmill (c) (Derby County), Dalglish (Celtic), Jordan (Leeds United), E. Gray (Leeds United) [Johnstone (Rangers)]

Scorers: Masson (18), Dalglish (49)

England: Clemence (Liverpool), Todd (Derby County), Mills (Ipswich Town), Thompson (Liverpool), McFarland (Derby County) [Doyle (Manchester City)], R. Kennedy (Liverpool), Keegan (Liverpool), Channon (Southampton), Pearson (Manchester United) [Cherry (Leeds United)], Francis (c) (Queens Park Rangers), Taylor (Crystal Palace)

Scorer: Channon (11)

Attendance: 85,165

18

Heart of Midlothian 3-4 Celtic

*20 November 1976, Scottish First
Division, Tynecastle Park*

THREE DAYS after the game with England, Kenny was at Celtic Park to play in the joint testimonial for Bobby Lennox and Jimmy Johnstone against Manchester United. Before the match, there was a Celtic Old Crocks versus The All Stars game. The match featured players such as Billy McNeill, Bobby Murdoch, Jim Baxter, Bobby Collins and Bobby Charlton. It was refereed by Billy Connolly.

Speaking in 2025, Connolly recalled Jock Stein kitting him out for the occasion. 'He gave me a blue tracksuit and a Rangers scarf and hat,' said Connolly. 'I had to lead Celtic on to the park dressed like this. You went on and the building facing you was the Jungle. It was corrugated iron and people who were in there had never been out of there. And they booed like you never heard a boo in your life. So I sent them off. I blew my whistle and they went berserk. They sang, "You can stick your f****** wellies up your arse." And it was the joy of my life.' (As well as being a world-famous stand-up comic, Connolly had had a hit single in 1974 with 'The Welly Boot Song'.)

In the match proper, with Jock Stein back in the dugout, Bobby Lennox put Celtic 1-0 up in the first half. Four minutes into the second half, remarkably, Kenny scored a carbon copy of the goal he scored against England. United goalkeeper Alex Stepney had Dalglish's shot covered, but then it trickled underneath his body and over the line. For Kenny's second, he took the ball from a Jimmy Johnstone backheel and lobbed it over Stepney. His hat-trick was completed in the 80th minute as he stunned the United defence with a quick change of direction.

On 25 October 1976, Celtic met Hearts in the League Cup semi-final. It was the first of two outstanding performances by Dalglish against the Edinburgh side in less than a month. The semi was played on a rain-drenched Monday night at Hampden Park.

Hearts opened the scoring in the 42nd minute when Jim Brown struck a perfect shot that flew low into the corner of the net. Celtic equalised just two minutes later. From the second successive corner Celtic had won, Dalglish rose and sent a superb header into the net.

Going into the last 20 minutes, Dalglish got into a tussle with centre-half John Gallacher at the edge of the Hearts box. Referee Hugh Alexander pointed to the spot. The Hearts players were livid, suggesting it should have been a foul against Dalglish, but the referee was unmoved.

Dalglish took the penalty himself and smashed the ball into the net.

With the red mist now swirling around the heads of the men from Tynecastle, Rab Prentice, who had been on the ground staff at Celtic a few years earlier, flew into a challenge on Celtic's Johnny Doyle, which saw him ordered off.

In the *Glasgow Herald*, Ian Archer wrote of, 'A connoisseur's performance from Kenny Dalglish.'

The win saw Celtic into their 13th League Cup final in a row. In the final, played less than two weeks later, Dalglish scored, but Aberdeen won 2-1 after extra time. Despite playing in six League Cup finals, Dalglish's only winners' medal came in the 6-3 win over Hibs in October 1974. 'I am honoured and very proud to have so many final appearances under my belt,' Dalglish wrote in his *Soccer Annual 1980* while reflecting on this solitary win from six. 'I know hundreds of players would give their eye teeth to be in such a position to complain.'

On 17 November, Dalglish and his clubmate Danny McGrain were part of the Scotland team which defeated Wales 1-0 in a World Cup qualifier at Hampden. The result put Scotland back in contention to qualify for the 1978 World Cup finals in Argentina after an opening group defeat to Czechoslovakia and Dalglish told the press he was desperate to make it happen again, for the fans as much as anything.

By the time Celtic met Hearts in the league in November, they were sitting fourth in the ten-team Premier League, still unbeaten but with five draws from nine games. Hearts only had one win from ten.

At club level, Dalglish had been playing in a more forward role. Ronnie Glavin took up space in the midfield alongside a young Roy Aitken. Joe Craig, a bustling centre-forward with height and strength, had been purchased from Partick Thistle in September.

The Celtic team who faced Hearts wore black armbands as a mark of respect for Jimmy Gribben, who had died aged 81. In 1951, Gribben had been working as Celtic's chief scout when he was asked by manager Jimmy McGrory and chairman Bob Kelly to help them find a player/coach to guide some of the younger players. Gribben only had one name for them – Jock Stein.

Stein regarded Gribben as a mentor. 'No one knew more about football than Jimmy Gribben,' he said in 1978.

Celtic got a real shock early on, finding themselves 2-0 down after ten minutes. Drew Busby punted the ball long and as Peter Latchford in the Celtic goal came racing out to meet it, Willie Gibson got in ahead of him and toe-poked the ball over his head and into the net for 1-0. Two minutes later, it was Gibson again when he redirected a 25-yard shot from Park past the wrong-footed Latchford.

Then Celtic came back. With 21 minutes gone Johnny Doyle hit a free kick which Dalglish nodded on for Roddie MacDonald to head past Brian Wilson.

With 33 minutes played, Hearts restored their two-goal advantage. Brown crossed and Prentice headed back across goal and Gibson was on hand to stab the ball in for his hat-trick. Just six minutes later it was 3-2 when Bobby Lennox pounced on an error by Wilson.

From then on it was always Celtic that were going to win. The equaliser arrived on 61 minutes. Danny McGrain went on a marauding run up the wing going past three defenders, sending in a cross for Dalglish to sweep into the Hearts net.

There were only three minutes remaining when Celtic got the winner. Wilson made a great save from a Dalglish shot but couldn't hold on to it. The ball broke to Ronnie Glavin, who fired it past a ruck of players and into the net.

In the *Sunday Post*, Bill McFarlane wrote, 'With the superb Danny McGrain setting the lead from the back, Ronnie Glavin and Roy Aitken ceaselessly pushing forward, and Kenny Dalglish threatening to score with every kick, Jock Stein's men just deserved the full share of what was going.'

Dalglish wrote of the game in his *Shoot!* 'Tartan Talk' column: 'My heart went out to Willie Gibson who scored a hat-trick and finished on the losing side. But that's show business and quite frankly I'm glad it was him rather than me.'

Wisla Krakow knocked Celtic out of the UEFA Cup in October's first round, but it was a different story in the league as Celtic lost only four games all season. They secured the inaugural Premier Division trophy with four games remaining when they beat Hibs 1-0 on 16 April 1977. Joe Craig scored the goal. As captain, Kenny led his colleagues down to the away end to hail the travelling Celtic support. Afterwards, his team-mates carried Kenny shoulder-high around Easter Road.

The Celtic side that season was very different from the one Dalglish had come into, borne out by the fact that for everyone in the squad bar Kenny, Bobby Lennox and Danny McGrain, it was their first league title medal. In the dressing room afterwards Kenny refused to allow the press to take any photographs until Lennox, who had broken his ankle against Rangers in November, had joined the players.

Looking back at the season in his *Shoot!* column Kenny highlighted the 5-1 win over then league leaders Dundee United in October as the turning point. Ever appreciative of the fans, he wrote that as the players were doing their Easter Road lap of honour he began thinking that it should have been the supporters taking a bow and the players standing on the terracing to applaud them.

Hearts: Wilson, Brown, Gallacher, Clunie, Kay, Jefferies, Shaw, Park, Busby, Gibson, Prentice

Scorer: Gibson (8, 10, 33)

Celtic: Latchford, McGrain, Lynch, Stanton, MacDonald, Aitken, Doyle, Glavin, Craig, Dalglish, Lennox

Scorers: MacDonald (21), Lennox (36), Dalglish (60), Glavin (87)

19

Celtic 1-0 Rangers

6 May 1977, Scottish Cup Final,
Hampden Park

KENNY DALGLISH and Rangers' Sandy Jardine were among the first Scottish players to have an agent. Tony Meehan represented both players, his first clients in a roster that by 1977 included Scotland manager Ally MacLeod, goalkeeper Alan Rough and singer and TV presenter Isla St Clair.

'We opened shops and supermarkets, made an advert for beer and even cut a record together,' Jardine recalled in his 1987 autobiography *Score and More*. The record was called 'Each Saturday'. They launched it in May 1975 ahead of Celtic and Rangers meeting in the Glasgow Cup Final. It was supposed to signify friendly rivalry on and off the field.

The Radio One DJ John Peel became one of Kenny's biggest fans after he joined Liverpool, and in August 1979, he began asking his listeners if one of them could send him a copy of the single. Listener Jim McCormack in Whins of Milton, Stirling, sent one in. 'Mind you, he wants some fairly rare records by way of exchange,' Peel said on his 5 September 1979 show. 'I must admit it's not the best record I've ever heard in my life,' Peel said as he introduced the song. Peel would play it again in March and September 1981.

In 1987, the *Daily Record*'s music writer Billy Sloan rated 'Each Saturday' as number one in his turgid top ten ahead of 'Agadoo' by Black Lace, 'The Birdie Song' by The Tweets and Terry Wogan's infamous 'Floral Dance'. 'It was a hit,' Jardine insisted, stretching the meaning of that term a little. 'It got to number 18 in the Radio Clyde charts.'

At the World Cup in West Germany in 1974, the players' eyes had been opened to commercial possibilities. 'Both Kenny and I saw what could be achieved,' Jardine wrote, 'and with the assistance of Tony Meehan got on well together.' The duo's friendship extended to playing golf together. 'Our commercial activities drew attention to that friendship, and I always reckoned that if it helped the supporters understand that there was no enmity between the clubs off the field then it was a good thing.'

In an Old Firm derby in the early 1970s, Dalglish hit a cross-field pass out to Celtic's right wing. Jardine blocked the cross, but in the process took the ball full in the face, falling to the floor. The ball went straight back to Kenny, who, recognising Jardine needed assistance, turned around and hammered it out of play.

In his book, Jardine rated Kenny as the best Scottish player of his generation. 'A better all-round footballer than Billy Bremner or Jim Baxter, Dalglish's ability was something else,' Jardine wrote. 'He had a marvellous football brain which actually got better as his career went on.' Jardine also rated Dalglish's passing as 'shrewd, accurate and incisive'.

Celtic didn't have the smoothest route to the 1977 Scottish Cup Final. In January's third round they drew 1-1 with Airdrieonians, but won the replay 5-0 with Joe Craig scoring four. In the fourth round there was another 1-1 draw, this time with Ayr United who scored a late equaliser at Celtic Park. At the Somerset Park replay Celtic won 3-1. The quarter-final was more straightforward with a 5-1 win over Queen of the South, Dalglish notching the fifth with a minute to go. Dundee were the opponents in the semi-final at Hampden. A late Joe Craig double gave Celtic a 2-0 win.

The final was live on television, the first Scottish Cup Final to be broadcast live since Celtic met Clyde in 1955.

In his *Shoot!* column ahead of the match, Kenny wrote that although he hoped the crowd would be around 70,000, as an Old Firm final deserved to fill any stadium, he felt the live coverage would put many spectators off attending.

That coverage and the pouring rain were considered factors in the lowest post-war final attendance of 54,252. 'TV kept the fans away,' Celtic chairman Desmond White said in the press. 'A crowd as small as that detracts from the spectacle of a cup final. We want spectators in the ground, not at home.'

A controversial penalty decided the game in the 20th minute. Roddie MacDonald met a corner with his head. The ball dropped on the six-yard line, where Jóhannes Eðvaldsson scooped it up towards the Rangers goal. Derek Johnstone blocked the weak shot on the goal line. 'The ball struck my knee,' Johnstone said later. 'My hands were down, but I didn't make contact.' Referee Bob Valentine disagreed, judged that Johnstone cleared the ball with his hand and awarded Celtic a penalty.

Kenny was typically pragmatic over the controversy, telling the *Evening Times*, 'It is not for me to say one way or the other, but the fact is the referee gave a penalty and we scored.'

Dalglish, who had scored seven penalties for Celtic that season, was later revealed to be the nominated penalty taker and, as captain, the player who would have the final say on the pitch. Surprisingly, though, it was Andy Lynch who stepped forward. Lynch, it was revealed, had only ever taken two penalty kicks in his senior career, both when he was with Hearts. Both had been missed.

The day before the final, at Seamill, the team had held a penalty competition where Lynch was the last player remaining after others missed and were eliminated. When Lynch and Kenny entered the hotel reception where Jock Stein was sitting, Kenny informed him that 'Kipper' (Lynch's nickname) would be taking penalties in the final.

At the pre-match meal Lynch was keen to assert that it wasn't just a fun competition. He sat beside Kenny and told him if Celtic were awarded a penalty kick he would step up to take it. Lynch wanted there to be no ambiguity or uncertainty if the moment arrived. When Celtic were awarded the penalty Kenny approached Lynch and offered him the opportunity to take it. Lynch felt his previous misses were of no concern, feeling he had matured as a player and had grown in confidence.

Although Stewart Kennedy guessed right and dived to his left, Lynch's kick was well-struck and beat him to put Celtic in front. Speaking to the *Daily Record* in 2017, Lynch, who had played with Dalglish at Glasgow United, described Kenny as a creative, courageous, consistent and confident player, an excellent team-mate who constantly encouraged others in the team.

'He read the game so well,' Lynch said. 'He was the guy who could create something out of nothing.'

It wasn't a classic cup final, as defences nullified attackers. Eðvaldsson and Roddie MacDonald were on top of Rangers' strike force Derek Johnstone and Derek Parlane. Rangers had assigned Jardine to shackle former Ranger Alfie Conn, signed earlier that year from Tottenham Hotspur, while Alex MacDonald was detailed to prevent McGrain from making any attacking forays. Tom Forsyth won man of the match for preventing Paul Wilson from making a significant impact.

'It was not a good final,' Jock Stein said. 'It was a game in which we tried to curtail Rangers, and they tried to do the same with us. Our planning paid off.'

Rangers' Johnstone was a fan of Kenny's, writing in his *Shoot!* column that any club in Britain would want to sign him. 'He combines all the skills, is extremely difficult to force off the ball, and he is a constant threat to defences … You can keep him quiet for lengthy spells, but lose concentration for one second and he will punish you.'

The SFA had banned laps of honour at Old Firm cup finals after the October 1965 League Cup Final when hundreds of Rangers fans swarmed the pitch as Celtic players carried the trophy around. Celtic, though, did a 'half-lap of honour' when they took the trophy down to their supporters. 'I saw some lads in wheelchairs by the side of the pitch and decided to take my medal over to show them,' Dalglish recalled in the *Kenny Dalglish Soccer Annual*. 'Just as I held it out for the lads to see, one of my team-mates bumped into my back and the medal flew out of its box and disappeared.'

Dalglish and goalkeeper Peter Latchford began searching the turf for the medal, while their team-mates carried on with the trophy. 'The police tried to get us to move on, promising that they would find it. But I was bitterly upset, convinced that I had become the shortest-ever holder of a Scottish Cup winners' medal.' Kenny had wanted to give his medal to his son Paul who had been born three months earlier. As Dalglish sat despondent in the dressing room a policeman knocked on the door and came in clutching the medal which had fallen into the folds of a fan's umbrella.

Celtic's Double, their tenth, left Rangers without any of the three domestic trophies they had won the previous season. With the Parkhead side back on top, the mood around the club was growing that they could return to another era of total dominance. However, they would have a massive setback to come.

Celtic: Latchford, McGrain, Lynch, Stanton, MacDonald, Aitken, Dalglish, Eðvaldsson, Craig, Conn, Wilson

Scorer: Lynch (20 pen)

Rangers: Kennedy, Jardine, Greig, Forsyth, Jackson, Watson [Robertson], McLean, Hamilton, Parlane, MacDonald, Johnstone

Attendance: 54,252

20

England 1-2 Scotland

4 June 1977, Home Internationals, Wembley Stadium

ON THE occasion of his 41st cap, in April of 1977, Kenny captained Scotland for the first time in a friendly against Sweden. Modestly, Dalglish wrote in his *Shoot!* column that he was only made captain due to English-based players' injuries and club commitments.

He scored the second goal in a 3-1 win, Scotland's first victory over the Swedes in four attempts. In the act of scoring, Kenny's boot came off, and as his team-mates rushed to celebrate with him, he hopped into the penalty area to retrieve it. The match was most memorable for Joe Craig in his first – and it would turn out only – international, scoring without having kicked the ball when he headed in Sandy Jardine's cross four minutes after coming on as a substitute.

The match turned out to be Willie Ormond's last game in charge of Scotland, as he left soon after to manage Hearts. Ormond was in charge for 38 games, of which Dalglish missed only one, that match against Wales which would have equalled George Young's consecutive caps record.

Dalglish would captain an Ormond team one more time when a Glasgow Select played an English Football League team at Hampden in front of the Queen in honour of Her Majesty's Silver Jubilee celebrations. The Glasgow squad was made up of players from Celtic, Rangers, Partick Thistle, Clyde and Queen's Park. Thistle's Alan Hansen was in the party, but didn't play in the game. The strip encompassed all those teams' colours, making for one of the most atrocious kits any team has ever worn. The Glasgow side won 2-1 with Kenny scoring the winner.

In the search to replace Ormond the SFA first went to Jock Stein, who turned the job down. They then turned to Aberdeen boss Ally MacLeod, who was appointed in the middle of May. MacLeod told the *Daily Record* that he aimed to prove he was 'the best manager in the world'. Dalglish wrote in *Shoot!* that he was sure MacLeod would relish the challenge.

MacLeod's first match in charge was the Home Internationals opening game, a 0-0 draw with Wales at the Racecourse Ground. In the other match, England beat Northern Ireland 2-1 in Belfast.

England then lost to Wales with a Leighton James penalty at Wembley, while Scotland beat Northern Ireland at Hampden 3-0. Kenny scored twice. Towards the end of the match, the Scots fans sang, 'Why are we so good?'

Northern Ireland and Wales drew 1-1 ahead of the England–Scotland game at Wembley.

On the morning of that game the sports pages of the newspapers announced that Liverpool's Kevin Keegan had sealed a £500,000 move to SV Hamburg. He was missing from the England line-up due to an injury.

The match was live on both BBC and ITV. John Motson commentated for the BBC while Brian Moore took mic duties on the commercial channel, with Alf Ramsey co-commentating.

Dalglish wrote in his fortnightly *Shoot!* column, that playing in a Scotland–England game was like no other experience. While crowds at Old Firm matches were split primarily 50/50, Dalglish observed that when Scotland played England, Scotland fans will always outnumber or at least out-sing their English counterparts.

Kenny was not wrong. After the match, the minister of sport, Denis Howell said, 'It seems all the tickets found their way to Scotland – it was difficult to find a single Englishman there.' Hector Munro, the shadow minister of sport, said that the Scots had shown 'jolly good initiative in finding tickets'.

Frank McGhee in the *Daily Mirror* said the reason Scots fans obtained more tickets than their English counterparts was simple: 'They care more.'

It was to be a day when despite the result, despite the performance and the grit, the heart, skill and persistence from the Scottish team, it was to be the Scottish fans who made all the headlines.

Scotland were 12/1 with Mecca and Ladbrokes to win 2-1.

It was just before the interval when the game sparked into life. Dalglish pressured Phil Neal at the edge of the box and the Liverpool player handled, giving Scotland a free kick on the left. Asa Hartford took the kick and put it high into the penalty area. Leaping above everyone in a white and dark blue shirt was Gordon McQueen, who sent a majestic header into the goal past Ray Clemence.

Liverpool boss Bob Paisley said to the *Sunday Mirror*, 'England should have known all about Gordon McQueen and set pieces. He'll snake his head around any defender if allowed.'

With just under half an hour of the match remaining it was 2-0. Hartford caught Neal out with a pass for Willie Johnston, who took the ball for a run then sent it to the far side of goal for Bruce Rioch. His header went to Macari and suddenly there was a scramble inside the six-yard box and Dalglish fought to get his foot to the ball and send it over Clemence's goal line.

'Kenny Dalglish was the ultimate professional, a manager's dream,' Willie Johnston wrote in his 2009 autobiography. 'Next to Denis Law and Jim Baxter he is probably one of Scotland's greatest players of all time. I can give him no higher accolade than that.'

There were three minutes left when McQueen pulled down Mick Channon in the box, the striker going on to score from the penalty spot.

As the final whistle sounded, Dalglish shook hands with Emlyn Hughes. As he turned to approach another England player he saw the rush of Scottish supporters on to the pitch and decided to get himself into the dressing room fast.

The Scots fans couldn't contain their joy and descended on the Wembley turf to rip it up, pull the goalposts down and dance around in a state of sheer joy.

In the *Sunday Telegraph* Colin Malam wrote, 'Scotland's second goal was a beauty, but with the notable exception of McGrain's superlative contribution from right-back, they rarely rose above the level of mere competence – whatever their ecstatic supporters, who flooded the pitch and smashed both goals to pieces at the end, thought.'

It might be hard for those who didn't see McGrain play, as he spent all his long career in Scotland, to comprehend just how good he was as a full-back. Just like Dalglish, who he had shared his football education with, he was modest and simply got on with the job in front of him. Malam's match report speaks of McGrain's 'pace, judgement and imagination' which gave him 'complete mastery of the right-hand side of the pitch'.

McGrain was always dependable, read the game well, had pace and vision to turn defence into attack and although a quiet and unassuming man, could inspire others in his team. He also suffered major injuries and health issues that he overcame to continue playing at the top level. Widely regarded as one of the finest full-backs in world football, McGrain stepped down from the Scotland team after the 1982 World Cup. However, he continued to play for Celtic until 1987, finishing his career off with a season at Hamilton Academical.

Also at Wembley that day was Hugh McIlvanney of *The Observer* who wrote, 'The one island of excellence amid the surge and eddy of ordinariness was McGrain, who once again demonstrated the composure, judgement of space and time and the wide repertoire of skill that make him surely the finest right-back in the world. Whether covering, tackling, jinking forward past embarrassed challengers or releasing the ball long or short with superb effect, he looked what he is: a master at the height of his powers.'

Of Dalglish, McIlvanney wrote, 'Dalglish, whose unselfish industry and sense of where he could be most worrying discomforted the English players all afternoon.'

Jock Stein said of Don Revie's team, 'If you've only got players who can run about, you've got nothing.'

Referee Károly Palotai of Hungary spoke to the *Daily Mirror* about how surprised he was that the game was such a punishing contest. 'Here were two teams both facing South American tours at the end of a long hard season,' he said. 'I thought players would be anxious to avoid injury – not to try to hurt each other as they were.' Palotai was an Olympic gold medal winner, captaining the Hungarian football team at the 1964 Tokyo Olympics. He would later take charge of the 1981 European Cup Final.

Dalglish was certainly not ashamed of the antics of the Scots fans that day. He used his 'Tartan Talk' column in *Shoot!* on 9 July to write a tribute to them, calling them 'the heart and soul of football itself', and insisted that they took a lot of stick they didn't deserve, particularly from the English press.

'What happened at Wembley was no more than a display of unashamed emotion,' Dalglish said.

Talking with the *Daily Mail* in 2021, Kenny said, 'The pitch was getting re-laid that summer. Well, if it wasn't, it certainly needed relaying after it! Half of it ended up back in Scotland.' He explained how fans saved up, week by week, for their trips to Wembley. 'It was a few quid away so they had enough for the game, the transport, the ticket and everything. There was always 40,000 travelling down. If the team had been as good as the Tartan Army, we'd have been very successful.'

Of his goal, Kenny said, 'I thought it unbelievable last year when I scored the winning goal for Scotland against England. I told everyone then that it was a once in a lifetime feeling. But how wrong can you be? Scoring the winning goal over the English at Wembley eclipsed even that.'

Scotland won the Championship with five points, Wales were second with four. Kenny was the tournament's top goalscorer with three.

One night in May, Kenny settled down to watch an episode of the BBC's flagship sports show, *Sportsnight*. On the show that night was Richard Dunn v Billy Aird fighting for the Heavyweight Championship of Great Britain, and a look at Lord Hesketh, the flamboyant aristocrat who gave James Hunt his first drive in Formula One, returning to the Grand Prix circuit with a new car and a new driver.

More importantly, there was a 17-minute filmed report narrated by John Motson on Liverpool FC, who were aiming for a Treble of league championship, FA Cup and European Cup. Kenny watched, knowing that his time with Celtic was coming to an end, and thinking that here was a club that he might like to join.

England: Clemence (Liverpool), Neal (Liverpool), Mills (Ipswich Town), B. Greenhoff (Manchester United) [Cherry (Leeds United)], Watson (Manchester City), Hughes (Liverpool), Francis (Birmingham City), Channon (Southampton), Pearson (Manchester United), Talbot (Ipswich Town), R. Kennedy (Liverpool) [Tueart (Manchester City)]

Scorer: Channon (87, pen)

Scotland: Rough (Partick Thistle), McGrain (Celtic), Donachie (Manchester City), Forsyth (Rangers), McQueen (Leeds United), Rioch (Everton), Masson (Queens Park

Rangers) [Gemmill (Derby County)], Dalglish (Celtic), Jordan (Manchester United) [Macari (Manchester United)], Hartford (Manchester City), Johnston (West Bromwich Albion)

Scorers: McQueen (42), Dalglish (63)

Attendance: 98,103

21

Liverpool 0-0 Manchester United

13 August 1977, Charity Shield,
Wembley Stadium

'WHAT A waste of money!' Manchester United's fans were keen to welcome Kenny to English football in the traditional season opener between the league champions and the cup holders at Wembley.

There was an inevitability about Dalglish leaving Celtic. Jock Stein was adamant that he was going nowhere only weeks before the deal was done. Dalglish had been pushing for a move for some time, and refused to go on Celtic's pre-season tour to Singapore and Australia, although Stein called him to say he had decided not to take him as he only wanted players who wanted to play for Celtic.

In his *Shoot!* 'Tartan Talk' column dated 13 August 1977, Kenny was previewing the new Scottish season and contemplating facing Premier League new boys St Mirren and Clydebank. He took the time to congratulate his Celtic colleagues on their results on their tour, but added, 'For reasons that I hope I will be able to reveal to you soon I did not make the trip.'

Liverpool had won the European Cup in May 1977, to go along with their English First Division title. They had missed out on a Treble by losing 2-1 to Manchester United in the FA Cup Final. Their talismanic forward Kevin Keegan had decided he wanted a fresh challenge and took the unusual step at that time of moving abroad, signing for SV Hamburg for £500,000.

Keegan would be a big loss for the club. He had joined from Scunthorpe in 1971, and scored 100 goals in 323 games. He had helped the club to three league titles, the FA Cup, two UEFA Cups and the European Cup. Who could replace him? Liverpool's boss Bob Paisley knew exactly who could.

On the evening of Monday, 8 August, Paisley called Stein after Liverpool returned from playing Ajax and Barcelona in a tournament in Amsterdam. Stein, who had promised to let Liverpool know if Dalglish was for sale, said he wanted to keep the player. 'Then on Tuesday he phoned to tell us to come up and talk about it,' Paisley said.

On 9 August Celtic were away to Dunfermline in the last pre-season friendly before the start of the new Premier League. It would be Dalglish's last match in the hoops. Despite turning down all Celtic's financial offers, and indicating he wanted a move, Dalglish was still club captain. 'We were in the dressing room just before the game,' he told Archie Macpherson for the broadcaster's biography of Stein. 'Jock started to talk to us and finished up by turning to Danny McGrain and saying, "Right Danny, lead the boys out on to the park." He didn't say a word to me. That's when I knew I was finished.'

In front of 4,500 fans, Celtic won 4-1. In his *Evening Times* match report, Shearer Borthwick wrote, 'His shrewd generalship, delicate passes, and consummate skill was in evidence, although he did not break sweat. That level of skill cannot be replaced overnight, if ever.'

The Celtic fans were aware of the rumours, but not that the deal was being done that night. Rumours were around Liverpool too, although other names were also being mentioned. Birmingham's Trevor Francis, Arsenal's Liam Brady and Peter Sayer of Cardiff City were mentioned as signing targets, with the *Liverpool Echo* writing that Dalglish was likely to follow Keegan to the continent. Paisley himself told the *Echo* that ahead of his meeting about Dalglish in

Glasgow on the Tuesday evening, he had not expected to clinch the deal immediately.

Stein and Paisley met alongside Desmond White and other Celtic board members at Celtic Park at 10.30pm. Celtic wanted the discussions to be done on the quiet as if the talks fell through they didn't want word to get out they were prepared to sell.

Liverpool weren't natural big spenders. Their biggest outlay to this point had been £200,000 for Ray Kennedy from Arsenal in 1974 and the same figure for David Johnson from Ipswich Town in 1976.

Celtic turned down bids of £330,000 and £360,000 for Dalglish, but when Liverpool reached £400,000, they were told that another ten per cent would seal the move. The fee of £440,000 would be a new high between English and Scottish clubs, and beat the record of £350,000 that Everton paid Birmingham for Bob Latchford three years earlier, when Howard Kendall and Archie Styles also went in the opposite direction.

Once the figure was agreed upon Dalglish was called in. Paisley told him that the two clubs had agreed a fee and it was now up to him. Dalglish and Paisley talked for not more than a few minutes. The deal was agreed. Dalglish was amazed by how swiftly negotiations were concluded.

He was sad to leave Celtic, but he knew the new challenges that lay ahead. He was signing for the English and European champions, a team who were set on retaining those trophies. That ambition was what Kenny wanted to hear. He couldn't possibly turn the chance down.

'We did everything we could to keep him at Parkhead,' Stein said to the press. 'But the boy felt that his career would progress further elsewhere and we could not stand in his way.' Stein said if Dalglish had wanted to stay there wasn't an amount of money he wouldn't have turned down. 'It's all right saying we've got £400,000 but where do you find another player like him?' Stein asked.

He wanted to make it clear to fans that it was Kenny's decision. 'I think it was obvious he wanted to play elsewhere,' he told the *Evening Times*. 'I'm disappointed ... we asked if there was any way he would stay. The answer was, "No."'

The *Evening Times* went out on to the streets of Glasgow and canvassed both Celtic and Rangers fans for their opinions on Kenny's transfer. Unanimously, everyone agreed that his departure was a loss for Scottish football. Celtic fans were mainly despondent at losing such a talent. When you speak to Celtic fans who remember Dalglish in the hoops today, the first thing they say is how heartbroken they were when Kenny left. Some say they never got over it.

Dalglish wasn't the first star at Celtic Park; every generation of Celtic fans saw great players; Patsy Gallacher, Jimmy McGrory, Charlie Tully, the list is endless. He wasn't even the first player fans could argue was the greatest in Britain; Jimmy Johnstone gave Celtic fans plenty of ammunition for that discussion. But Kenny's ability, charm, modesty and looks saw him become the favourite player for the majority of fans of that era, albeit that in Billy McNeill's 2004 autobiography he asserts that Dalglish wasn't loved the same way as Johnstone, or a later hero like Henrik Larsson, suggesting that there was always a suspicion that he was a Rangers fan at heart. While Celtic were fighting for European honours every season, many Celtic fans couldn't understand why Dalglish would want to play elsewhere.

Frank McAvennie would later play alongside Kenny for Scotland and become a Celtic idol himself, but in 1977, he was one of many on the terracing. 'I thought my world had ended,' he said in 2025 of Kenny's transfer.

Simple Minds frontman Jim Kerr was a young Celtic supporter in 1977, just starting to play in bands. He idolised Kenny, watching him play in the reserves and seeing him progress into the first team. 'We loved the story of how he'd supported Rangers and Sean Fallon had nicked him from under their noses,' he told *The Scotsman* in 2014. 'But when he was transferred to Liverpool I was distraught and had to spend three days in bed. "F*** it," I told myself, "music's the thing now."'

A year later, Celtic fans would take their opportunity to tell Dalglish how they felt about his departure.

But Kenny had won everything there was to win in Scotland. There were further challenges elsewhere and what he wanted most of all was to win the European Cup. Liverpool, the new European champions after their 3-1 victory over Borussia Mönchengladbach, gave him that opportunity.

Dalglish collected his boots at Parkhead the next morning before Jock Stein drove him down to a hotel in Moffat where Bob Paisley and Liverpool chairman John Smith were staying under the assumed names of the Smith brothers. Smith called the deal 'An historic occasion for the club.' Jock Stein said he was looking forward to seeing the Kop's reaction to Dalglish's boyish grin when he scored.

Speaking to Macpherson, Kenny recalled a warm moment with Stein. 'Before he left me that day he suddenly grabbed me in a big bear hug and just said, "Good luck, ya wee bugger." It was affectionate, and I felt quite moved by it.'

'Kenny is used to silverware. He responds to it,' Paisley said. 'I bought him because he has so much ability. He's similar to Keegan insofar as he can play many positions. Kevin had a dual role and I think Kenny can do this too. He has a penchant for scoring goals and I'll be looking for him in that area ... If you want to keep at the top, as we do, you have to be prepared to buy the best. I think that's what we've done.'

Paisley and Smith drove Kenny to Anfield. There he had a medical. The assessor declared, 'He is one of the fittest men I have ever examined.' Once that was completed Kenny signed his contract.

That night John Toshack, Kenny's new striking partner, picked him up in his car and drove him to Bill Shankly's home in West Derby, close to Melwood, Liverpool's training ground. Although Shankly, who stood down as manager in 1974, was no longer on the Liverpool staff he was still a figurehead of the club, and Toshack had so much reverence for him he wanted the new signing to spend some time with him. Shankly reminisced with Kenny about his trial in 1966. Then he offered him two pieces of advice. 'Don't over-eat in that hotel and don't lose your accent.'

On Thursday morning, Kenny went into training and played in a bounce game. On Friday he travelled down to London with the team. On Saturday, he made his debut.

Dalglish denied he had moved for the money, telling the *Daily Record*'s Ken Gallacher he was looking for fresh challenges. Dalglish was keen to pay tribute to Celtic and the fans, wishing he could have had a farewell in front of them. 'I've left now but I won't forget the supporters – and I won't forget the club or the people there.'

He was, though, now looking forward to playing for Liverpool. 'Liverpool are very special. They have, as I say, the same magic which surrounds Celtic.'

Liverpool were due to return thousands of unsold Charity Shield tickets, but Dalglish's signing prompted them to go back on sale and 1,500 fans bought £7 tickets for the British Rail Wembley Special trains.

'We all knew Dalglish had special qualities,' Phil Thompson wrote in his 2005 autobiography, 'but we didn't have a complete understanding about his ability because we simply did not see enough of Scottish football at that time. It was very rarely on our TV screens and while we knew Kenny was star quality north of the border, the big question was whether he could translate that to the English top flight.' Thompson recalled that it took about 30 seconds of his first training session to understand what a unique footballer Kenny was.

Dalglish came out of the Wembley tunnel chatting with his former Celtic team-mate Lou Macari, who was playing for United, although he said later he had no recollection of what they chatted about.

The Liverpool fans gave him 'the sort of welcome I couldn't even have dreamed about', he wrote in *Shoot!* 'They chanted my name and made me more relaxed immediately. The part they played in my debut cannot be minimised.' Dalglish enjoyed a great relationship with supporters of all the clubs he played for and managed, and he was always keen to acknowledge their contribution.

'Within ten minutes we realised what a player we had,' Liverpool midfielder Terry McDermott wrote in his 2017 autobiography. 'He was unbelievable. Everything he did in the opening few minutes was bang on. He was so physically strong and would stick his backside into everybody – that was his forte – but no one could have forecast that he would be held in the same high esteem as Kevin, that he would be adored so much by the Kop.'

After half an hour Dalglish created a great chance for himself when he controlled the ball on his chest, lost Buchan and Greenhoff and fired a shot just wide.

The game was entertaining with both sides showing flashes of skill and grit, although it finished goalless, with the sides sharing the Shield.

Kenny felt that he fitted in quickly to Liverpool's style. He said that the lasting memory he had of the match was the scarf which a Liverpool supporter draped around his neck. 'I have many trophies already, but the scarf will always hold a special memory for me. A memento from the Kop of my first match for the Reds.'

Liverpool: Clemence, Neal, Jones, Thompson, R. Kennedy, Hughes (c), Dalglish, Case, Fairclough, McDermott, Callaghan

Manchester United: Stepney, Nicholl, Albiston, McIlroy, B. Greenhoff, Buchan, Coppell, J. Greenhoff [McCreery], Pearson, Macari, Hill

Attendance: 82,000

22

Middlesbrough 1-1 Liverpool

20 August 1977, English First Division,
Ayresome Park

THE OPENING league fixture for 1977/78 for Liverpool was away to Middlesbrough. Jim Platt, the Middlesbrough goalkeeper, had faced Dalglish before. In July 1975, Celtic went on a pre-season tour to Ireland, where they took on Dundalk. Platt, who had been ever-present for Boro in the English First Division the previous season, played for Dundalk as a guest. Celtic won 6-0 with six different goalscorers. Dalglish was, of course, one of them. In the *Daily Record*, Hugh Taylor contended that no one would score a better goal all season. Kenny brought down a through ball, looked up and lobbed the ball into the top corner.

'That was the greatest goal that has ever been scored against me,' Platt said to the *Record*. He now got the chance to face Kenny on his English league debut.

Willie Maddren was in the Middlesbrough defence. Nearing the end of his ten seasons there, he was nursing a knee injury and had only 45 minutes in two friendlies as preparation for the new season.

'Of all the players I might have been marking after such minimal preparation one of the last I would have chosen was Kenny Dalglish,' Maddren wrote in his 1998 autobiography. 'Dalglish, full of twists and turns to test the turning circle of even the fittest defender. The game kicked off at a white hot pace and it was immediately apparent Liverpool were in irresistible form.'

Dalglish had Liverpool in front after only six minutes. Receiving the ball from Terry McDermott, he drew Platt, waited until the Northern Irishman had committed, and then slotted the ball past him with precision.

Maddren was horrified when Liverpool went ahead. 'As I tracked an opponent out to the left flank they played the ball from midfield into the heart of our defence, and I could only look on in dismay as Dalglish raced through unmarked to beat Jim Platt.'

Dalglish looked a constant threat during the first half as his midfield provided him with balls on the ground. In the second half, however, Liverpool opted to play the ball in the air, where Stuart Boam was imperious in the centre of Boro's defence. Kenny couldn't get a look in.

Middlesbrough's equaliser came four minutes into the second half when McDermott was weak with a header back to Clemence, allowing David Armstrong to nick in and finish.

Liverpool were quite pleased with the draw away from home, which Kenny was surprised about. Celtic expected a win everywhere they went, and Dalglish thought that Liverpool should have a similar outlook.

In the *Liverpool Echo*, Michael Charters wrote of Liverpool, 'They have one of the finest match-winners in British football in Kenny Dalglish but they must play to his strengths. This lesson is clear – give Dalglish the ball on the deck, and he'll score a lot of goals.'

It wasn't so much Dalglish forming an understanding with his new team-mates; he had proved by this stage of his career that he could play with any player of quality; it was more that his new team-mates had to understand how best to play him into the game.

'For the 1977/78 season Bob opted for a heavier midfield,' Jimmy Case wrote in his 2015 autobiography, 'with a more fluid, pacier attack formation, preferring David Johnson to John Toshack up front, and it took time to adjust.'

Quite quickly Dalglish realised Liverpool was the perfect place for him. Kenny and Marina found the people there very friendly. They initially moved into the Holiday Inn in Paradise Street in Liverpool city centre, where the Liverpool One shopping precinct now resides. The innkeeper happened to be a friend of Marina's dad Pat, and the staff looked after the Dalglish children, Paul, who was six months, and Kelly, who was 18 months old. It helped the family settle in, and they found Liverpool very similar to Glasgow. The players too were welcoming and happy to show Kenny and Marina around the city. 'We walked into a club that had its arms open to receive us,' Dalglish said in 2017.

In his 1993 biography of Liverpool midfielder Ray Kennedy, Dr Andrew Lees wrote about Kennedy's assessment of Kevin Keegan's replacement. 'He felt ... Dalglish was a far better player. In training Ray found that if he just stood still Kevin would be unable to go past him and would be forced to pass, whereas Dalglish was deceptive and could get round without parting with the ball.'

Three days later, Dalglish made his home debut at Anfield in a game with Newcastle United. 'Nothing since has ever come up to that night for me,' Dalglish said in 1993. He felt the pressure of the occasion, but the reception from the Liverpool fans was unforgettable. 'It was the start of a long relationship I had with them.'

'Straight away everyone knew this boy was special,' Phil Thompson wrote in his 2005 autobiography. 'Memories of Kevin disappeared all in the space of 90 minutes against Boro. Here was a new star for the next few years in more ways than one. Dalglish scored in five of his first six league games. Immediately, he was dubbed the new "King of the Kop".'

Kenny netted against Newcastle in a 2-0 win, using a burst of pace to beat Irving Nattrass to a pass from Kennedy, then touching the ball past Steven Harwick in goal. The fans gave him the most brilliant reception, among them the Radio

One DJ John Peel, who was standing on the Kop and wrote in *The Guardian* in 1994, 'We warmed to him in a way that we had never really warmed to Keegan.'

Kenny scored again when West Bromwich Albion visited Anfield on 27 August. Steve Heighway added a second, and Dalglish set up Jimmy Case for the third in a 3-0 win.

Dalglish's fourth goal in four games arrived in a 2-0 win over Chelsea in the League Cup. Goals against Coventry in a 2-0 win and Ipswich in a 1-1 draw followed. Kenny's fellow Scot Alan Hansen made his debut in the 1-0 win over Derby County as Liverpool sat third in the league, level on points with Manchester City and Nottingham Forest.

The match against Chelsea on 8 October was Hansen's fourth game for Liverpool. In his autobiography *A Matter of Opinion*, he recalled, 'I was sitting next to Kenny in the dressing room before the game, and as we were chatting Bob came across and said to Kenny, "Watch out for John Phillips [Chelsea's goalkeeper] straying too far off his line."' In the second minute, Kenny scored with a long-range chip over the Shrewsbury-born goalkeeper's head.

The 2-0 win gave Kenny the perfect send-off as he prepared for Scotland's away World Cup qualifier against Wales. At Anfield.

Middlesbrough: Platt, Craggs, Cooper, Souness, Boam, Maddren, Mahoney, Mills, Woof, McAndrew, Armstrong

Scorer: Armstrong (49)

Liverpool: Clemence, Neal, Jones, Thompson, R. Kennedy, Hughes (c), Dalglish, Case, Heighway, McDermott, Callaghan

Scorer: Dalglish (6)

Attendance: 31,000

23

Wales 0-2 Scotland

12 October 1977, World Cup qualifier,
Anfield

IN THE qualifying campaign for the 1978 World Cup in Argentina, Scotland were placed in a three-team group with Wales and Czechoslovakia, where only the winners qualified.

Dalglish played in the 2-0 loss to Czechoslovakia in the opening group game in October 1976. It was a match in which Andy Gray and Anton Ondrus were sent off in the first half for fighting. Another four Scots were booked.

In November 1976, Dalglish earned his 40th cap in the 1-0 win over Wales at Hampden – a win that was down to an Ian Evans own goal.

In May of 1977, Wales and Scotland had drawn 0-0 at the Racecourse Ground in front of 14,468 spectators in the Home Internationals.

In September 1977, with Kenny now a Liverpool player, the Czechs came to Hampden, where 83,679 were in attendance. Wales had beaten them 3-0 in Wrexham, and so the Czechs desperately needed the win. It was a classic Scottish performance. Joe Jordan put the Scots in front after 18 minutes, with Manchester City's Asa Hartford doubling the lead on 35 minutes. Kenny would make it 3-0 nine minutes into the second half. Although Miroslav Gajdusek pulled one back with ten minutes remaining, Scotland achieved a famous win, which meant that if they could beat Wales in the last game in October, the Scots would take the one qualification spot.

Ninian Park in Cardiff was the original choice of venue for the match. However, the 1975 Safety of Sports Grounds Act saw the ground be deemed unsuitable, as South Glamorgan County Council could only provide a safety certificate for a 14,000 capacity. Wrexham's Racecourse Ground had a similar restriction imposed by Clywd County Council. The Welsh FA knew that the match would attract an attendance of around 50,000, so they couldn't risk playing it at a venue with only a third of that capacity.

Many retrospective accounts of why the game was played at Anfield erroneously state that Wales were ordered to play the match away from Cardiff due to crowd trouble in a game with Yugoslavia in May 1976. In fact, the ban was imposed by UEFA, who ordered Wales to play all home matches in the 1978–80 European Championship qualifiers on grounds at least 124 miles (200km) from Cardiff (so World Cup qualifiers were not affected). Their home European qualifiers were all played at the Racecourse Ground, around 139 miles from the capital.

Villa Park in Birmingham was briefly considered an option for the Scotland clash, but ruled out as it was deemed a 'no man's land' between north and south Wales, making it difficult to get to from both regions. On 30 August, Anfield was confirmed as the venue. Liverpool striker John Toshack was delighted, saying, 'This is great news. Anfield is just the place for Wales and both Joey Jones and I can guarantee the crowd will give us tremendous support.' He perhaps had forgotten that Anfield was currently falling in love with a new hero. That night, Dalglish scored an almost impossible goal against Chelsea in the League Cup when, after collecting a Phil Neal pass on the byline, he hit a shot just as he turned. Taken by surprise, goalkeeper John Phillips allowed the ball to slip through his hands, under his body and into the net. Jimmy Case made it 2-0 and sent Liverpool into the third round.

Welsh FA secretary Trevor Morris said Anfield was designed to attain as much home advantage as possible for the Welsh players. 'Anfield is just as acceptable to many people from north Wales as Wrexham. They can easily get there in less than an hour.' Liverpool's home was around 28 miles away from the Welsh FA's Wrexham headquarters.

It would be the first full international at Anfield in 46 years since England beat Wales 3-1 in the Home Internationals on 18 November 1931.

Ally MacLeod and the Welsh boss Mike Smith were happy with the venue. Smith had quickly ruled out the suggestion that the game could be played at Wembley as he felt the Scots would outnumber the Welsh fans and turn the match into a Scottish home game. Wales planned to train at Wrexham, while MacLeod had booked hotel accommodation in the Wirral and would use Tranmere Rovers' Prenton Park to train.

In *The Observer*, Peter Corrigan wrote, 'I fear Wales have made a mistake in transferring the game to Anfield. They will surely make a great deal of money, and the game will be granted a suitable atmosphere. Yet the sort of hysterical atmosphere we can expect is more likely to stir the Scots than the Welsh.'

Cardiff chairman Stefan Teraelski was furious, 'If it had been a rugby matter, there would have been debates in Parliament,' he said, 'protests in the media, and the Welsh Office would have been called in. Because it is soccer, there have been no signs of any MP, Jim Callaghan the Prime Minister or Denis Howell intervening.'

Ahead of the game at Hampden in November the previous year, Welsh captain Terry Yorath, speaking to the *South Wales Argus*, said, 'I always reckon they [Scotland] play better away from home. With a large crowd behind them, they seem to become nervous. They sense that the goals must come quickly to keep the crowd happy and this prevents them from playing their true game.' Yorath was about to get a sense of how Scotland played both away from home and with a large crowd behind them.

Trevor Morris said that Scots fans would not get more than their allocation, which at 12,000 was a quarter of the ground. However, Scots fans made day trips to Wales to get tickets and even went to the headquarters of the Welsh FA in Wrexham to secure them.

Prices for the game ranged from £1.50 to £5. Turnstiles opened at 4.30pm, three hours ahead of kick-off. BBC Scotland had the whole game live from 7.25pm; however, BBC Wales only had highlights at 9.55pm.

In the run-up to the game, the Scots and Welsh at Anfield were having a great time. Dalglish, Alan Hansen, who was just staking a claim in Liverpool's first team and had yet to make his Scotland debut, along with Scottish coach Reuben Bennett, were winding up Toshack and Joey Jones. Their game was being played out at the Melwood training ground on a daily basis.

Jones said he'd helped Kenny settle in at Anfield and they had become good pals. 'I'm not expecting any favours from Kenny and he won't be expecting any from me. I've played against him already a few times in internationals and we've exchanged words – unrepeatable. He's kicked me, I've kicked him, but it's all forgotten afterwards.'

Scots fans who arrived in Liverpool without tickets tried everything they could think of to get some. Several even knocked on the door of former Liverpool boss Bill Shankly. 'I don't know where they got my address from,' Shankly said to the *Echo*, 'and I had no tickets to give them.'

Dalglish recalled, when speaking to the *Glasgow Times* in 2017, 'I just remember the thousands and thousands of Scotland fans who were there. The car park was packed, not with cars, but Scottish punters. Unbelievable.'

Trevor Morris wrote an address in the match programme, criticising the restrictions that led to Cardiff being ruled out as the venue. He stated that the Safety of Sports Ground Act was 'pushed through Parliament without proper consultation with football and other sporting authorities'. However, he stressed the Act was commendable and necessary. 'So rigid was the application of the guidelines by the local authority responsible for issuing the certificate that restrictions imposed made Cardiff out of the question.' There was no realistic alternative but to play outside Wales, he wrote. It was 'absurd', he said, to have the game played in front of only 14,000 spectators.

The crowd was recorded as 50,850, although there's little doubt many without tickets managed to get in. The famous Kop was designated as a Welsh end, but by kick-off, it was 90 per cent Scots.

In his autobiography Wales goalkeeper Dai Davies recounted his experience. 'Arriving at Anfield a few hours before the game was incredible, almost frightening. Liverpool was literally a sea of Scottish flags, and thousands and thousands of supporters, most of them apparently intoxicated.'

'It became our home game,' recalled Joe Jordan in 2012. 'The Anfield crowd was dominated by Scots, and that was important for us. We knew we were playing a very good Welsh team, but seeing the number of fans we had and hearing them gave us the edge. I don't know how so many of them got tickets, but we took over Liverpool that night.' Lou Macari said he had no fears of a Scotland defeat once he saw the supporters in the ground.

The game's turning point was a wonderful save Alan Rough made from a John Toshack volley in the second half. Rough, yards off his line, leapt backwards and turned the goal-bound shot over the bar as Toshack sank to the ground in disbelief. Over the years, Rough has been reluctant to call it his greatest save, but speaking to Aidan Smith of *The Scotsman* in 2022, he said, 'The saves you remember are the most important, and the one from big Toshack was certainly that.'

'Scottish goalkeeping was a bit of a joke back then, but Rough had the game of his life,' Welsh midfielder Brian Flynn recalled.

'There was far too much passion in the place for anyone to be able to play cool, controlled football,' Davies wrote. 'Even keeping a cool head and a clear mind was an effort.'

With 12 minutes remaining, Scotland were awarded a penalty. A long throw from Willie Johnston went into the Welsh box. Jordan rose alongside Norwich City's David Jones. A hand went up in the air. Referee Robert Wurst pointed to the spot. Captain Don Masson took responsibility and fired the penalty home.

Much debate has raged since that award as to whose hand played the ball. Was it Jones? Or, as most Welsh people believe, was it actually Jordan? When Dalglish was asked years later he was non-committal, saying he didn't know what had happened at the time and still couldn't see clearly when watching back on television.

In *The Guardian*, Paul Fitzpatrick said he doubted Jones would have reacted so meekly to the decision if he had been innocent.

'As far as I know, the ball did not touch me,' Jordan said directly after the match. 'I did not feel it and was surprised when the penalty was given.' Joe has remained tight-lipped since that day over the incident, accepting that Welsh people want to quiz him on it but feeling that saying nothing is the best thing to do.

Mike Smith said afterwards, 'There's disagreement among my players as to why the kick was given, but the referee gave it for a foul.'

Searching for an equaliser, the Welsh left gaps at the back, and with three minutes remaining, Scotland exposed them. Buchan was in acres of space on the right, and he put in a perfect cross for Kenny Dalglish to leap and head into the net for 2-0. Scotland had done it. They had qualified for Argentina. Now, the expectations had really begun.

As for the Welsh, due in no small part to that match, the FAW made a record profit of £60,000 in 1977.

The 1978 World Cup finals in Argentina became one of Scotland's most infamous disasters. In the match against Iran, Dalglish broke Denis Law's Scottish caps record when he made his 56th appearance for his country. He would say that he was 'genuinely thrilled' with the honour but felt a slight tinge of regret that he had taken the record from his hero. Dalglish hit an opportunistic goal in the 3-2 win over the Netherlands, which allowed Scotland to at least go out of the tournament with their heads held high.

Wales: Davies (Wrexham), Thomas (Derby County), Jones (Liverpool), Mahoney (Middlesbrough), Jones (Norwich City), Phillips (Aston Villa), Sayer (Cardiff City) [Deacy (PSV Eindhoven)], Yorath (Coventry City), Flynn (Burnley), Thomas (Wrexham), Toshack (Liverpool)

Scotland: Rough (Partick Thistle), Jardine (Rangers) [Buchan (Manchester United)], Donachie (Manchester City), Masson (c) (Queens Park Rangers), McQueen (Leeds United), Forsyth (Rangers), Dalglish (Liverpool), Hartford (Manchester City), Jordan (Leeds United), Macari (Manchester United), Johnston (West Bromwich Albion)

Scorers: Masson (78, pen), Dalglish (87)

Attendance: 50,850

24

Liverpool 3-0 Borussia Mönchengladbach

12 April 1978, European Cup semi-final second leg, Anfield

LIVERPOOL BEGAN their defence of the European Cup with a 5-1 win over Dynamo Dresden in the second round first leg. John Toshack set up three of the goals, but by February of 1978, he would become Swansea City's player-manager. A 2-1 defeat in Dresden took Liverpool through 6-3 on aggregate.

Dalglish recalled that Dresden was the best side he'd come up against in Europe at that time. He especially remembered Hans-Jürgen Dörner hitting 60- and 70-yard passes out to his wingers, which caused Liverpool a number of problems.

Before March's third round, Liverpool would lift the European Super Cup in an interesting two-legged affair against Hamburg, the European Cup Winners' Cup holders, with Kenny Dalglish facing Kevin Keegan. In the first leg in West Germany, Kenny would set up Liverpool's goal for David Fairclough, cancelling out Ferdinand Keller's strike for Hamburg.

Anfield's second leg in December was a night to remember for the 34,931 fans in attendance. Keegan called the game 'a total disaster' and recalled that although he received a great reception from the Liverpool fans, by the end of the night they were singing 'you should have stayed at Anfield'.

Phil Thompson opened the scoring on 21 minutes, but the night belonged to Terry McDermott. Bob Paisley had told McDermott he should be getting forward more and linking with Kenny Dalglish. McDermott paid heed that evening and hit a hat-trick. He would say his performance led to a rise in his confidence, and his goals for Liverpool increased every season from then on. Fairclough added a fifth with Kenny netting to make it 6-0 with two minutes remaining.

After the match, Keegan told the *Daily Mirror*, 'We were diabolical. From what I had heard about Liverpool I didn't think they would play that well. I didn't see much wrong with them from where I stood watching.'

It was Kenny's first European honour.

In March, Benfica were the opponents in the European Cup third round. Jimmy Case and Emlyn Hughes scored the goals in a 2-1 win at a muddy Estadio Da Luz, after Nené had opened the scoring. In the second leg at Anfield, Ian Callaghan scored after six minutes, with Dalglish adding the second after 17 minutes. Nené pulled one back on the half hour, but further goals from McDermott and Neal gave Liverpool a 6-2 aggregate win and a place in the semi-finals.

The semi-final was a repeat of the 1977 final, with Borussia Mönchengladbach the opponents. In the first leg, Wilfried Hannes put the home team 1-0 up in the Rheinstadion after 28 minutes. With two minutes remaining, Dalglish crossed for David Johnson, who headed in despite being pulled back by Berti Vogts. There was a shock to come for the Reds, though, as a minute later Rainer Bonhof cracked home a free kick to give the West Germans a 2-1 win. Despite the disappointment of defeat, the away goal gave Liverpool the confidence that they could get the job done in the second leg a fortnight later.

Eight of Borussia's starting line-up at Anfield had played in the 1977 European Cup Final. Additionally, Vogts,

Bonhof, Wimmer, Kulik and Heynckes played in both legs of the 1973 UEFA Cup Final when Liverpool won 3-2 on aggregate.

Several reports indicate that the German players looked nervous when they met the fantastic roar from the Kop and all around Anfield, and the one-goal deficit was wiped out after only six minutes. Graeme Souness, bought from Middlesbrough in January 1978 for £352,000, threaded a ball through for Dalglish, who caught it just at the byline. He put in a perfect cross for Ray Kennedy to head home. Liverpool were now ahead on away goals, but they wouldn't leave it there.

The lead was increased in the 35th minute. Emlyn Hughes launched the ball towards the penalty spot, where Ray Kennedy headed it down into the path of Dalglish. Kenny hit a shot just inside the post.

In midfield, Souness, a player Vogts admitted later the Germans knew little about, overshadowed Bonhof. It was notably his best game for the club up until that point, and afterwards, he said the occasion was the greatest night of his life.

Along with Dalglish, Scottish international Graeme Souness was probably Liverpool's most important signing of the late 1970s. Beginning with Tottenham Hotspur as a teenager, he moved on to Middlesbrough in the Second Division without ever establishing himself at White Hart Lane. Although Souness was signed by Stan Anderson for Boro it was under Anderson's successor, Jack Charlton, that he really began to flourish. He also benefitted from playing in midfield alongside one of Kenny's former team-mates in Bobby Murdoch, learning a great deal from him.

With Souness and Murdoch in midfield, Middlesbrough won the Second Division in 1974. Souness's abilities in the First Division brought interest from Liverpool, Leeds United and Manchester City. One morning he was told to report to a hotel in Leeds to speak to an interested club, although he wasn't told who. On the way, Souness made up his mind that he wouldn't sign for anyone else but Liverpool. He found John Smith, the Liverpool chairman, was there, and he quickly agreed to Middlesbrough's price, and Souness was off to Anfield.

Liverpool played against Mönchengladbach with four men across the midfield, which might have looked like a negative tactic, but wasn't, as those midfielders moved into attacking positions when gaps appeared. Ray Kennedy was particularly effective and Udo Lattek, the Borussia manager, named him as the man of the match.

At half-time Kennedy reported to Bob Paisley that he was suffering from a groin strain. It wasn't troubling him when he played the ball with his left foot, but it gave him pain to play it with his right. Paisley pondered substituting him but left the decision to Kennedy, who felt he was enjoying himself so much he'd like to continue. 'Imagine what the crowd's reaction would have been if I had taken him off!' Paisley said afterwards.

Steve Heighway had the measure of Berti Vogts, who resorted to clattering the Irish international repeatedly.

The third goal was made by Kennedy. The former Arsenal striker played a pass across the corner of the German penalty area. The ball found Jimmy Case, who dummied Hannes, cut inside and rocketed a shot past Kleff.

Vogts gave his assessment of Dalglish to the *Record* after the match. 'Kenny Dalglish is a very good player, and we have known that for some time,' Vogts began. 'But since he has joined Liverpool he has improved ... The way he has taken over from Kevin Keegan proves he is also confident of his ability.'

'He's very quiet on the pitch,' Tommy Smith said about Dalglish to the *Daily Post* in 1979, 'and he takes the stick from defenders very well, just as a highly paid professional should.

He prefers to let his feet do the talking, and sometimes after beating a defender who had kicked him and then scoring, he would just give a little V-sign ... He has fitted into the Liverpool system very well and is probably more of a Liverpool player than Kevin was.'

At the final whistle, the German players gathered in the centre circle and applauded Liverpool as the home players ran around the ground in a lap of honour.

'It was a psychological thing with us,' Udo Lattek said afterwards. 'Some of our players clearly didn't like the atmosphere.'

It took until four minutes from the end of extra time for Belgian side Club Brugge to beat Juventus to seal their place in the final. 'After knocking out Juventus we don't need to fear anybody,' their manager Ernst Happel said.

This had been Kenny's third European Cup semi-final, and now he had finally got to where he wanted to be, the main reason he left Celtic: he was in the European Cup Final.

Liverpool: Clemence, Neal, Smith, Thompson, R. Kennedy, Hughes (c), Dalglish, Case, Heighway, McDermott, Souness

Scorers: R. Kennedy (6), Dalglish (35), Case (56)

Borussia Mönchengladbach: Kleff, Vogts, Hannes, Wittkamp, Wohlers [Schäfer], Bonhof, Wimmer [Lienen], Nielsen, Kulik, Del'Haye, Heynckes

25

Liverpool 1-0 Club Brugge

10 May 1978, European Cup Final,
Wembley Stadium

ALTHOUGH THEY could only achieve second place, Liverpool had a wonderful run-in to the league season in 1977/78. Their last defeat was on 8 March when Derby County won 4-2 at the Baseball Ground. They then went on a 12-game unbeaten run. Nottingham Forest, though, had wrapped up the title with a few weeks to spare. Liverpool finished their league season with a goalless draw against the new champions. The XI who lined up for that game would be the same starters at Wembley. David Fairclough was the only surprise, as it was anticipated that the fit-again Steve Heighway would get his place back. Bob Paisley, though, had felt Fairclough earned his spot with his performances since Heighway had been injured.

In the early rounds, Club Brugge beat KuPS of Finland and Greece's Panathinaikos. In the quarter-final, they faced Atlético Madrid, beating them 4-3 on aggregate. Juventus were their opponents in the semi-final. Brugge lost 1-0 in Turin in the first leg, but a 1-0 victory at home took the tie to extra time, where René Vandereycken hit the winner.

For the final, Brugge were missing injured midfielder Paul Courant and striker Raoul Lambert, who had scored against Liverpool in the 1976 UEFA Cup Final. While Courant missed out completely, Lambert was fit enough for a place on the bench. Both were important players, and with them out, Club Brugge's tactics were to employ man-to-man marking and use an offside trap. Or as Steven Scragg wrote in *These Football Times*, they had set out to envelop Liverpool 'within a matrix of defensive strangulation'.

Rather than ballooning the ball upfield impatiently, as a Liverpool side of the past may have done, this group had the elegant Souness in midfield and the intelligent movement of Terry McDermott to call upon. Ray Kennedy also shut down the Brugge midfield, while up front, Fairclough harried and made a nuisance of himself.

In the first half Dalglish set up Souness, who fired a volley over the bar. Alan Hansen had a great header tipped over.

The game-winning moment came in the 65th minute. Phil Neal had the ball near the right-hand corner flag. Neal played it to McDermott, who chipped the ball along the byline and into the penalty box for Dalglish. Kenny flicked the ball over his head, but De Cubber cleanly headed it away. It fell to Souness at the edge of the area. He chested the ball down, then took a touch. 'Will he get a shot in?' Brian Moore asked in commentary. As two Brugge defenders descended on him from either side, Souness side-footed a right-foot pass between them to Dalglish, who typically had his back to goal. Kenny turned and ran on to the ball. As Jensen in goal came out to the corner of the six-yard box Kenny lifted it over him and into the net.

On the 7NWA podcast in 2020, Kenny talked through the goal. 'What was going through my head [when the ball was played in by McDermott] was, "Just knock it back in towards the middle of the goal." Just to keep it alive … there should be somebody there. Then the next bit, the guy goes to header it out. You're trying to keep onside. It goes to Graeme, so I've got to get half-turned. Because there's a chance I'm going to get it, and he went into a tackle with a guy, and it broke to me.'

Dalglish had noticed that Brugge's Danish goalkeeper Birger Jensen had gone down early a couple of times in the game, particularly in a one-on-one with Terry McDermott. 'And I thought, "I hope he's going to do it again." So I just dipped the shoulder a wee bit and chipped it in.'

'The goal was pure Dalglish,' Jimmy Case wrote in his 2015 autobiography, 'and proof indeed, if ever it was needed, of what a great player he was, certainly the best I ever played with.'

As Kenny raced away to celebrate with the Liverpool fans in the corner, something entered his head as he leapt over the advertising hoarding. He recalled that Alan Pascoe, the 1974 Commonwealth Games gold medal hurdler, had, after he won a race, attempted to leap over a set of hurdles on his way to take the acclaim of the crowd, but fell over them. He thought better of trying to leap back over the advertising hoarding a second time as he made his way back on to the pitch.

'How he got his arse above those advertising hoardings I will never know,' Phil Thompson wrote in his autobiography.

Brugge had an excellent chance to equalise when Jan Simoen went round Ray Clemence. He fired the ball towards the open goal, only for Thompson to get back and kick it off the line.

'It takes two teams to make a game into a spectacle and Brugge only seemed to be concerned with keeping the score down,' Bob Paisley said afterwards on why the game was a poor one.

Kenny's greatest ambition at the time was to win a European Cup. He had tried hard at Celtic, but it wasn't to be, but here now, after only one season at Anfield, he had achieved his aim. But he wasn't content with that. He wanted more, and he knew Liverpool wanted more as well.

A feature of the win Kenny greatly enjoyed was finally getting to go on an open-topped bus tour of Liverpool with the trophy. In Glasgow, neither Celtic nor Rangers were allowed to tour the city after a trophy win.

Dalglish finished his first season on Merseyside as Liverpool's top goalscorer with 31 in all competitions. In the league he'd scored 20, with one in the FA Cup in the 4-2 third round defeat to Chelsea, six in the League Cup, where they lost to Nottingham Forest in the final after a replay, and four in Europe. David Fairclough was next in the club's scoring charts with 15 in all tournaments. Dalglish also supplied ten assists, second only to Ray Kennedy, who chipped in with 15.

Although they went out of the FA Cup at the first hurdle, it was a busy season for Liverpool, with Kenny and Phil Neal being the only two ever-presents with 62 appearances.

Liverpool: Clemence, Neal, Thompson, Hansen, Kennedy, Hughes (c), Dalglish, Case [Heighway], Fairclough, McDermott, Souness

Scorer: Dalglish (65)

Club Brugge: Jensen, Bastijns, Krieger, Leekens, Maes [Volders], Cools, De Cubber, Kü [Sanders], Vandereycken, Sørensen, Simoen

Attendance: 92,500

26

Celtic 2-3 Liverpool

14 August 1978, Jock Stein Testimonial,
Celtic Park

LIVERPOOL'S 1978/79 pre-season schedule was hectic. They began August by playing a League of Ireland team in Dublin, then travelled to Switzerland to play FC Basel, before a game in Munich against Bayern, then a match versus FC Austria in Vienna on 11 August. Paisley had initiated an increase in 'training tempo' due to what he called their 'cup final in September'. The defending European champions had been drawn against the new English champions, Nottingham Forest, in the first round of the European Cup.

Plans for Jock Stein's testimonial match were revealed on 6 July 1978. Dalglish's return was the big talking point. Scottish and Newcastle Breweries put up a trophy for the occasion.

Billy McNeill was now the Celtic manager with Stein stepping down in May of 1978. Celtic's first season without Dalglish had been their worst in many years. They went out of all cup competitions, and finished only in fifth place in the league, not even qualifying for Europe.

The match was all-ticket, with no cash being accepted at the turnstiles, which was unusual for the time.

Danny McGrain had succeeded Dalglish as Celtic's captain and Kenny would skipper Liverpool for the night. 'This should be a marvellous occasion for Jock Stein ... it will be special returning to Celtic Park,' he told the *Evening Times* ahead of the game.

Before the match Liverpool paraded the European Cup.

'I know that Celtic don't play friendlies,' Bob Paisley said ahead of the match, 'and that suits us, because neither do we.'

Before kick-off, Stein was joined on the pitch by the Lisbon Lions, and the legendary manager ended his 13 years in charge in tears. In the stand, the invited guests included Sean Connery, Billy Connolly, Southampton manager Lawrie McMenemy and former Secretary of State Willie Ross.

The Celtic fans cheered both teams on to the pitch before the whole ground sang 'You'll Never Walk Alone'.

However, the reception was not so friendly for Dalglish individually. In his 1982 autobiography, Dalglish recalled his disappointment at being booed. He had thought that the relationship that he built over the years with the Celtic fans would be eternal. It was a shock for him. Far from being a homecoming, he suddenly felt alienated.

Dalglish had heard rumours that he was in for a torrid time from the punters in the Dart Inn, the pub his father-in-law ran in Rutherglen. He told his team-mates there was a chance he would get stick. They couldn't believe that would be the case, but on running out of the tunnel they realised it was worse than Dalglish had dared fear.

Although Dalglish could understand the strong feelings Celtic fans had for their team, and how many couldn't imagine any player, especially one as idolised as Kenny would want to play for someone else, deep down he was hurt.

Celtic took the lead after referee Brian McGinlay awarded a free kick when Souness pulled down Tommy Burns. Ronnie Glavin hammered the kick past Clemence.

Liverpool equalised when Ray Kennedy sent a ball through the middle for new signing from Newcastle, Alan Kennedy, to latch on to. Kennedy drew Peter Latchford, then tucked the ball in.

Five minutes before half-time, Liverpool went 2-1 in front when Dalglish headed in a Steve Heighway cross.

Four minutes later, Celtic were level. Alan Sneddon launched a long ball to the back post. Tom McAdam waited for it to drop and timed his volley to perfection to fire the ball past Clemence.

Ten minutes into the second half, Kenny shot from the corner of Celtic's box, and the ball flew into the top corner of Latchford's goal. Liverpool won the match 3-2, and Stein presented the trophy to Dalglish at the end.

Kenny would have better receptions from Celtic fans in later years. In August 1987, he brought his Liverpool team to Parkhead for Tommy Burns's testimonial. Burns was a great admirer and the Celtic fans gave Dalglish a big welcome on that occasion. A few months later, Kenny guested for Celtic in Davie Provan's testimonial.

In April 1989, Liverpool returned to playing football two weeks after the Hillsborough tragedy. The venue was Celtic Park. Dalglish wrote in the programme, 'To come back to football among friends will be good for everyone.' The specially arranged match was an emotional but uplifting occasion as Celtic and Liverpool fans sang 'You'll Never Walk Alone' together. All 57,437 fans applauded at the end of a 4-0 Liverpool win in a match where Kenny, then aged 38, played for an hour and scored the opening goal. 'The scoreline was irrelevant. This was all simply about easing us back into the game and Celtic were quite magnificent in their help,' Kenny told the *Evening Times*.

Celtic: Latchford, Sneddon, Lynch, Aitken, MacDonald, Eðvaldsson, Conn, Glavin, McAdam, Burns, Wilson

Scorers: Glavin (21), McAdam (44)

Liverpool: Clemence, Neal, A. Kennedy, Thompson, R. Kennedy, Hughes, Dalglish, Case, Heighway, McDermott, Souness

Scorers: A. Kennedy (32), Dalglish (40, 55)

Attendance: 62,600

27

Liverpool 7-0 Tottenham Hotspur

*2 September 1978, English First
Division, Anfield*

DALGLISH'S REPUTATION had now spread throughout
the English game with defenders realising what a handful he
could be. Ron 'Chopper' Harris spoke to the *Topical Times
Football Book*. 'The greatest player I ever marked was Denis
Law,' Harris said of Kenny's hero. 'Of current players I'd say
Kenny Dalglish is much the same.' Harris had marked Kenny
in an FA Cup tie in which Chelsea won 4-2, but Dalglish
still scored one and assisted the other. 'He was so much like
Denis Law. You never knew what he was going to do next.
We had a tremendous battle – and shook hands at the end.'

While Liverpool had won their opening three league
fixtures of the 1978/79 season, they had gone out of the
League Cup at the first hurdle a few days before Tottenham
visited Anfield. While Liverpool dominated Second Division
Sheffield United, they couldn't find a goal and conceded with
ten minutes remaining to lose 1-0.

It may not have been surprising, then, that Tottenham
were about to feel a backlash. Spurs had spent the previous
season in the Second Division, having lost their First
Division place in 1976/77. They were promoted in third place
and haven't been out of the top flight since [at the time of
writing].

The White Hart Lane club were still looking for their
first win of the season, having drawn with Nottingham
Forest and Chelsea and lost to Aston Villa.

Early on, Tottenham could have taken the lead. John Duncan burst through and went down the right side of the penalty box, where Ray Clemence dashed out to meet him. Had Duncan squared the ball to his left, Ricky Villa or Glenn Hoddle would have had a tap-in from the edge of the box. However, Duncan attempted to take the ball around Clemence, only for the ex-Scunthorpe man to smother it.

Liverpool took the lead after eight minutes when Jimmy Case drilled the ball into the penalty area for what may have been a mishit shot. However, it landed at the feet of Dalglish. Kenny, with his back to goal, was marked tightly by John Lacy, but he took the ball on his right, turned outside Lacy, and as Steve Perryman attempted a sliding tackle, drove the ball under him and past Barry Daines in goal.

The second goal came on 20 minutes. Tottenham cleared a shot, and the ball cannoned around the penalty area. It fell to Souness, who at the penalty spot played the ball out to Case. Dalglish was able to remain standing on the edge of the six-yard box, as in addition to goalkeeper Daines, Spurs had three men on the goal line, ensuring Kenny was well onside. When the ball came in, he redirected it into the net for 2-0.

Ray Kennedy claimed the third as his header seemed to be put into the net by Lacy's thigh. It was four, three minutes into the second half, when substitute David Johnson followed up on Daines's block from Dalglish's shot.

It was Johnson again for number five, Dalglish taking his time on the ball and allowing him to run into space before sweeping the ball through the middle for Johnson to slam it through Daines's legs.

Steve Heighway was pulled down to give Liverpool a penalty. While Phil Neal's kick was saved by Daines, the referee, Mr Flint, ordered the kick to be retaken, saying that the keeper had moved before the ball was struck. Neal fired the retake into the net.

The seventh goal really showed up Liverpool's superiority. Tottenham had a corner which was cleared by Clemence, who played the ball out to Ray Kennedy, who nodded it on to Dalglish. Kenny swept it out on the right to Johnson, who found Heighway on the left with a long ball. Terry McDermott, who had been on the post defending the corner, chatting to Alan Kennedy about where they were going to go for a drink that night, had run up the pitch to be on the right side of Tottenham's box, and when Heighway fired over the cross first time, McDermott headed in from the six-yard line.

'That must be the best goal Anfield has ever seen,' Bob Paisley said.

'It was an unbelievable ball, I don't know how he picked me out,' McDermott wrote in his 2017 autobiography.

'Liverpool played the game the way it should be played,' spectator Bill Shankly said. 'Simple. They made themselves available when they had the ball. It was the easiest thing to find each other with passes. That's what the game's all about.'

In his 1983 autobiography, Ossie Ardiles wrote that he wasn't fit for the game but felt obliged to take the field. 'So I played at Anfield,' he wrote. 'Afterwards, I felt that I never wanted to play anywhere again. We'd been awful. All of us. Liverpool, though, had played like men from another planet.'

'That thrashing at Anfield was a crushing experience,' Ricky Villa wrote in his 2010 autobiography. 'We were awful, and Liverpool were so much better than us. I don't remember losing any other game 7-0 in my life. It was embarrassing, and the dressing room was silent after the game.'

Villa was another opponent who rated Kenny highly. 'In Kenny Dalglish [Liverpool] had the best player I faced during my spell in England. Dalglish possessed great control, he used his body so well, and in front of goal he never seemed to miss.'

Liverpool continued their good form in the league, but were knocked out of the European Cup in the first round by Nottingham Forest.

The Reds had some measure of revenge when Forest came to Anfield in December when two Terry McDermott goals gave them a 2-0 win. During the match Phil Neal recognised that his England colleague Viv Anderson, playing at right-back for Forest, was becoming increasingly frustrated as Kenny was getting the better of their every encounter. Using this to his advantage, Neal made sure that when he moved the ball forward it wasn't just randomly into Forest's penalty box. He played the ball in to Kenny's feet, so that he could turn Anderson.

Three minutes into the second half with Liverpool already one up, Dalglish turned Anderson in the box, the covering Archie Gemmill slid in and pulled Kenny down. McDermott put the resultant penalty kick away. 'We drove them to commit the foul by the sheer frustration of being tormented by constant pressure,' Neal wrote in his 1981 autobiography. '[Kenny] was able to do that because of his team's awareness that he was the man tormenting their defence most effectively. Once we had become aware of that it was our job to deliver the ball to him in the most effective way, the way he likes to receive it. We did just that and Kenny did the rest.'

Derby County, managed by Tommy Docherty, came to Anfield in October and were also handed a footballing lesson. Dalglish scored twice and set up another two in a 5-0 win.

December brought defeats in the league to Arsenal and Bristol City and an aggregate loss in the European Super Cup to Anderlecht.

The Reds, though, maintained their position at the top of the league and Manchester United manager Dave Sexton hailed them as a cert for the title after the Jimmy Case-inspired team had beaten Manchester United 3-0 on Boxing Day.

Liverpool: Clemence, Neal, A. Kennedy, Thompson, R. Kennedy, Hughes (c) [Johnson], Dalglish, Case, Heighway, McDermott, Souness

Scorers: Dalglish (8, 20), R. Kennedy (28), Johnson (48, 58), Neal (64, pen), McDermott (76)

Tottenham: Daines, McAllister, Naylor, Hoddle, Lacy, Perryman, Villa, Ardiles, Taylor, Duncan, McNab

Attendance: 50,705

28

Liverpool 6-0 Norwich City

*21 February 1979, English First
Division, Anfield*

SOUTHEND UNITED were Liverpool's opponents in
the third round of the FA Cup, and the Third Division side
held the European champions to a goalless draw on a snow-
covered pitch at Roots Hall. In the replay, which Liverpool
won 3-0, Dalglish scored his first goal since netting the
second in the 2-0 win over Chelsea on 21 October, having
failed to score in 13 consecutive games.

Kenny scored the only goal of the match in the fourth
round as Liverpool knocked out Blackburn Rovers. He hit
another in the 2-1 win over West Bromwich Albion in the
league on 3 February.

The league match with Norwich was postponed due
to heavy snowfall; only one First Division game survived
that Saturday, where Southampton beat Everton 3-0. The
rearranged game was the following Wednesday. Before
the match, Norwich boss John Bond said Liverpool were
certainties to win the title.

Going into the match, Liverpool were one point ahead
of Arsenal, but with three games in hand. Everton and
West Bromwich Albion had both been top of the league for
a period.

Liverpool went in front after only three minutes when
Dalglish headed in a Souness volley. The visitors got in at
half-time without conceding another, despite Kevin Keelan
in goal looking suspect on a few occasions.

In his *Kenny Dalglish Soccer Annual*, Kenny noted that Norwich came to Anfield intending to shut Liverpool out with a close marking system. While it worked for most of the first half, in the second 45, Liverpool took command of the match.

It was only a minute into the second half when David Johnson made it 2-0 when he met Steve Heighway's cross at the back post.

Dalglish flicked in another header from Ray Kennedy's cross to make the score 3-0 with only three minutes of the half gone. Johnson notched the fourth on 51 minutes when Keelan dropped a Heighway corner at his feet.

It was the 70th minute before Norwich had a shot at goal.

Keelan made two great saves from Ray and Alan Kennedy, but then both scored against him. First, Dalglish assisted Alan Kennedy with ten minutes remaining. Then in the last minute, Dalglish set up Ray Kennedy, who hammered a shot in off the post to make the score 6-0. Dalglish rated him as 'probably the best finisher at Liverpool'.

The crowd gave Liverpool a standing ovation at the end.

Avi Cohen, the Israeli international defender, watched the match having completed a week's trial with Liverpool. 'I have never seen such football,' he told the *Daily Express* afterwards. 'Liverpool must be the best team in the world. It is an honour to be in with even a remote chance of getting into this team.'

Norwich's manager John Bond called Liverpool, 'Magnificent.'

'We could have had 26 tonight and that's no disrespect to Norwich,' Bob Paisley said. 'I've never seen so many goal-line clearances and near misses in all my life.' Paisley, though, acknowledged that Keelan had a poor game. 'He's always been brilliant against us in the past but this is the first time he's dithered.'

In Liverpool's next eight matches, they only conceded one goal, in the 1-1 draw with Everton at Anfield.

They played in a classic FA Cup semi-final with Manchester United at Maine Road at the end of March. Dalglish opened the scoring. Jimmy Case knocked the ball through to him in the penalty box. Defenders Arthur Albiston and Martin Buchan were both on him. 'Kenny wriggled through with the most amazing hip movement I have ever seen,' Phil Neal wrote. Dalglish raised his right arm in order to get around Albiston. His movement saw Buchan race straight past him. Free from the defence, he touched the ball past the diving Gary Bailey in the United goal, and then as he lost his balance he slid a left-foot shot into the far corner.

Joe Jordan would later equalise. Terry McDermott missed a penalty kick before Brian Greenhoff made it 2-1 to United in the second half. Liverpool's equaliser came eight minutes from time when Alan Hansen got on the end of a rebound from six yards out. Liverpool lost the Goodison Park replay 1-0.

Out of all the cups, in the league, it was a different story. Liverpool were unstoppable. Arsenal were defeated 3-0 in Phil Thompson's first game as captain. Dalglish scored the first in a 2-0 win over United at Anfield ten days after the FA Cup loss. It wasn't about *if* Liverpool would win the title, it was about how great the margin would be.

Liverpool: Clemence, Neal, Hughes (c), A. Kennedy, R. Kennedy, Hansen, Dalglish, Johnson, Heighway, McDermott, Souness

Scorers: Dalglish (3, 48), Johnson (46, 51), A. Kennedy (80), R. Kennedy (90)

Norwich City: Keelan, Bond, Forbes, Ryan, Hoadley, Powell, Neighbour, Symonds, Chivers, Lythgoe, Peters

Attendance: 35,754

29

Leeds United 0-3 Liverpool

17 May 1979, English First Division,
Elland Road

LEEDS UNITED entered the English record books in 1969 when they won the First Division with 67 points, the most in a season. Now Liverpool had the chance to take that record from them, but the fixture list allowed Leeds the opportunity to stop them. Liverpool had been runners-up in 1968/69 on 61 points. Leeds had passed them in February, and Liverpool couldn't catch up.

It was a different story a decade later. While Leeds were heading for fifth place in the league, Liverpool had already wrapped up the title. A 3-0 win over Aston Villa on 8 May, 40 years to the day after Bob Paisley arrived at the club, sealed their 11th league championship. The win left second-placed West Bromwich Albion unable to overhaul them. Dalglish scored the second, racing through the middle on his own to gather a header from Phil Neal and shoot past the advancing goalkeeper Jimmy Rimmer from 20 yards. It was Dalglish's 25th goal of the season.

On Radio One, DJ John Peel paid homage to Kenny. 'I've been going to see Liverpool since I was seven years old, so mine may not be a totally unprejudiced view, but I think Kenny Dalglish is the best football player I have ever seen.'

Of the players in that record-breaking 1969 Leeds team, Paul Madeley and Eddie Gray were still at the club and in the starting XI at Elland Road. Maurice Lindley, Leeds' assistant manager, had described Liverpool as 'breathtaking' when he saw them beat Bolton 4-1 a few weeks earlier. 'The only side I've seen come near to their incredible standards was United ten years ago,' he said ahead of the game.

A week earlier, Kenny, who had now scored 53 goals for Liverpool in 108 appearances, had picked up the Football Writers' Player of the Year award. The ceremony took place at London's Cafe Royal and Sir Stanley Matthews, who won the award in 1948 and in 1963, when he was 48, presented Kenny with it. Matthews was then living in Malta and made one of his rare visits to England for the occasion.

Dalglish said that he found this award particularly satisfying as 'it showed I had established myself in the English League'. He had polled more than 60 per cent of the votes.

'When accepting the award I made the point that I was receiving it on behalf of an outstanding Liverpool team,' Kenny said in the book *Golden Heroes: Fifty Seasons of Footballer of the Year.*

The PFA award, selected by the players, was won by Arsenal's Liam Brady. Dalglish hadn't even been placed in their top six. No one from Anfield was recognised. Club officials diplomatically suggested that Liverpool were so good it was difficult to single out individual players. The Liverpool players were disgusted. Tommy Smith, who had moved to Swansea City at the start of the season, said it was nothing more than jealousy and Ray Kennedy told the *Northern Echo* that the players were so disgusted that Dalglish wasn't recognised that they were considering boycotting the PFA award.

Graeme Souness said of Dalglish, 'His vision is incredible. Trevor Francis cost £1m but cannot compare with Dalglish. Francis is a player of potential whereas Kenny has proved himself. Some of his goals have been out of this world. Apart from that Kenny is such a good professional. He just gets on with his job.'

Ron Greenwood brought his England team over from Manchester to Elland Road to watch the Liverpool game, with Leeds' Tony Currie, who was left out of the team.

Liverpool took the lead when David Johnson pounced on a rebound after David Harvey had saved Terry McDermott's shot. The second goal began when Hansen brought the ball out from defence. He gave it to Dalglish, who went on a run across the pitch. He turned in and passed to Jimmy Case, who smacked a shot into the roof of Leeds' net.

In his book *Kennedy's Way*, Alan Kennedy wrote, 'Dalglish's ego-free willingness to chase apparently lost causes also meant that early clearances from the Liverpool rearguard were often converted into valuable Liverpool possession in the opposing third, especially when the striker got his backside stuck into opposing defenders. The Scot had amazingly powerful thighs and hips and a low centre of gravity, which invariably allowed him to wrap his body around the ball, viewing it as a personal affront if he was refused possession. Alan Hansen said that Liverpool defenders learned to give the ball to Kenny simply to avoid an argument.'

In the 55th minute, Harvey again blocked a shot from McDermott. This time, the ball fell to Phil Neal, who lofted it to the far post. Dalglish headed it on for Johnson to nod in Liverpool's third of the night and their 85th league goal of the season. The win gave Liverpool 68 points for the season and a new record.

'Kenny had the biggest arse in football, or it seemed that way to defenders when he leaned forward and pushed it back to prevent them getting anywhere near the ball,' Phil Thompson wrote in his book. 'It gave him the space to guide the ball right or left. When he had made his mind up, the pass was perfect, or he would turn people on a tanner, to use an old expression, and then bend the ball into the back of the net.'

Liverpool finished that season conceding only 16 goals, a new Football League record, beating Southampton's return of 21 in the 1921/22 season[4]. Twelve goals had been conceded

---

4 Preston North End conceded only 15 goals in 1889, but in a season consisting of only 22 league games.

away from home and a mere four at Anfield, where they hadn't lost a league game all campaign. They finished on a goal difference of plus 69.

Liverpool: Clemence, Neal, A. Kennedy, Thompson (c), R. Kennedy, Hansen, Dalglish, Case, Johnson, McDermott, Souness

Scorers: Johnson (21, 57), Case (42)

Leeds United: Harvey, Hird, Madeley, Hart, F. Gray, Flynn, Cherry, E. Gray, Graham, Hawley, Harris

30

Liverpool 3-1 Arsenal

11 August 1979, Charity Shield,
Wembley Stadium

ARSENAL HAD defeated Manchester United in a classic FA Cup Final in May, so they were the opposition for the opening match of the 1979/80 season. For the beginning of that campaign, Liverpool only made two signings – Israeli international Avi Cohen and St Mirren's Frank McGarvey. Former captain Emlyn Hughes left to join Wolves at the start of August and Liverpool warmed up for the season with a tour of West Germany.

At Wembley, the first chance came when Dalglish played Johnson in, pulling the ball back from the byline, but Johnson hit his shot over.

Dalglish played a one-two with Ray Kennedy and, despite David O'Leary's close attention, managed to fire a shot which Jennings saved. In his 1988 autobiography, O'Leary wrote, 'Dalglish could look after himself. I have marked him often enough. I should know. Kenny was tough. He couldn't be intimidated. Dalglish, I would have to say, is the best all-round footballer to have played in the First Division in my time. I found him a bit of a moaner, but his work-rate was phenomenal, and he was a winner. He had this acute awareness. He could see a situation in a split second and take advantage of it. While he wouldn't knock his own players, he still demanded perfection from those around him.'

Arsenal had a chance to take the lead, but Clemence made a great save from Frank Stapleton's flying header.

The opening goal came with seven minutes of the first half remaining. Terry McDermott ran freely through the middle of the park and collected Ray Kennedy's through ball as Dalglish's decoy run took Arsenal's attention out to their right. McDermott latched on to the ball and hit a shot from 20 yards out that screamed home.

Liverpool's second goal was a superb piece of play. Alan Hansen nipped in ahead of Alan Sunderland to collect Graham Rix's through pass, which was intended for the man who scored the winner in the 1979 FA Cup Final. He then decided to break out of defence with the ball. Hansen in full flow was a tremendous sight. With pace and vision, he carried the ball up the field and slid it to his left, where Dalglish collected. Kenny took the ball to the edge of the Arsenal box where he turned Paul Walford, who ended up on his backside, and fired the ball into Jennings's far corner. 'That was absolutely world-class,' said John Motson in his BBC commentary.

It was another Arsenal attack which led to Liverpool's third goal. Liam Brady brought the ball just inside Liverpool's half of the centre circle. Dalglish waited for him and took the ball off the elegant midfielder's toe. He played it on to Johnson. As the Liverpool number 9 brought the ball forward, Kenny moved towards him to indicate he wanted it back. Johnson gave it to him, and Dalglish muscled past a defender and laid it off to McDermott, who smashed the ball into the net.

Sunderland scored Arsenal's consolation with two minutes remaining.

In *The Guardian*, David Lacey noted that with Liverpool's consistency over the past few years, it would be easy to think there had been no changes to their team. He noted, however, that only five of the starting XI here had played in the 1977 European Cup Final and Dalglish had been the most important recruit. '[He] reminded everyone of this fact at Wembley, with one masterly goal and significant contributions to the others.'

'Kenny was an absolute pleasure to play with, to train with and have a laugh with,' Phil Thompson wrote in his 2005 autobiography. 'Like many of the lads, he came from a modest background, and it seemed to make him doubly determined to succeed.'

Liverpool's early league form included a couple of defeats to Southampton and Nottingham Forest, which left them ninth at the end of September. Worse was to come in the European Cup when Liverpool went out in the first round for the second successive year. A 2-1 win over Dinamo Tbilisi at Anfield wasn't the best result to travel to the away leg with. In the Georgian capital, with the rain pouring down, David Kipiani gave a masterful performance for the Soviet Top League champions.

Second-half goals from Vladimir Gutsaev, Ramaz Shengelia, and a penalty from Aleksandr Chivadze gave Tbilisi a 3-0 win.

From there, Liverpool went on a 19-match unbeaten run, including a 4-0 win over Manchester City with Dalglish netting a brace and setting up another, a 2-0 victory over Manchester United and a 5-0 romp over Grimsby Town in the FA Cup third round.

Dalglish had scored a wonderful goal against Crystal Palace in Liverpool's 3-0 win in December 1979. He juggled the ball past three defenders inside the box, then hooked it back across the goal into the net.

Former Liverpool and Scotland defender Ron Yeats was at the match and spoke with the *Daily Record*. 'I often wish I was back playing,' the man who appeared more than 400 times for Liverpool said. 'Then I watch Kenny Dalglish and start to get nightmares about trying to mark him.'

Palace's defender Jim Cannon, who had recently been called up into the Scotland squad, said of Dalglish, 'He is just magnificent.'

A double-header against Nottingham Forest, the European champions and League Cup holders, came along at the end of January. In the first leg of the League Cup semi-final, Liverpool fell to a last-minute John Robertson penalty.

In the FA Cup fourth round four days later, again at the City Ground, it was a different story. In the 31st minute, goalkeeper Peter Shilton dropped Phil Neal's cross at the feet of Kenny Dalglish, who stuck out his left boot and prodded home the opening goal.

'Kenny Dalglish was a formidable opponent, touched with football genius,' Shilton wrote in his 2004 autobiography. 'He was at his most dangerous when the ball was played up to him in or around the penalty box and he had his back to goal. He could turn the best defenders and was one of the best shielders of a ball I ever came across.' Shilton felt that this made a goalkeeper's job difficult. 'Instead of turning and firing off a shot, more often than not Kenny would hold the ball at his feet, then suddenly force me to change position by laying the ball square for an oncoming team-mate to have a shot at goal. His ability to hold on to the ball then lay it off was one of the reasons why Liverpool midfield players scored so many goals, and why Kenny was held in such high esteem by managers and his fellow professionals.'

The second came when, under pressure from Dalglish, David Needham handled in the penalty box. Terry McDermott put away the resulting penalty kick. Brian Clough called the result 'extremely fair'.

Liverpool's next match was a classic for the ages.

Liverpool: Clemence, Neal, A. Kennedy, Thompson (c), R. Kennedy, Hansen, Dalglish, Case, Johnson, McDermott, Souness

Scorers: McDermott (38, 68), Dalglish (65)

Arsenal: Jennings, Rice, Nelson [Young], Talbot, O'Leary, Walford, Brady, Sunderland, Stapleton, Price [Hollins], Rix

Scorer: Sunderland (88)

Attendance: 92,000

31

Norwich City 3-5 Liverpool

*9 February 1980, English First
Division, Carrow Road*

THE GAME against Norwich City in February 1980 was a remarkable match, not primarily remembered for Dalglish's outstanding display, David Fairclough's hat-trick, or even the performance of Martin Peters, now playing in his 19th season. The match will be forever remembered for the stunning goal scored by Justin Fashanu.

Graeme Souness was out of the side through suspension, while David Johnson had picked up a head injury playing for England the week before. The young Sammy Lee came into midfield, while the perennial super sub, 23-year-old David Fairclough, started up front.

The goalscoring began in the first minute after Norwich forced a corner on Liverpool's left. It was a textbook set-piece goal. The corner was whipped where Kevin Reeves rose to meet it on the edge of the six-yard box. He leapt and spun in the air, sending his header into the middle where Peters arrived completely unmarked to head in from two yards out. Clemence looked around, bewildered.

The equaliser came after only four minutes. With Norwich on the attack, the ball was played into Fashanu, who was midway into Liverpool's half. With his back to goal, he attempted to play the ball back out to a team-mate, but McDermott nipped in to intercept the pass. He carried the ball and then sent it long down to Fairclough on the right wing. He played it square for Lee, who gave Fairclough the return ball. The red-headed striker made his way into the Norwich penalty area and struck a left-footed shot past Keelan.

At the halfway line in the 18th minute, Hansen picked the ball up from Lee. He went on a run with no Norwich player seeming like they wanted to challenge him. The ex-Partick Thistle man then slid the ball into Fairclough, who shot first time into the net.

Kevin Reeves made it 2-2 with 37 minutes gone. The ball was swung into the Liverpool box, headed on, and Reeves lunged in with an outstretched foot and put the ball over Clemence.

There were no more goals until the last 15 minutes of the game, which served up another four of them. Fairclough completed his hat-trick when Dalglish charged forward on the left, then put a terrific low cross across the Norwich six-yard box for Fairclough to get on the end of.

Fashanu had already tried the spectacular earlier in the game when his overhead kick put Peters in, with the World Cup winner just hitting the ball past the post. With nine minutes of the game remaining, Fashanu displayed the skill which made his name.

With Norwich on the attack, Kevin Bond played the ball into John Ryan on Liverpool's right around 25 yards out. Ryan knocked a left-footed pass in first time to Fashanu, standing on the edge of the box, being marked tightly by Alan Kennedy. Fashanu flicked the ball up with his right foot, which gave him space away from the defender. As the ball dropped, he smashed it with his left, and it curved up and down past Clemence. 'Oh what a goal!' exclaimed Barry Davies, commentating for *Match of the Day*. 'Oh that's a magnificent goal.'

Dalglish himself rated it as 'simply superb' in a round-up of great goals for *The Kenny Dalglish Soccer Annual*. 'It was very much an instinctive goal,' Dalglish wrote. 'It moved about four ways in the air before beating Ray Clemence – in itself something of an achievement – and Justin has every reason to treasure that goal.'

Match of the Day viewers chose Fashanu's goal as the goal of the season. The commentator John Motson chose the game as his match of the season and Dalglish as player of the season.

Fairclough had a great chance to grab his fourth, but Keelan made an unorthodox save by catching the ball between his knees.

Liverpool went in front with two minutes remaining when Phil Neal played the ball to McDermott, who got to the byline and crossed low, under the body of the diving Keelan. Dalglish was waiting in the middle of the six-yard box, and he bent down to send a header into the net.

A minute later, it was 5-3. Dalglish and Case exchanged passes, and Case made his way into the box and fired past Keelan.

The win saw Liverpool go two points ahead of Manchester United with a game in hand.

Nottingham Forest were a hurdle too far in the League Cup, a 1-1 draw ensuring a 2-1 aggregate victory for Brian Clough's team, meaning Liverpool's search for a first trophy win in the competition went on to another year.

In April, the *Sunday Mirror* reported that Hamburg, who were set to lose Kevin Keegan at the end of the season, had their sights set on Dalglish as his replacement. They had sent a scout to watch Kenny in Scotland's 4-1 win over Portugal at Hampden.

In the FA Cup, Liverpool lost to Arsenal after a third replay in the semi-final.

Liverpool had been top of the league since December, and their 12th title was confirmed with a 4-1 win over Aston Villa at Anfield on 3 May 1980 in front of 51,541 fans.

Scottish striker Frank McGarvey was frustrated by his lack of opportunities to get into the Liverpool team, and by

March 1980, he had returned north to join Celtic, where he had a wonderful career. During the season, youngsters Ronnie Whelan from Home Farm and Ian Rush from Chester City joined, both of whom would make a massive contribution to the club in the years to come.

At the end of the season, Kenny and Kevin Keegan played in the same team. On 14 May, Liverpool were presented with the league championship trophy by the league's vice-president Bob Lord ahead of Ray Clemence's testimonial against Anderlecht. Keegan was among a handful of former Liverpool players who guested. The legendary goalkeeper's cause wasn't helped by the TUC's Day of Action, which resulted in no public transport, but 18,800 fans still turned up.

With six England internationals who had played against Argentina 24 hours earlier, Liverpool found themselves 6-2 down at half-time. In a high-scoring game, which was a hallmark of testimonials at the time, Liverpool eventually lost 8-6. Howard Gayle scored twice, Keegan, Money, Jones with a penalty and the biggest cheer of the night, Ray Clemence also scored from the spot.

At the end of the season, Kenny won *Shoot!* magazine's Most Exciting English League Player for the third season in a row, as well as the *Daily Star*'s First Division Player of the Year. With the £500 prize from the *Star* Kenny bought sets of strips for two boys' club teams. He was selected in the PFA's First Division Team of the Year, alongside Terry McDermott and David Johnson.

Norwich City: Keelan, Bond, Downs, Ryan, Brown, Jones, Mendham [McGuire], Reeves, Fashanu, Paddon, Peters

Scorers: Peters (1), Reeves (37), Fashanu (81)

Liverpool: Clemence, Neal, A. Kennedy, Thompson (c), R. Kennedy, Hansen, Dalglish, Case, Fairclough, McDermott, Lee

Scorers: Fairclough (4, 18, 75), Dalglish (88), Case (89)

32

Liverpool 10-1 Oulun Palloseura

*1 October 1980, European Cup, first
round, second leg, Anfield*

FOR THE first round of the European Cup Liverpool had been drawn against Finnish champions Oulun Palloseura. This was Liverpool's 17th consecutive season in Europe, and the first time they had drawn a side from Finland. Seeded for the draw in Zurich, Liverpool had been knocked out at the first round stage the past two seasons, losing to Nottingham Forest in 1978 and to Dinamo Tbilisi in 1979.

Liverpool should have been at home for the first leg, but after discussions with the Finnish officials, the legs were switched. Oulun, 200 miles away from Helsinki was 100 miles south of the Arctic Circle, so the feeling was that the weather would be more favourable for September's first leg.

The tie, against a team of amateurs playing in the first European match of their 50-year history, was largely presumed to be almost a walkover for the English champions. There were two Brits in the Oulun team: Keith Armstrong started his career at Sunderland, where he played 11 times in the league in 1977/78, while Hugh Smith played with Airdrie and Stranraer.

The first leg didn't go quite according to plan. The game started well as Liverpool with Dalglish up front alongside David Fairclough, took the lead through Terry McDermott in the 15th minute. The Reds dominated the game, but the Finns' tactics were well practised and Liverpool found themselves caught offside 19 times. The pitch, which earlier that day had been used for training by javelin throwers and shot putters, was bumpy and uneven. It all added up to Liverpool being unable to make their vast possession count. Bob Paisley later called it a Sunday League surface and suggested the home club should invest in a groundsman.

With ten minutes remaining, welder Soini Puotiniemi rammed home an equaliser. The goal delighted the record 10,000 crowd, which was 4,500 more than the previous record, although some were found on the roof of the stand and around the running track. The draw kept Oulun's near two-year unbeaten home record intact.

A report in the *Liverpool Echo* gives an indication of how much the modern-day iteration of Europe's premier cup competition has moved on, in terms of the financial rewards on offer. In the first leg the *Echo* reported that Liverpool lost £20,000. *The Guardian* even suggested that Liverpool could be tempted to lose the match, as a comfortable win would see a poor attendance for the second leg at Anfield, in a city of 100,000 unemployed. If the attendance at Anfield was under 20,000 Liverpool would have lost money on the tie as a whole. According to the *Sporting News* in the 2024/25 season a drawn match in the Champions League group stage would bring each club €700,000.

The second leg was a fantastic example of Kenny Dalglish's ability to set up chances for his team-mates. While Kenny didn't score himself, he set up five of Liverpool's goals. The first came after only five minutes. Kenny ran through on a panicked defence, which opened up enough to allow Graeme Souness to find himself in plenty of space inside the box. As goalkeeper Jukka Rantanen raced out to meet him, Dalglish slipped the ball through for Souness to open the scoring with his first goal in European competition.

The second came 19 minutes later. Kenny found himself crowded out inside the penalty area so he slipped the ball out to the edge of the box to Souness, who side-stepped a defender and hit a low shot which spun in off the goalkeeper's outstretched foot.

In the 29th minute, Terry McDermott tapped in the third from close range after Kenny had cut the ball back from the byline. Four minutes before half-time it was 4-0. Dalglish ran the defence ragged and knocked the ball to the left of a goalkeeper determined to rush out of his goal to meet each attack. While it was clearly trundling into an unguarded net McDermott thought he should make sure and bashed it in on the goal line. 'I thought it was going wide, or the wind was going to hold it up or something,' McDermott said in his post-match TV interview. 'So I just wanted to make sure. I don't score too many in European matches and Kenny's got so many he wouldn't mind me having that one.'

Just after half-time, Armstrong scored with a nice finish to make it 4-1. Souness was pulled down inside the box in the 52nd minute. He lifted the ball to indicate he would be taking the penalty himself. McDermott, though, asked him to think again and reluctantly, Souness hurled the ball at him, while Dalglish, walking in between his colleagues, laughed. The Liverpool crowd intervened, and McDermott stepped aside to let Souness hit the penalty and score his hat-trick. It was the second of his career, having netted three in April 1974 when Middlesbrough beat Sheffield Wednesday 8-0 in the Second Division. McDermott suggested afterwards that the Kop may have thought Kenny had scored the earlier goal and didn't realise he was also looking for a hat-trick.

It was the second season in a row that the midfield pair had a £25 bet on which of them would score the most goals throughout the season. McDermott had won in 1979/80 with 14 to Souness's two. Souness would say that they made the bet every pre-season and every Christmas, knowing McDermott already had him beat, he would pay up.

Sammy Lee and Ray Kennedy added goals to make it 7-1. In the 68th minute, Fairclough headed in the eighth after a dummy run by Dalglish had pulled defenders away from him. With nine minutes remaining Dalglish crossed from the right for Fairclough to rise at and the back post and head in the ninth. McDermott cracked in a 20-yard volley to make it 10-1 with two minutes left.

In *The Guardian*, Paul Fitzpatrick rated Oulun as 'one of the most ill-equipped [teams] ever seen in the European Cup'. He said if the Finns hadn't been so good at employing the offside trap, Liverpool would probably have broken all the European Cup scoring records. As it was, they were caught offside 25 times.

Holders Nottingham Forest were knocked out the same night after a 2-0 aggregate defeat to CSKA Sofia.

It was back to the league the following Saturday with a trip to Maine Road to face Manchester City. Dalglish got the scoring started, incurring the ire of City's outspoken manager Malcolm Allison in the process. Avi Cohen played the ball into Dalglish's feet with Kenny in his classic back-to-goal position. City's young defender Tommy Caton was tight to him, but Dalglish's jinks, turns and twists had Caton beaten. Kenny turned and shot with his left foot. The hit was soft and low. Joe Corrigan in the City goal saw it late and went down reaching for the ball with his right hand, which the ball bounced over and nestled in the net. Allison told reporters afterwards that Dalglish's reputation had deluded them into thinking it was a great goal. 'A schoolboy could have saved it. It was a crap goal,' he said. Souness and Lee also netted to give a dominant Liverpool a 3-0 win.

Allison said that Dalglish was one of the greatest players he had ever seen, comparable to Pelé and Di Stefano. He told the *Daily Mirror* in 1994, 'I wanted to sign Kenny Dalglish from Celtic when I was at Manchester City, but we couldn't come up with the asking price, and Liverpool did. I lived to regret it.'

Liverpool: Clemence, Neal, Cohen, Thompson (c), R. Kennedy, Hansen, Dalglish, Lee, Fairclough, McDermott, Souness

Scorers: Souness (5, 24, 52 pen), McDermott (29, 41, 83), Lee (53), R. Kennedy (66), Fairclough (68, 81)

Oulun Palloseura: Rantanen, Lahtinen, Ahonen, Heikkinen, Kemppainen, Puotiniemi, Houtsonen, Smith, Jalasvaara, Armstrong, Himanka

Scorer: Armstrong (47)

Attendance: 21,013

33

Liverpool 4-0 Aberdeen

*5 November 1980, European Cup,
second round first leg, Anfield*

THE EUROPEAN Cup second round draw gave Liverpool a plum tie. They came out of the hat with Aberdeen, who had defeated Austria Memphis in the first round. It would be the first meeting between the English champions and the Scottish champions since Leeds played Celtic in the 1970 European Cup semi-final. 'This is a marvellous draw for everyone connected with our club,' Dons manager Alex Ferguson said. 'Liverpool are a magical name throughout the world of football. They have earned a unique position in the game.'

Ferguson and his assistant Archie Knox went to Anfield to see Liverpool take on Middlesbrough. McDermott scored within a minute, but the match didn't catch fire until the last half hour when Craig Johnston equalised for Boro before Ray Kennedy and McDermott with a penalty made it 3-1. Bozo Jankovic got one back for the visitors before Dalglish made the final score 4-2 with four minutes remaining. Liverpool had now scored 26 goals inside two weeks.

The *Daily Record* reported that Aberdeen could have sold 80,000 tickets for the 24,000-capacity first leg at Pittodrie. 'Liverpool are human beings,' Dons midfielder Gordon Strachan told the *Record*. 'We think there are ways to beat them.'

Dalglish was aware how desperate Aberdeen would be to beat Liverpool and made sure his team-mates knew it.

Dalglish, Souness and Hansen were all acutely aware that if Liverpool didn't do the business they would hear about it each time they crossed the border.

Ferguson set Aberdeen up in a 4-4-2 to mirror Liverpool, but Terry McDermott had Liverpool in front within five minutes. Ferguson wrote in 1985, 'The Liverpool players had a bit of grit and nastiness about them, good qualities when you need them.' Liverpool would take a 1-0 lead into the second leg. It was the first time in 16 European ties that Aberdeen had failed to score at Pittodrie, with Liverpool being only the third side to claim a European victory there.

Dalglish noted that it could have been more but for the reflexes of the young Jim Leighton. He also thought that Bob Paisley's pre-match praise of Gordon Strachan might have resulted in the midfielder's quiet game.

At Anfield, Ferguson was in awe of Liverpool. 'They demonstrated possession of the ball, delicate passes and deft touch control. All the qualities that great sides had.'

Early on, Dalglish set up Alan Kennedy, who had a fizzing long-range drive well saved by Jim Leighton. Aberdeen's Mark McGhee made a great run when he turned Phil Thompson and drove forward only to shoot straight at Clemence.

Aberdeen were holding out at 0-0 with eight minutes of the first half remaining when Dalglish played a short corner to Avi Cohen, who centred for Alan Hansen to head the ball on. Aberdeen captain Willie Miller, who had been a ball-boy at Pittodrie the night of Dalglish's Scotland debut, attempted to clear, but only succeeded in turning the ball into his own net.

Liverpool's second goal two minutes before half-time was sublime. Phil Thompson started the move, playing the ball into Dalglish, who was around 25 yards out. Instinctively, Dalglish backheeled the ball inside Miller and into space inside the area for Phil Neal to run on to. Leighton came out to meet him and narrowed the angle, blocking off the possibility of a right-foot shot. Neal countered by switching the ball from his right foot to his left and shot neatly inside the far post.

Liverpool's defence wasn't your typical English back line of the time that would feature two hard-as-nails centre-backs intent on lumping the ball forward and heading it away. At the back Liverpool had ball players, defenders who were comfortable with the ball at their feet and happy bringing it forward.

The Scotland striker Andy Gray had played against Liverpool in his time with Aston Villa, Wolves and Everton. In his 1999 book *Flat Back Four: The Tactical Game* he looked at what made the Liverpool defence so formidable at that time. 'When I was playing we would decide which of the opposition's defenders to leave with the ball – the one least likely to hurt us. And we would invariably find someone at the back, usually a centre-back who we felt didn't have the passing ability to cause us any problems, and then we would go and mark all the other players so that he would have to play it long. But when we played against Liverpool we couldn't leave any of them with the ball because they were all so good. Consequently the play nearly always started from the back with Liverpool. They had players able to build up from the back, to keep possession, to probe and wait for a chance to pounce.'

The third goal came when Avi Cohen attempted to chip the goalkeeper, succeeding only in hitting the crossbar. The rebound fell to Sammy Lee on the byline, who turned the ball back and into the air for Dalglish to head into the unguarded net.

It was a lovely team passing movement that created the fourth. The ball was headed out of defence by Alan Kennedy, to be collected by David Johnson on the left side of Liverpool's half. He played it into Cohen around 30 yards out. With one touch, he knocked the ball back to Johnson, who squared it to McDermott, the midfielder losing his balance and he played it first time backwards to Souness. Again with only one touch, Souness found Dalglish on Aberdeen's left. Kenny took a touch to make space as Miller shadowed him. He took another touch with his right as his Scotland team-mate kept his eye on the ball, Dalglish played it past him with his left to McDermott, who was charging into the box unnoticed. As Leighton went out to meet him, McDermott cut the ball back for Alan Hansen to slip the ball into the net with his right foot from six yards.

It ended 4-0 and although Aberdeen had a handful of chances to score, the gulf in class was apparent.

Appearing on the 7NWA podcast in 2022, Dalglish was asked if Liverpool's outstanding teamwork was a result of intensive work on the training field. 'No, it's just intelligence,' Kenny replied. 'If there's not an opposition player there, run into the space, if you're playing with somebody that's half-decent, he'll pass it to you … Fortunately for us, there were a lot of players that could do that.'

The result made Ferguson and Aberdeen take stock. They had gone into the tie thinking they could beat anyone on their day, but found they were completely outclassed and Liverpool were leagues ahead of them. Ferguson has acknowledged that the games were educational for him. Without the experience, perhaps Aberdeen may not have become the force in Europe that they went on to become later in the 1980s.

The 4-0 win put Liverpool into the quarter-final for the first time since 1978, where they were drawn against CSKA Sofia.

Liverpool had reached the League Cup Final, defeating Manchester City 2-1 on aggregate in the semi-final with Dalglish getting the goal in the second leg. They had lost in the FA Cup fourth round to Everton in January, the first game in a six-match winless run. On 28 February, in the last game before the first leg against Bulgaria's CSKA Sofia, Liverpool got back to winning ways.

The match against Southampton was Kevin Keegan's first league game at Anfield since a 0-0 draw with West Ham in May 1977. Liverpool won 2-0 with Ray Kennedy and Terry McDermott scoring. David Johnson departed at half-time with a thigh injury, which gave Bob Paisley a dilemma for the CSKA game.

'I quite like playing here,' Southampton's Charlie George said after the match, 'even although I usually chase around and never get the ball.' Keegan said that Liverpool could play even better and he tipped them to win the European Cup.

Steve Heighway came in for Johnson in only his third start and fifth appearance of the season. It would be the Irish international's 65th European match.

This was CSKA's 12th consecutive season in Europe and their 20th overall. They had defeated Nottingham Forest in the first round and Dalglish and Souness were given a rundown on their abilities when the Liverpool duo went to Israel on Scotland duty with Forest's Frank Gray, Kenny Burns and John Robertson. Patience, Dalglish said, would be the key.

Scotland boss Jock Stein was in the crowd to see how his three Scots players would fare against a side he expected to play defensively. The *Daily Record* predicted that the Bulgarians wouldn't be at their best after their winter shutdown. Dalglish also felt that the opposition could be rusty at this point in the season.

The game was played on Dalglish's 30th birthday, but it would be Graeme Souness's night. The opening goal came in the 16th minute. Hansen took the ball from the halfway line and played it to Dalglish on the right. Kenny attempted to play a first-time ball with his left foot into the box, but a defender blocked it. The ball came back to Dalglish, who, although losing his balance, toe-poked it with his right into the path of Souness, who had run from the halfway line to collect it. Souness took the ball into the box, evaded a challenge and struck it powerfully from 12 yards into the net. It was the first goal CSKA had conceded in their fifth European tie of the season.

Dalglish missed a golden chance when Georgi Iliev headed a McDermott cross back towards his own six-yard box. Dalglish took the gift with his right foot on the half-volley but hammered it over the crossbar. He held his head in disbelief.

Sammy Lee scored on the stroke of half-time to make it 2-0. Six minutes into the second half, Heighway set up Souness for his second. Georgi Velinov in the CSKA goal stood still as Souness's shot torpedoed into the top right corner. Tzvetan Ionchev pulled one back before McDermott made it four. With ten minutes remaining, Ray Kennedy knocked the ball to Souness at the edge of the box and this time Souness shot into the top left-hand corner of the net.

In the second leg, David Johnson scored after ten minutes to give the Reds a 6-1 aggregate win and set up a semi-final tie with Bayern Munich.

Liverpool: Clemence, Neal, A. Kennedy [Cohen], Thompson (c) [Irwin], R. Kennedy, Hansen, Dalglish, Lee, Johnson, McDermott, Souness

Scorers: Miller (og 37), Neal (43), Dalglish (58), Hansen (71)

Aberdeen: Leighton, Dornan, Rougvie [Cooper], Watson, McLeish, Miller, Strachan, Bell [Hewitt], McGhee, Jarvie, Scanlon

34

Liverpool 2-1 West Ham United

1 April 1981, League Cup Final Replay,
Villa Park

THE LEAGUE Cup was first played for in the 1960/61 season. Liverpool lost in that inaugural campaign to Southampton in the third round. It was the one competition that had eluded them so far. They had lost the 1978 final to Nottingham Forest after a replay, while the same club had ended Liverpool's campaign at the semi-final stage in 1980.

This time, Dalglish had scored twice in the first round, a 4-1 aggregate victory over Bradford. He had also scored in subsequent wins over Swindon Town, Portsmouth and Birmingham City. In the semi-final, the Reds met Manchester City. A late Ray Kennedy goal gave them a 1-0 win in the first leg at Maine Road, while another goal from Kenny helped them to a 1-1 draw in Anfield's second leg to take the tie 2-1 on aggregate.

The final against Second Division West Ham at Wembley went to extra time after a goalless 90 minutes. With two minutes remaining of the 120, the match livened up. Liverpool had a free kick 20 yards out. Jimmy Case's shot was cleared but came back out to Phil Neal, who launched the ball forward. Colin Irwin headed it on into the box where Sammy Lee went up for a header with Billy Bonds. Both missed the ball, but Lee came crashing to the floor and stayed there. The ball fell to Alvin Martin, who, facing his own goal, kicked it behind him, only for it to fall at the edge of the box to Alan Kennedy, who belted it into the net.

The linesman quickly raised his flag as Lee was lying in an offside position when Kennedy's shot came flying over the top of him.

Referee Clive Thomas ran towards his colleague but, without actually consulting him, awarded the goal. Thomas would later concede this was 'bad refereeing', but was happy that awarding the goal was the correct decision.

In 1980 Kenny was asked what he disliked in football. 'Referees who are inconsistent,' was his reply. 'One game you get the official who works in harmony with his linesmen and all goes well. The next, you get the referee who ignores his linesmen's every signal and it's chaos.'

Just when it looked like the cup had finally been won, West Ham won a corner. From Jimmy Neighbour's kick, Alvin Martin sent in a header that arced over Ray Clemence and was about to drop under the crossbar when Terry McDermott jumped and tipped the ball on to the bar with his hand. The Hammers' penalty expert, Ray Stewart, stepped up and tucked the kick away to level the scores.

In a radio interview, Thomas said that West Ham boss John Lyall had come on to the pitch to call him a cheat. 'No one, in England or anywhere else in the world, calls me a cheat,' Thomas said, adding he intended to report Lyall to the FA. The Hammers manager said what he actually said was, 'I feel we have been cheated.' The FA later exonerated Lyall.

The replay was set for Villa Park more than two weeks later. Liverpool had worn all red for the Wembley match, so they would now wear their change kit of white shirts, black shorts and red socks. 'We've got something to prove to the nation tonight, and perhaps we'll do that,' Ray Clemence said in an interview with ITV before the match.

West Ham took the lead after only ten minutes. Trevor Brooking brought the ball out of defence, then played it down the right to Jimmy Neighbour. The experienced former

Tottenham and Norwich winger went on a run, jinking past Alan Hansen's tackle to get to the byline, where he put over a superb cross to the near post. Paul Goddard dived ahead of Phil Neal to head the Hammers in front.

It took Liverpool 15 minutes to draw level. West Ham were defending well, stopping Liverpool from having possession in the final third. As Liverpool tried to build an attack, the ball was pushed out to McDermott at around the 35-yard mark, with the Hammers' defence back in numbers. McDermott perfectly weighted a long ball with his right foot, which dropped on the edge of the six-yard box. Dalglish got in between two defenders, swivelled and met the ball low on the volley, crashing it over Parkes and into the net.

'An absolute beautiful goal,' Brian Clough said in his co-commentary. '[McDermott] delayed his pass, it was taken before it reached the floor. Phil Parkes had no chance whatsoever with that.'

Three minutes later, it was 2-1. Dalglish turned his marker and sent in a shot that Parkes turned round the post. 'He really is looking something special tonight, this Liverpool number 7 Kenny Dalglish,' Brian Moore said in his commentary. Jimmy Case took the resultant corner. The ball came over to the far post, where Hansen rose above Alvin Martin. His header came off Bonds' knee and into the net.

Ian Rush was playing in only his second match for Liverpool. Signed from Chester in May of 1980, he made his debut against Ipswich in December of that year, where he wore the number 7 shirt in place of Dalglish, who had been injured against Spurs the previous week. Tonight was the first time they had played together.

After his debut the young Welshman had gone back into the reserves, where Paisley insisted that he learn his trade. This was frustrating for Rush as he knew he was good enough for the first team, but he began to realise that it made sense. He told *The Guardian* in 2008, 'In the reserves you were allowed to make mistakes … [in] the first team that was unacceptable.'

Rush had been at the Wembley match with the rest of the reserve team. By the time of the replay, he had been added to the squad but hadn't expected to play. Steve Heighway had picked up a groin injury and David Johnson had been out injured for a few weeks. Rush told the *Daily Post* on the eve of the match, 'The thought of possibly playing in the final does not worry me a bit, in fact I could not wish for anything more.'

At half-time, former Liverpool striker Ian St John was asked to summarise Rush's performance. 'He's linked up well with Dalglish, who's playing marvellous,' St John said, 'and between the two of them they're looking a terrific partnership.'

Dalglish's relationship with Rush began in the dressing room when he saw a gangly teenager with a pencil-thin moustache wearing drainpipe corduroys. The young Welshman was welcomed by becoming the central point for Kenny's and the dressing room's jokes. 'Taking the mickey, as we did, was our way of welcoming the new boy,' Kenny wrote in the foreword for Rush's 1996 autobiography. 'It's when colleagues ignore you, when there is an edge in the dressing room, that's when you need to feel worried.'

It would take a little time for Rush to come round to accepting the dressing room banter, and to warm to Dalglish.

There were no goals in the second half. Liverpool had won their first League Cup. It was Bob Paisley's ninth major trophy since taking over from Bill Shankly in 1974.

St John felt Dalglish was the man of the match. 'I think he had an outstanding game,' he said. 'He led the line. He used his experience to help young Ian Rush up front. And of course Dalglish scored an outstanding goal. I thought it was a magnificent goal. I think he was the outstanding player, in a display where all the Liverpool players played well.'

Paisley was delighted with the performance of Ian Rush. 'His control is good. He is difficult to knock off the ball and he can pace people into the game which is Kenny's asset. And he can turn them like Kenny. He's got a long way to go, and the lad will know that, but it is pleasing when he starts off like that.'

Liverpool: Clemence, Neal, A. Kennedy, Thompson (c), R. Kennedy, Hansen, Dalglish, Lee, Rush, McDermott, Case

Scorers: Dalglish (25), Hansen (28)

West Ham United: Parkes, Stewart, Lampard, Bonds, Martin, Devonshire, Neighbour, Goddard, Cross, Brooking, Pike [Pearson]

Scorer: Goddard (10)

Attendance: 36,693

35

Liverpool 1-0 Real Madrid

27 May 1981, European Cup Final,
Parc des Princes

IN THE first leg of the European Cup semi-final, Bayern Munich visited Anfield and left with a 0-0 draw. Dalglish had two great chances both saved by Walter Junghans in goal. Much of the British press felt that Liverpool's prospects of becoming the first British club to play in three European Cup finals had slipped away by virtue of not taking a lead to Bavaria for the second leg.

Before he departed Liverpool, Bayern midfielder Paul Breitner, who had won the European Cup in his first spell with the club in 1974, said: 'We have a great opportunity [in the second leg] and I think we will attack, dominate and win.' It wasn't the most controversial thing that he said, as in an interview with an Italian journalist he was reported to have called Liverpool 'dull and unintelligent'.

'Breitner's decision to shout his mouth off to the newspapers wound the lads up,' Dalglish wrote in his 1996 autobiography. The Liverpool players were eager to play the second leg, and had the newspaper clippings pinned up in the dressing room.

Bill Shankly had acclaimed Breitner as the best man on the pitch at Anfield, but Bob Paisley made sure that wouldn't be the case in the Olympiastadion. Sammy Lee had been tasked to follow the World Cup winner everywhere, and he stuck to his task admirably. 'Sammy Lee put Breitner out of the game and they had no one else with enough imagination,' Paisley said afterwards.

With only seven minutes of the game gone, Dalglish was the target for a rough tackle from Karl Del'Haye, who caught his left ankle from behind. Kenny tried to run the injury off, but soon he fell to the ground again. Ronnie Moran came on with his magic sponge, but nothing was going to keep Kenny in the game. He had to come off.

Perhaps nobbling Liverpool's best player was the masterplan, but it proved to be counter-productive. Dalglish was replaced by Howard Gayle. It was a surprising decision as Ian Rush or Jimmy Case would have been the more obvious choice. Earlier in the day, the official UEFA observer had come over to Bob Paisley with the team list. 'Who is this?' he said, pointing to Gayle's name, as if he were an ineligible player. It got Paisley thinking. If the UEFA man had no clue who Howard Gayle was, then chances were that Bayern Munich would know nothing of the Liverpudlian winger, who had made his only previous Liverpool appearance in October of 1980 against Manchester City.

If Bayern knew nothing of Gayle before the match, they certainly knew all about him at the final whistle. Gayle ran their defence ragged. He tormented the Bayern right-back Wolfgang Dremmler, although he and his team-mates Klaus Augenthaler and Hans Weiner kicked and pulled at Gayle, in their attempts to stop him. 'I know I have Bayern's defenders on toast,' Gayle told the *Morning Star* in 2019. 'The only way they can get to me is by fouling.' The reaction of the German crowd spurred Gayle on. 'Every time I got the ball I heard monkey chants,' Gayle told lfchistory.net. 'They made me even more intent to be good at what I had to do.'

Ray Kennedy was thrown up front. Kennedy had been a striker when he was at Arsenal and had only been converted to a midfielder when he joined Liverpool. With seven minutes to go and extra time on the horizon, David Johnson played the ball into Kennedy. He controlled it and launched a shot that flew into the Bayern net.

With three minutes left Karl-Heinz Rummenigge drew Bayern level again. However, the final score of 1-1 was enough for Liverpool to win on away goals and go into the European Cup Final to face Real Madrid, who had beaten Inter Milan 2-1 on aggregate. Paisley hailed the match as Liverpool's greatest performance in Europe.

'Paul Breitner called us stupid but he was too cocky,' Kennedy said after the match. 'You can't do that to Liverpool and get away with it.'

'I never said Liverpool were stupid,' Breitner said. 'I merely said the team played simple football.' David Lacey was open to giving Breitner the benefit of the doubt, saying he was a 'sensitive, intelligent man'.

The final was Liverpool's 63rd competitive match that season. They had been top of the league at the turn of the year, but by the end of February, the Reds were eight points behind Aston Villa, having played a game more. The season would end with Villa winning the league, nine points ahead of Liverpool in fifth. That meant Liverpool would only have UEFA Cup football to look forward to in 1981/82 unless they could win the European Cup.

The match in Paris came eight days after Liverpool's final league match of the season, a 1-0 win over FA Cup finalists Manchester City. Real Madrid also had a full week's rest. They had played the first leg of their Spanish Cup quarter-final with Real Sporting Gijón a week earlier. Their league season had also ended in disappointment, losing out on the La Liga title to Real Sociedad on head-to-head goal difference, so they too knew that they wouldn't be in the European Cup next season unless they won the trophy.

Real won the first European Cup in Paris in 1956, the first of five in a row. However, they hadn't appeared in the final since their last win in 1966.

Dalglish was doubtful to play due to the injury sustained in that tackle by Del'Haye. He hadn't played since, missing all Liverpool's league games and Scotland's World Cup qualifier with Israel and the Home Internationals against Wales, Northern Ireland and England. He had treatment and trained with the hope that he'd be healed for the final. Despite having no match time, Kenny was determined to play so long as he passed all the fitness tests. He did, and when the team arrived at the Parc des Princes and Bob Paisley announced his team, Kenny was named in the starting line-up.

Alan Kennedy had broken a wrist in the first match with Bayern and was reported at the time to have played his last game of the season. However, he too was on the team sheet. 'I had a metal cast strapped to my wrist,' Kennedy told the BBC in May 2018. 'It was a bit cumbersome and heavy and would undoubtedly be classed as dangerous in today's football world.'

This was Liverpool's first-ever meeting with Real Madrid. Laurie Cunningham had played against the Reds four times for his previous club, West Bromwich Albion. Uli Stielike had also faced Liverpool before, playing in the Borussia Mönchengladbach team that had lost 3-1 in the 1977 European Cup Final. It was Ray Clemence's save from his 55th-minute shot when the match was poised at 1-1 that was the turning point of the game.

Liverpool were forced to deal with a distraction when TV broadcasters insisted that they cover up the Umbro logo on their shirts. Horst Dassler, the head of Adidas, who supplied Real Madrid's kit, wanted Liverpool for his roster. He had attempted to court the club, much to Umbro's chagrin. The occasion of the European Cup Final was an opportunity for Dassler to cause a little bit of chaos. He managed to convince UEFA that advertising such as the Umbro logo should not be visible. Real Madrid had already taken steps to cover up their Adidas logo, although the three stripes that adorned the shirts' sleeves, shorts and socks were universally known as Adidas's trademark. It was the first time in 79 years that Real had deviated from plain white shirts, the new style being introduced for this match.

UEFA went with it, and so Liverpool's players looked around for something to cover up the Umbro logo. They used medical tape and spent crucial pre-match time applying it to each other's kits and tracksuit tops.

'The Fonz is Cool. Kenny Dalglish is Cooler', a fan's banner read, referencing Henry Winkler's character in the US hit TV show *Happy Days*.

In the first half, Dalglish, held back by his shirt the first time he twisted away from García Cortés but seldom held thereafter, was a constant danger in the Real penalty area, and this advantage ought to have brought Liverpool an earlier goal. In the second half, Dalglish was utilised a little deeper, seeking to draw defenders to maximise McDermott's long runs deep in the Real cover.

The tension built as Liverpool were unable to capitalise on all their pressure, and the breakthrough finally came with nine minutes remaining.

'I wasn't thinking about scoring a goal, I was thinking that if I could make a run here it might create a bit of space for Souness, McDermott or Dalglish,' Kennedy told the BBC. 'But Dalglish had come to the byline so I ran into the space that had been left open for me.' García Cortés swung a boot at Kennedy but missed. That put Kennedy through against the goalkeeper, and when he noticed the keeper had moved slightly to his left, Kennedy decided to drive the ball to his right. His shot found the net. The match had suddenly come to life.

Cramp got the better of Dalglish late in the game, and with four minutes remaining, Jimmy Case replaced him. He might not have been on the pitch at the final whistle in Paris, but Kenny got to enjoy another of his favourite cup-winning experiences a few days later, as half a million people lined a 17-mile route in Liverpool for an open-top bus parade.

He ended the season winning *Shoot!* magazine's Most Exciting English League Player award for the fourth time. 'I'm a bit taken aback,' a typically modest Dalglish told the magazine. 'From a personal point of view I hardly set the heather alight last season.'

Paisley, who had now become the first manager to win the European Cup three times, would refresh his Liverpool team over the summer. Ray Clemence left for Spurs, with Jimmy Case joining Brighton. In their place came Bruce Grobbelaar, who experienced much criticism early on due to his hesitant start, and Mark Lawrenson, who signed for a record £900,000 from Brighton. Ian Rush would begin to establish himself as a regular. Irishman Ronnie Whelan had made his debut in a late-season game against Stoke in April 1981, but he would become a fixture in the number 5 shirt playing in midfield in 1981/82.

Midfielder Craig Johnston joined from Middlesbrough. 'Kenny Dalglish wasn't the captain, but he was a leader in the dressing room,' Johnston said to author Simon Hughes. 'Within the first 24 hours of me being there he took me around Southport to look for property and went out of his way to make me feel at home and comfortable.' The South Africa-born Australian would soon become a pivotal member of the Liverpool team.

Liverpool: Clemence, Neal, A. Kennedy, Thompson (c), R. Kennedy, Hansen, Dalglish [Case 86], Lee, Johnson, McDermott, Souness

Scorer: A. Kennedy (81)

Real Madrid: Agustín, Cortes [Pineda], Camacho, Stielike, Sabido, Del Bosque, Ángel, Santillana, Navajas, Juanito, Cunningham

Attendance: 48,360

36

Liverpool 3-1 Everton

*7 November 1981, First Division,
Anfield*

BOB PAISLEY was asked by Alex Cameron of the *Daily Record* what price he would put on Dalglish's talents. Paisley replied that he wouldn't sell him for £2m.[5] He said he felt he was better than Kevin Keegan, although they had different styles, with Keegan moving in fast bursts and being dangerous near goal, while Dalglish was more graceful, a thinker, and more likely to lay the ball off for team-mates, as well as scoring goals himself. 'People have said I should be in jail for stealing him from Celtic,' he quipped.

In his 1981 autobiography Phil Neal compared how the players requested different service from their team-mates. Neal said that Keegan liked a low driven ball, while Kenny preferred the ball played into his feet, so he could turn his marker.

Paisley told the *Liverpool Echo* he didn't think any player was worth £1m and revealed he had been criticised over the transfers of Keegan and Dalglish, by someone 'high in the game' who had said it set a trend which others then followed. Paisley said, 'I replied that the Keegan/Dalglish deals were an exchange, with Liverpool making the best part of £100,000 into the bargain.'

Liverpool lost on the opening day of the 1981/82 season 1-0 to Wolves at Molineux. It was their first loss on the

---

5 The British transfer record was broken in October 1981 when Manchester United paid West Bromwich Albion £1.5m for midfielder Bryan Robson.

opening day since a 2-0 defeat to Queens Park Rangers in August 1975.

Oulun Palloseura were again opponents in the European Cup. In Finland, Liverpool managed a 1-0 win with Dalglish netting the goal. By the time of the second leg on 30 September, the city of Liverpool was in mourning. Bill Shankly had died the morning before. Phil Thompson was the only player in the Liverpool team who had played under Shankly, but everyone in a red shirt felt the loss.

There was a minute's silence before kick-off, and the teams wore black armbands. Kenny scored the first goal in a 7-0 rout, while the Liverpool fans sang Shankly's name throughout the second half. 'Anybody who's got any allegiance towards Liverpool in any way, shape or form whatever that is, you just look back and he's the guy that everybody's got to thank,' Dalglish said in an interview with Peter Hooton for BT Sport in 2022. 'Even the ones who succeeded him and were hugely successful – Bob, Joe, Ronnie, anybody, even right up to the present day, it's because of Shanks and of what he did and the things he installed. Without Shanks Liverpool wouldn't have been the same.'

Liverpool were ninth in the league by the time of the Merseyside derby in November, while Everton were one place above them. Days earlier, Liverpool had defeated AZ 67 Alkmaar 5-4 on aggregate thanks to a late Alan Hansen goal.

Everton hadn't won at Anfield since Joe Royle and Alan Whittle gave them a 2-0 win in March 1970.

Both sides had chances to score in the first half. McDermott, Rush and Dalglish came closest for Liverpool, with McDermott also having a goal ruled out. O'Keefe brought out a great save from Grobbelaar.

Just before half-time, Dalglish had his name taken when referee Peter Willis from County Durham decided he'd had enough of Kenny's trademark complaining. Willis, a policeman, had played as an amateur for Newcastle United before taking up refereeing in 1963.

Before this match, Dalglish had not scored a league goal at Anfield since the double he hit in a 2-1 win over Aston Villa on 22 November 1980. 'People start talking about you playing in midfield because you're not scoring goals and because you're getting older,' Dalglish wrote in *Shoot!* 'But Bob Paisley still thinks that I'm most use to him up front and I go along with that.' He was confident his lean spell would end because his goalscoring instinct was still there.

In *The Guardian*, Patrick Barclay suggested that Dalglish's reflexes were no longer as sharp as they once were, and perhaps a move back into a role behind the strikers, like he had occupied at Celtic Park, might favour him. It would be the position from which he netted his brace after moving back to accommodate substitute David Johnson.

In the days of only one player on the bench, a straight swap wasn't available when Ray Kennedy went down injured under Steve McMahon's challenge. To the cheers of the Kop, Kennedy carried on after going off the pitch for treatment, but a few minutes later, he had no choice but to leave the pitch for good. Johnson, an ex-Everton man, went up front, Ronnie Whelan moved over to the left and Kenny slotted into the centre of midfield.

With Dalglish further back, Everton neglected to assign a marker to him. Barclay observed that Dalglish initially seemed a little puzzled about finding himself without a chaperone in blue.

Liverpool started the second half quickly, winning a corner on the right. McDermott whipped it in for Whelan to hit a volley that Arnold could only parry. Dalglish was there to slam the ball into the net.

The second goal was only a few minutes behind. It was another corner from the left. Souness took the kick to McDermott, who threaded a pass through Everton's back four for Dalglish to run on to. Kenny placed a low shot wide of Arnold to make it 2-0.

McMahon was booked for a foul on Neal, while Johnson had the ball in the net, only to see it disallowed. Dalglish also found his name in referee Peter Willis's notebook for dissent.

Eamonn O'Keefe was sent off for, according to Barclay, 'an act of vandalism' on Whelan. O'Keefe claimed it was the worst moment of his life and suggested the Liverpool players had influenced the referee.

Liverpool continued to press, and the result came in the 75th minute. Dalglish found Johnson on the edge of the Everton box. Jim Arnold blocked the substitute's shot. Gary Stevens attempted to clear the ball but could only hit it off the incoming Ian Rush, and the ball flew into the net for Liverpool's third.

Everton pulled one back in the 83rd minute, Mick Ferguson jumping between two Liverpool defenders to head in.

Rush was now settling in well to Liverpool's first team and developing a relationship with Kenny, despite the Scotsman's teasing of his young colleague rankling the Welshman. 'Kenny Dalglish, whom I had disliked so much, was brilliant towards me,' Rush wrote in his 1996 autobiography. 'He was forever giving me advice on the field, making me aware of situations, spotting weaknesses in the opposition defence, telling me when and how to make my runs off the ball.'

'It was like Kenny had radar,' Mark Lawrenson told *The Athletic* in 2021. 'His partnership with Ian Rush was extraordinary. They knew exactly where the other one wanted it. Kenny seemed to know where Rushie was even when he couldn't see him and delivered the perfect pass.'

Dalglish quipped in the *Liverpool Echo* in 2017 that Rush could run, while he couldn't. He said Paisley had taken a gamble, paying £300,000 for him as an 18-year-old, but it paid off. 'He was fantastic for us. He didn't score for a few games at the start, but after that he was prolific. He was easy to play with. Really easy.'

Rush reflected in *The Guardian* that the partnership with Dalglish just worked straight away. 'I had the pace and he had the football brain.' However, he added that they didn't really mix off the pitch, which wasn't surprising as there was a ten-year difference in age between them and they didn't exactly live close to each other. Dalglish lived in Southport and centred a lot of his leisure time around the golf course while Rush was based in north Wales. Rush spent his social time with Ronnie Whelan, Jan Molby and Terry McDermott. 'It's funny, but Kenny and I get along brilliantly now, much better than we ever did when we were playing together,' he said in 2008.

In December, Liverpool had a chastening experience when they went to Tokyo to play in the Intercontinental Cup. They hadn't previously played in the annual match between the European champions and the South American champions. Dalglish wasn't enthused about going. Despite the match being established in 1960, it wasn't a trophy that was coveted by players or fans the way the European Cup was.

Historically, there had been violence on the pitch during these games. Celtic, Manchester United and AC Milan had been involved in games almost resembling wars in the late 1960s. Liverpool's players had been cautioned not to get involved, and they didn't. After the 3-0 defeat to Brazil's Flamengo, Paisley felt that his team didn't get involved in much at all. 'I've never seen the team so dull physically and mentally. We were lacking in ideas and aggression.'

Liverpool hadn't shaken the defeat off by the time of their next league game, when they were beaten 3-1 by Manchester City on Boxing Day. The game was marred by a wine bottle thrown from the Kop hitting City's goalkeeper Joe Corrigan. The defeat left Liverpool in 12th place, nine points behind the surprise league leaders Swansea City. Bob Paisley reacted by taking the captaincy from Phil Thompson and handing the armband to Graeme Souness. Paisley believed that the extra responsibility was affecting Thompson's game, and while the England international didn't agree, he accepted the decision with humility.

Souness's first game as captain was a 4-0 win over Swansea in the FA Cup. 'Liverpool played us off the park,' Swansea keeper Dai Davies wrote in his 1986 autobiography. 'That painful thorn in my side, Kenny Dalglish, possibly the most talented player I ever played against, was the mastermind.'

That win started an 11-game unbeaten run, only ended by Chelsea in the FA Cup fifth round. By the time of a 5-1 win over Stoke City in March, Liverpool were fourth in the First Division, six points behind leaders Southampton.

Tottenham Hotspur were Liverpool's opposition in the Milk Cup Final (the League Cup was now sponsored by the Milk Marketing Board, and so had this new name). It was Ronnie Whelan's day as he scored two goals in Liverpool's 3-1 extra-time win. Whelan recalled that Dalglish had sat down beside him on the occasion of his debut against Stoke in April of 1981, and told him that he'd obviously been doing things right to get his chance in Liverpool's first team, so just keep on doing what he'd been doing. The advice settled the 19-year-old, who went on to score in a 3-0 win.

'Dalglish was no speed merchant,' Whelan wrote in his 2011 autobiography, 'but between his ears he was lightning quick; he could spot a defence-splitting pass that no one else would have seen and execute it in the same moment.'

Two days after that Milk Cup win Paul McCartney sat down at Air Studios in London to do an interview with the French journalist Freddy Hauser. 'Do you have any idols?' Hauser asked the ex-Beatle. 'Not just musically but in any field?' McCartney paused and pondered the question.

'Musically I've got a lot. Not in music? Footballers. Kenny Dalglish is pretty good. [He plays for] Liverpool. A good team. We just won you see, so we're very up at the moment.'

None of the Beatles were particular football fans although McCartney admitted to having a leaning towards Everton, as his father was born there, and his family were all Evertonians. However, he told *The Observer*, 'After a concert at Wembley Arena I got a bit of a friendship with Kenny Dalglish, who had been to the gig and I thought "You know what? I am just going to support them both because it's all Liverpool and I don't have that Catholic–Protestant thing."'

Liverpool: Grobbelaar, Neal, Lawrenson, Thompson (c), R. Kennedy [Johnson], Hansen, Dalglish, Whelan, Rush, McDermott, Souness

Scorers: Dalglish (47, 52), Rush (75)

Everton: Arnold, Stevens, Bailey, Higgins, Lyons, Lodge, McMahon, O'Keefe, Ferguson, Ainscow [Biley], McBride

Scorer: Ferguson (85)

Attendance: 48,861

37

Liverpool 3-1 Tottenham Hotspur

15 May 1982, First Division, Anfield

WITH TWO games of the season remaining, Liverpool were three points ahead of Ipswich Town at the top of the table, Bobby Robson's side being the one that had sustained a challenge for the title, while previous leaders Swansea and Southampton had dropped to fifth and seventh respectively. This was the first season of three points for a win. Ipswich had two home games left against Nottingham Forest and Tottenham, while Liverpool had Tottenham at home and Middlesbrough away. Liverpool's goal difference of plus 46 compared to Ipswich's plus 23 was as good as another point.

Remarkably, the last time Tottenham had beaten Liverpool at Anfield was in March 1912, when Tom Mason and Ernie Newman scored in a 2-1 win.

The Kop was full at 2pm and the gates at Anfield were closed half an hour before kick-off. Ray Clemence was given a warm welcome by the Liverpool fans behind his goal on his return to Anfield.

Dalglish missed a good chance early on. The ball was crossed into him, but it was just too close to his body to make a proper connection.

Tottenham shocked the Kop by taking the lead in the 27th minute. Ricky Villa played a square ball to Glenn Hoddle. There looked to be no danger when the England international suddenly unleashed a shot from 30 yards, which swerved past Grobbelaar and in.

Liverpool, though, didn't panic. There was little doubt in the players' minds that they would get back into the game, and there was no need to rush.

'The one thing they [the management team] would say to us before we went out on a Saturday at three o'clock was "Be together,"' Alan Hansen told the documentary series *Football's Greatest Teams*. 'And we always were. When you're under pressure you come under pressure as a team, not as an individual.'

In the second half, Whelan switched from the left of midfield into a central role, preventing Hoddle and his colleague Micky Hazard from having the control they had enjoyed in the first half.

Six minutes into the second half, Liverpool's equaliser came from an unlikely source; the man leaping highest to meet Sammy Lee's corner was defender Mark Lawrenson, who, from 12 yards out, netted his fourth of the season.

It was Lawrenson who set up Dalglish for the second. His overhead kick caught out the Spurs defence and Dalglish latched on to the ball. He made Clemence commit himself before shifting the ball from his right foot to his left and netting his 22nd goal of the season. In the *Daily Mirror*, Frank McGhee wrote, 'I can think of few players in the British game given so little time and room and facing as accomplished a goalkeeper as Clemence who could have slotted a scoring shot with such chilling efficiency.'

'Liverpool know how to get the best out of Kenny,' Spurs captain Steve Perryman told Ken Jones of the *Sunday Mirror*. 'He's a great team player and he's quite happy not to get the ball as long as he's taking defenders into bad places. Kenny has got a marvellous first touch. He kills the ball dead, and if you are too close, he'll do you on the turn. He's alert and always looking for ways to punish you.'

Over at Portman Road, Ipswich were one down thanks to a Peter Davenport goal. He would go on to net a hat-trick in a 3-1 Forest win, which killed Town's hopes for the title. His manager, Brian Clough, bizarrely told the press after the match he would sell Davenport back to the Birkenhead club, Cammell Laird, if he didn't do better than that.

Meanwhile, at Anfield, Ronnie Whelan sealed the match and the title with his 14th goal of the season. He brought the ball down 20 yards out, carried it a few steps, and then hammered it into the net.

Since the defeat to Manchester City on Boxing Day, Liverpool had taken 62 points from a possible 72.

Spurs legend Jimmy Greaves was one of Dalglish's many admirers: 'Kenny is the finest of Britain's present-day strikers,' Greaves said. 'He is always composed and controlled in the penalty area, no matter how great the pressure, and is continually a thought and deed ahead of the defenders. His finishing is mercilessly accurate, and he plays without fuss or unnecessary theatrics. A pro from his head to his toes.'

'Whatever success I have gained playing in England is equally shared by my colleagues at Anfield,' Kenny said in 1980. 'Not just the lads on the field but the entire staff who have given so much help. While individualism is always a necessary asset, we must never lose sight of the fact it's a team game.'

Grobbelaar played in every game that season. In fact, he made 317 consecutive appearances for the club from the opening league game at Wolves until the Charity Shield match against Everton on 16 August 1986.

The title win also meant that 1982/83 would be Liverpool's seventh successive season in the European Cup. Paisley said he was proudest of this title out of the five he had won, because 'there was so much more to do'.

Liverpool: Grobbelaar, Neal, Lawrenson, A. Kennedy, Whelan, Thompson, Dalglish, Lee, Rush, Hansen, Souness (c)

Scorers: Lawrenson (51), Dalglish (55), Whelan (87)

Tottenham: Clemence, Hughton, Miller, Roberts, Hazard, Perryman (c), Brooke, Falco, Villa, Hoddle, Crooks [Price]

Scorer: Hoddle (27)

Attendance: 48,122

38

Belgium 3-2 Scotland

15 December 1982, European
Championship qualifier, Heysel Stadium

DALGLISH HAD an underwhelming World Cup with
Scotland in the summer of 1982. He had led the line
alongside Alan Brazil in Scotland's opening match against
New Zealand, getting on the scoresheet in a 5-2 win. In the
second game against Brazil, he was relegated to the bench,
coming on in the second half as Scotland fell to a 4-1 defeat.
In the final group game against the USSR, Kenny wasn't even
picked as a substitute. It looked as if his days as a Scotland
international may have been coming to a close.

Kenny concentrated on his Liverpool career, opening
the season with a 1-0 Charity Shield win over Tottenham.
David Johnson left at the start of the season to join Everton.
In September Terry McDermott left Liverpool to join
Newcastle United, who had been fortified by the arrival of
Kevin Keegan. David Hodgson arrived from Middlesbrough
while Jim Beglin came in for £20,000 from Shamrock Rovers.

Liverpool's season was shaping up very well, with the
highlight of the autumn being a 5-0 win over Everton at
Goodison with Ian Rush scoring four. Scotland manager
Jock Stein was in the crowd.

Kenny had missed the two games Scotland had played
since the World Cup finals. For October's European
Championship qualifier at Hampden against East Germany
Jock Stein didn't select him in the squad. John Wark and Paul
Sturrock scored in a 2-0 win.

In the second week of November, ten days after Kenny had scored his first goals of the season in a 3-1 win over Brighton, he was selected for the Scotland squad for the match against Switzerland in Berne. 'This is not a backwards step,' Stein said, 'just practical. Dalglish has started scoring and playing well again. It will gee him up to be pulled into the squad again, and it might have a similar effect on the others.'

Bob Paisley felt Kenny had shown the right attitude, and was being rewarded for that.

A thigh injury prevented Dalglish from playing in the Milk Cup win over Rotherham. Less than a week later, Kenny aggravated the injury after scoring against Coventry in a 4-0 win and pulled out of the Scotland squad. Sturrock and Alan Brazil were up front as Switzerland won 2-0 in the Wankdorf Stadion.

At the start of December, Liverpool were top of the league, three points ahead of Manchester United and Aston Villa, and still retained interest in the European Cup and League Cup.

Stein decided against naming the in-form Celtic striker Charlie Nicholas in his Scotland squad for the match against Belgium, instead keeping the player who was becoming known as 'the new Dalglish' in the under-21s. Stein's forwards were Sturrock, Tottenham's Steve Archibald and Kenny.

The European Championship qualifier at the Heysel Stadium in Brussels against Belgium would be Kenny's 89th cap and a match in which he gave one of his greatest performances in a Scotland shirt. Archibald was his partner up front in a Scotland team lining up in a 4-4-2 formation, designed to come away with a draw.

'I admire every skilful, adventurous, attacking player and Kenny certainly comes into that category,' Steve Archibald said in the Scotland programme in 1981. 'It's an experience lining up with such a player. You can't help but pick up a hint or two just by playing alongside him.'

Belgium had not been beaten at home in five years and 16 internationals. Previewing the match in the *Daily Record*, Alex Cameron said the 'wily fox' Dalglish was key to the game, and hoped he could replicate his club form and turn the tide for Scotland.

The previous Saturday, Dalglish had ripped fourth-place Watford apart, Bob Paisley telling *The Guardian*, 'They didn't have a clue how to deal with him.' Dalglish made the first goal for Ian Rush, turning a Watford defender. The second came from a Phil Neal penalty after Kenny had been pulled down. Liverpool went on to win 3-1.

Gordon Strachan wrote that he learned an important lesson from Kenny while they were on Scotland duty together, and that was to have plenty of rest. 'You could not find a better example of any professional than Kenny,' Strachan wrote in his 1991 book *Strachan Style*. 'I used to see him go off to his bed in the afternoon. Most of the lads would be in the snooker room at the hotel ... watching the racing on the box ... having a game of putting or even taking a sauna. Not Kenny – none of that was for him. When he had free time, usually in the afternoon when the training and the team talks were over, he was off to his bed for a couple of hours.'

Scotland took the lead after 13 minutes with a wonderful team goal. Frank Gray won the ball on the left of Scotland's defence and played it on to Rangers' Jim Bett. The midfielder moved it on to Dalglish. Kenny took the ball from well inside his own half, turned and moved forward 15 yards. He spotted Archibald running through and slid a pass into him that the Spurs striker gathered just outside the penalty box. Archibald controlled the ball, brought it into the area and slid a square ball across to the inrushing Kenny, who from 12 yards chipped it over Jean-Marie Pfaff.

Erwin Vandenbergh equalised 12 minutes later after Jim Leighton missed a cross and the Anderlecht forward fired home.

In the 35th minute of the match, Dalglish created one of the moments of magic he would be remembered for in a Scotland shirt. Souness chipped a ball into him down the right, which Kenny gathered at the edge of the Belgian penalty area. He turned sharply to the right, controlling the ball with the outside of his boot, wrong-footing Eric Gerets. Moving towards goal, he jinked away from Walter Meeuws and bent the ball left-footed across the face of the goal and into the far corner.

It was so quick that Pfaff only had time to move his neck to watch the ball nestle in the net. In his commentary for STV Jock Brown said, 'Absolutely magnificent. Perhaps the only man in the United Kingdom who could have done this. If anyone cares to question his ability in a Scotland jersey, let them look at that goal again.'

Ian St John was on co-commentary and was equally impressed, remarking, 'Kenny Dalglish has been playing this season for Liverpool, as well as he's ever played in his life I should think. What a superb goal.'

The goal would win *Match of the Day*'s Goal of the Season for 1982/83.

The second was Dalglish's 28th goal for his country. It was the third brace he had scored for Scotland; the first occurred against Northern Ireland in June 1977, while the second came against Norway in October 1978.

Unfortunately though, West Ham's Francois Van der Elst soon had Belgium level, and in the 63rd minute the same player made the score 3-2 to Belgium.

With 13 minutes remaining Scotland took off Gordon Strachan and Jim Bett for Tommy Burns and Paul Sturrock. The 26-year-old Sturrock was one of many Scottish strikers who looked up to Dalglish. 'I always considered it a privilege to share the same football park as Kenny Dalglish and Danny McGrain,' Sturrock wrote in his 1989 autobiography *Forward Thinking*.

Dalglish was the player Sturrock likened himself to. He wrote, 'It is fairly unusual for a world-class player to be able to play at the highest level in several positions. Kenny Dalglish could perform in the highest company with many different numbers on his shirt. Rarely has a player been able to score goals from either side and with his head so effectively, and yet been a skilful, industrious midfield player as Kenny was. Indeed I can think of no other over the last two decades who has been so prolific in front of goal and so creative further back on the football field.'

'In his playing career Paul was unlucky that Kenny Dalglish was around, otherwise he would have won an awful lot more Scotland caps than he did,' Harry Redknapp wrote in the introduction to Sturrock's 2015 autobiography. 'He was a terrific footballer but no player would displace Kenny Dalglish in his prime.'

Scotland had a chance to level when Jan Ceulemans pulled Souness down in the box with 12 minutes remaining. Scotland's regular penalty-taker John Robertson was not playing. Dalglish was still on the field, though surprisingly he had never taken a penalty kick for Scotland. Leeds United's Frank Gray, who had scored against Holland earlier that year, stepped up to take the kick. Pfaff, very obviously a few steps off his line, dived to his left to save and condemn Scotland to a 3-2 defeat.

'It's unbelievable that Kenny Dalglish should score two such brilliant goals and still be on the losing side,' Scotland boss Jock Stein said after the match. Eric Gerets, who was then with Standard Liege, said of Dalglish, 'He's the best forward in the world.'

'His first hour was as good as any performance I've seen in an international,' said Stein. 'Both his goals were good, but the second was one of the finest ever. The way he turned the Belgium defender as he received the ball was out of this world.

'Dalglish has received a lot of criticism when playing for Scotland. Most of it has been undeserved. He's the kind of player who's always going looking for the ball and risks being caught with it rather than make an unfair pass. Kenny isn't just happy to take a chance on a near miss. He wants to be in on the game all the time. In Brussels he was like the youngster I remember, coming on as a sub[6] for Celtic at Kilmarnock and scoring six goals. He had the enthusiasm of a youngster but the skill which comes only from great experience.'

The second goal would be remembered long after the match itself. Years later, reflecting on that strike in his *Sunday Post* column in 2018, Dalglish showed his characteristic team-first mentality, 'For me, the goal meant zilch as we lost the game. I'd rather have tapped one in from half-a-yard out if it meant securing a victory.'

Belgium: Pfaff (Bayern Munich), Gerets (Standard Liege), Daerden (Standard Liege), Meeuws (Standard Liege), Baecke (KSK Beveren), Vercauteren (Anderlecht) [Verheyen (SK Lokeren)], Van der Elst (West Ham United), Vandersmissen (Standard Liege), Vandenbergh (Anderlecht) [De Schrijver (SK Lokeren)], Coeck (Anderlecht), Ceulemans (Club Brugge)

Scorers: Vandenbergh (25), Van der Elst (38, 63)

Scotland: Leighton (Aberdeen), Narey (Dundee United), Gray (Leeds United), Aitken (Celtic), McLeish (Aberdeen), Hansen (Liverpool), Strachan (Aberdeen) [Burns (Celtic)], Archibald (Tottenham Hotspur), Dalglish (Liverpool), Bett (Rangers) [Sturrock (Dundee United)], Souness (Liverpool)

Scorer: Dalglish (13, 35)

---

6 Put this down to Stein's recollection at that moment as the contemporary reports indicate that Dalglish was in the starting XI for Frank Beattie's testimonial.

The teenage Kenny with three of his Cumbernauld United team-mates and club mascot Fiona Gibb in 1968.

Kenny evades Dundee United's Archie Knox during Celtic's 1974 Scottish Cup Final win.

Dalglish at Celtic in 1974.

Kenny in action against Brazil in the 1974 World Cup.

Kenny playing for Celtic against Rangers in August 1976.

In his last competitive game for Celtic, Kenny and 1977 Scottish Cup Final referee Bob Valentine watch Rangers' captain John Greig toss the coin for kick-off.

Kenny engages the police to help him look for his dropped Scottish Cup winners' medal at Hampden in May 1977.

August 1977 and Kenny arrives at Anfield with Liverpool boss Bob Paisley to start life at his new club.

Kenny walks out at Wembley for his Liverpool debut in the 1977 Charity Shield against Manchester United.

Kenny celebrates scoring his first goal at Anfield for Liverpool against Newcastle United, August 1977.

In the dressing room at Anfield Kenny and Don Masson celebrate the win over Wales that qualifies Scotland for the 1978 World Cup.

Dalglish prepares to hit the winning goal in the 1978 European Cup Final.

Kenny with pals Rod Stewart and Sandy Jardine ahead of Scotland's departure for the 1978 World Cup.

Stanley Matthews presents Kenny with the Football Writers' Player of the Year Award in May 1979.

Kenny lines up for Scotland in May 1979.

Kenny celebrates with the 1980 Charity Shield.

A familiar picture of Liverpool's three 'Jocks' with another trophy. This time, the 1981 European Cup.

39

Aston Villa 2-4 Liverpool

18 December 1982, First Division,
Villa Park

THREE DAYS after the disappointment of defeat in Belgium, Kenny was back in a Liverpool shirt as, in their all-yellow change strip, they took on league champions Aston Villa.

Villa captain Dennis Mortimer grew up a Liverpool fan, watching them from the Boys' Pen alongside the Kop and accumulated a collection of players' autographs. He played alongside Terry McDermott in Kirkby. Indeed, when Football League clubs signed players from their team on S Forms, the pair – who both went on to win the European Cup – were the only two overlooked.

The Villa team had returned five days earlier from their Intercontinental Cup match in Tokyo, where they lost 2-0 to Penarol. Villa brought in 18-year-old Mark Walters for only his third start, in place of Tony Morley.

The game was first versus fourth, with Liverpool six points ahead of Villa and three ahead of second-placed Manchester United.

About two-thirds of the pitch was covered in ice and frost. The entire half Aston Villa had to defend at the Holte End was icy underfoot, which contributed to some of the terrible tackles the Villa players made.

Peter Withe made two ridiculous challenges on Dalglish in the space of 60 seconds, both resulting in free kicks, and the second causing referee MP Scott to have a word in the striker's ear. The resulting free kick was around 20 yards out. Sammy Lee cracked a shot that Rimmer saved, but Hodgson followed up and knocked the ball into the net.

Minutes later, a shot from Rush was tipped around the post by Rimmer. Kenny went over to take the corner kick. He sent the ball curling into the near post. Despite Rimmer and two of his defenders being closer to the goal and ball than any Liverpool player, it deceived them all and went straight into the net.

Liverpool had another free kick just outside the Villa area when Evans made a clumsy challenge on Rush. Souness hit a shot which the wall deflected, but only into the path of the onrushing Alan Kennedy, who tucked the ball away for 3-0 with 27 minutes gone.

Villa came back first of all with a goal from Gary Shaw in the 34th minute. One minute later, Dalglish fouled Walters out on Liverpool's right, although TV footage suggested that he took the ball. Cowans took the free kick and crossed the ball in for Withe, who headed in Villa's second.

In the second half, Grobbelaar brilliantly tipped a powerful Withe header on to the bar to prevent Villa getting an equaliser. The Zimbabwe international goalkeeper made another great save a moment later as the ball zinged around the penalty box. He saved again from a Ken McNaught header only minutes after that.

With two minutes remaining, Hodgson cut the ball back to Dalglish, who slotted a through ball to his right for Rush to run on to and slip the ball home to make it 4-2.

Peter Withe recalled the match in his autobiography, 'Half the pitch was frozen and would have been considered unplayable nowadays,' he wrote. 'I made a tackle on Kenny Dalglish – well, I went straight through him actually, although I'd gone for the ball, and he went tumbling over. Souness wasn't happy about my tackle and came over to make his point, and we had a bit of a tête-à-tête, shall we say. Then

Kenny got up and came over to me and gave me some verbal. I told him to "Keep it shut or I'll come and sort you out as well ..." or words to that effect. Ironically, they got a free kick and scored from it, so I learned my lesson that day. We lost the game 4-2.'

Liverpool's next match was nine days later, in a busy post-Christmas period. Manchester City had beaten Liverpool 3-1 on Boxing Day 1981, in a game which looked like it had ended the Anfield side's title hopes. It, of course, only spurred the Reds on as they won 20 of the remaining 25 league games to lift the title. City visited Anfield a year and a day later.

The match kicked off at 11.30am, with the turnstiles opening at 9.45am. The turnout was Anfield's biggest attendance of the season to that point. The gates to the Kop only closed half an hour after kick-off, with an estimated 6,000 of the 34,000-plus fans gaining entry to the ground after the game had begun. Anfield's capacity was down to 45,030, having been reduced from 50,307 in September 1981.

Dalglish had begun the season without a goal in the first 16 games. He ended this match having scored 11 in 11.

With 18 minutes played Kenny, playing behind the front two of Rush and Hodgson, hit a drive with the outside of his boot which rose into Joe Corrigan's net.

Three minutes later, Phil Neal stepped on to a harmless-looking ball around 30 yards out. He fired it towards Corrigan's goal, and it flew into the net.

It was only two minutes later when Dalglish lined up a free kick and smacked it straight through the wall to put Liverpool three up.

City got back into the game when a pass from Souness went astray and David Cross chipped Grobbelaar.

Into the second half, and Dalglish set up Ian Rush, who drew Corrigan and made it 4-1. Kenny had his hat-trick after Lee played a diagonal ball for Hodgson, who hooked it back for Dalglish to score. Late on, Grobbelaar made an outstanding save from Bodak's close-range volley. Tommy Caton headed in close to the end to make the final score Liverpool 5 Manchester City 2.

Trevor Francis played against Kenny's Liverpool with Birmingham City, Nottingham Forest and Manchester City. 'Up front they had such a cutting edge,' Francis said on the documentary series *Football's Greatest Teams*, 'the likes of Dalglish and Rush. Those two will go down as two of the all-time greats at Anfield.'

In *The Guardian*, Patrick Barclay suggested that Liverpool weren't so much marching to the title they were strolling, with Dalglish deserving a lot of the credit.

Liverpool: Grobbelaar, Neal, A. Kennedy, Lawrenson, Whelan, Hansen, Dalglish, Lee, Rush, Hodgson, Souness (c)

Scorers: Hodgson (5), Dalglish (9), A. Kennedy (27), Rush (88)

Aston Villa: Rimmer, Jones, Williams, Evans, McNaught, Mortimer, Bremner, Shaw, Withe, Cowans, Walters

Scorers: Shaw (34), Withe (35)

Attendance: 34,568

40

Liverpool 5-1 Notts County

1 January 1983, First Division, Anfield

'AS THE years roll by, the superlatives begin to pale somewhat as Liverpool – and especially Kenny Dalglish – get better all the time,' wrote Simon Inglis in his match report for *The Guardian*.

Liverpool had a rough festive period. Their win against Manchester City and the 0-0 draw with Sunderland were played on 27 and 28 December. Both opposing sides decided that a physical game would stop Liverpool, and Dalglish came in for most of the treatment.

'Teams are starting to get into us to see how we like it,' said Graeme Souness, a man who very much did like it. 'I wasn't conscious of it before, but I will be, now it has been highlighted.'

Bob Paisley defended his captain for a tackle on Sunderland's Shaun Elliott. 'That fellow had about five goes at our people but the referee said nothing to him,' Paisley said to the press. 'Graeme did not go over the top. He caught him on the shoulder and took the man's breath away. It was the crowd's reaction that got Graeme booked.' Elliott was stretchered off with stud marks on his knee, although Sunderland's manager, Alan Durban, speaking to the *Northern Echo*, also thought it was the crowd that got Souness booked.

Souness himself said, 'It was body contact and if he hadn't fallen on to the track he would have been all right.' Years later, though, quoted in journalist Phil Thompson's book *Do That Again Son and I'll Break Your Legs* Souness said of the body check, 'That, I admit was deliberate. I wanted him to know that I was there and that I also knew what he was up to.'

Bob Paisley told the *Daily Post* that he needed his players to keep calm. 'When you get involved in two successive games like this, players can't play their natural game.'

Since scoring that goal of the season against Liverpool for Norwich, Justin Fashanu had signed for Nottingham Forest in a £1m deal in the summer of 1981 and then been offloaded for a bargain £150,000 to Notts County in December of 1982.

This was a game where Liverpool's front three were absolutely dominant. The fact that County's manager Jimmy Sirrell was intent on his team playing attacking, entertaining football played right into Liverpool's hands. *The Daily Post*'s reporter reckoned that this was something of an off-day for the Reds.

The first goal came after 15 minutes when Sammy Lee swung in a free kick for Ian Rush to head in. But Notts County came back quickly, and they were level two minutes later. John Chiedozie received the ball from Ian McCulloch and found Justin Fashanu in the six-yard box. Fashanu, whose reputation had taken something of a battering during his time across the Trent at Forest, tucked the ball away.

With half an hour gone, Rush picked Pedro Richards' pocket and he played it on to David Hodgson. The former Middlesbrough man sent the ball to Dalglish, who comfortably slotted home.

Five minutes before half-time, Liverpool had a penalty when Mark Goodwin pulled down Alan Kennedy. Phil Neal, the regular taker, stepped up and fired his penalty high and wide.

With 73 minutes played, a flick by Hodgson allowed Dalglish to go one-on-one with Raddy Avramovic, and go round the goalkeeper to tap into the net.

Dalglish set up Rush for number four with 12 minutes left before Hodgson's third assist led to Rush completing his third hat-trick of the season with three minutes left. The 21-year-old Rush now had 20 goals for the season in all competitions. He had scored 50 goals in 77 Liverpool appearances.

'It's a terrible habit Ian's got into,' Dalglish said to the *Daily Express* afterwards, 'and I hope he doesn't break it.'

'I can't stop scoring,' Rush said to the *Sunday Mirror*. 'Kenny Dalglish is giving me great service by playing so brilliantly.'

'Dalglish was a genius,' Hodgson said to *Tribal Football* in 2024. 'His football brain was one step or two steps ahead of the others. He was a striker who looked after himself. For me, Souness was the greatest player I had the pleasure to play with, Dalglish was the most genius and Rush the greatest striker.'

The former Wolves player-turned-pundit Derek Dougan wrote of Dalglish, 'He is such a marvellous controller of the ball. He turns defenders so brilliantly in the penalty area, and he seems to have an inbuilt antenna, telling him when the others have taken up position.'

In an interview with lfchistory.net, Ian Rush spoke about his partnership with Kenny, saying Dalglish managed to put the ball into positions he had thought impossible, meaning Rush then had to make a run he wasn't quite expecting to.

The more they played together, Dalglish began to realise how quick Rush was, and although the pair didn't speak much off the pitch they started to understand what each other was good at. 'We just had a thing that was natural,' Rush said. 'Kenny wouldn't look up to see where I was, he would just put the ball into space and I just knew Kenny was going to put the ball there.'

The win put Liverpool eight points clear at the top of the league. They followed it up with a 3-1 win over Arsenal on

3 January. Patrick Barclay was again amazed by Dalglish's performance, writing in *The Guardian* that defender Peter Nicholas was 'left trailing miserably in his wake' and the Liverpool star played to a standard being set by Brazil's footballers. Kenny netted the third with Rush and Souness scoring the others.

Ken Jones of the *Sunday Mirror* asked Kenny what the difference was between his sensational form at this juncture of the season and the apparent slump he had been in early in the campaign. 'Only that I'm scoring more often,' Dalglish replied. 'It's what the punters understand. I get marvellous support from the team and I'm getting a bit of luck every player needs.' Kenny never gave away much in his interviews, and he was never big-headed.

'Kenny is running freely again,' Jock Stein told Jones, 'and I think it's ambition that makes him look stronger … he's getting to the time when men of his calibre want to prove that they can still make a job of it.'

Stein said that on the day Kenny left Celtic, he told Bob Paisley that they had signed a player better than Kevin Keegan. 'And I was right,' Stein said. 'One of the great things about him is that he wants to be out there every week. Kenny will play when he's only 80 per cent fit, and you can't say that about a lot of them.'

The Scotland manager could see that Kenny's current striking partner was adding something to his game. 'He's always liked to spread the play around. I feel that the boy Rush is good for him at Liverpool, making those sharp, angled runs in behind defenders.'

It was after that win over Arsenal that Paisley declared Dalglish 'the best player Liverpool have ever had'.

Kenny told Ken Gallacher of the *Daily Record* that he had taken a lot of stick from the players after that praise. Now 31 and in the form of his life, he added that he didn't know how long he would play on for, but he didn't agree with players being written off when they reached 30. Players suffered bad patches at any age, but Dalglish explained that good players with age add refinements to their game. They realise that some things they can do better than previously and they understand what they can no longer attempt. That didn't make them worse players than they were in their mid-20s.

Maybe surprisingly, though, despite his sensational form, Kenny told Gallacher that he didn't think he would add the 11 international appearances required to gain 100 Scotland caps.

In the FA Cup fifth round, Liverpool lost to Brighton, who were struggling at the foot of the First Division. The Anfield club had gone a remarkable 63 home cup matches without defeat. Their last home loss had been to Middlesbrough in the fourth round of the League Cup on 12 November 1974. The game was notable for being Liverpool's first ever match at Anfield played on a Sunday.

Kenny's celebrity was such that in February he was the subject of an episode of *This Is Your Life* which reached a viewing audience of 15.65 million.

In early March Liverpool went out of the European Cup in the third round after a 4-3 aggregate defeat to Poland's Widzew Lodz. Kenny missed the second leg with a stomach upset.

He hit two goals the following Saturday as Stoke were defeated 5-1 and Liverpool went 14 points clear of second-placed Watford in the league.

On 26 March, Liverpool met Manchester United at Wembley in the Milk Cup Final. They were behind from the 12th minute when Norman Whiteside scored. That was still the case with 15 minutes remaining until Alan Kennedy popped up to score a screamer from 25 yards out when he hit a diagonal drive past goalkeeper Gary Bailey.

The cup was won by Ronnie Whelan's memorable curling shot from the edge of the box in extra time.

The following night, Kenny was voted the PFA's Player of the Year and Ian Rush was awarded the Young Player of the Year. Bryan Robson was runner-up to Dalglish, and Norman Whiteside was second to Rush. Six Liverpool players were named in the All-Star First Division XI: Lawrenson, Hansen, Souness and Lee joining Dalglish and Rush. Bob Paisley was the guest of honour and received the PFA's Merit Award.

Kenny also collected the Football Writers' award for the second time. It was presented by Pelé, who was a surprise guest of honour. Decades later, following Pelé's death in 2022, Kenny reflected in his *Sunday Post* column, 'It was a great honour and thrill to meet him – and it's fair to say I was a bit starstruck. He spoke a bit of English – some said he spoke better English than me – and it was nice to have a wee conversation with him. Overall, he was a very humble person … He wanted to talk about others, and what they'd done.'

Albert Stubbins, who scored 24 goals as Liverpool won the First Division in 1946/47, told the *Liverpool Echo*, 'I'd have loved to have played up front with Kenny Dalglish and Ian Rush.' Stubbins was also notable for being one of the figures featured on the cover of The Beatles' 1967 album *Sgt. Pepper's Lonely Hearts Club Band*.

Despite being top of the league since October, Liverpool stuttered to the title, as in mid-April they lost to Southampton at the Dell and then Norwich at Anfield. The league championship was finally confirmed on 30 April at White Hart Lane. Despite Liverpool losing 2-0, Manchester United, with games in hand, could only draw 1-1 with Norwich, meaning that no one could catch Liverpool. Watford would finish second, 11 points behind. Shockingly, Liverpool failed to win in their last seven league games, losing five of them.

Bob Paisley stepped down at the end of the season. After the 2-1 defeat to Watford at Vicarage Road, he said,

'I'm fortunate in knowing this was my last game. There are managers of other clubs who haven't been told yet.'

Paisley said he would have loved to have Keegan and Dalglish on the same team, as great players could always play together. 'But if I had to choose one of them, it would have to be Kenny,' he wrote in his 1983 book *A Lifetime in Football*. 'As individuals, he and Kevin are on a par. But Kenny can make a team spark collectively with his gifted ability to read situations, and offers other players so many options with his wide-ranging distribution and vision.'

Paisley, who began his career with Liverpool as a player in 1939, ended his assessment with a glowing commendation. 'Of all the players I have played alongside, managed and coached in more than 40 years at Anfield, he is the most talented. When Kenny shines, the whole team is illuminated.'

Liverpool: Grobbelaar, Neal, A. Kennedy, Lawrenson, Johnston, Hansen, Dalglish, Lee, Rush, Hodgson, Souness (c)

Scorers: Rush (15, 78, 87), Dalglish (30,72)

Notts County: Avramovic, Benjamin, Worthington, Hunt [Hooks], Kilcline, Richards, Chiedozie, Fashanu, McCulloch, Goodwin, Mair

Scorer: Fashanu (17)

Attendance: 33,643

41

Ipswich Town 1-1 Liverpool

*26 November 1983, English First
Division, Portman Road*

IN SUMMER 1983, Kenny played celebrity golf for Great Britain against the US in the Duke of Edinburgh Cup at Royal Mid-Surrey. In the singles, he beat actor Fred MacMurray, star of *Double Indemnity* (1944) and *The Apartment* (1960), by six holes.

Joe Fagan had now taken over from Bob Paisley as manager: it was an internal appointment and not much was expected to change behind the scenes, although Paisley was arguably English football's greatest manager, so it was no easy challenge to replace him.

The players all thought it was a brilliant appointment. Fagan was well liked and well respected within Anfield. 'He didn't want to take over,' Kenny told author Tony Evans. 'But he knew if someone else came in everything would change.'

Fagan continued Liverpool's tradition of strengthening the side over the summer months. Defender Gary Gillespie was bought from Coventry City, and striker Michael Robinson was signed from relegated Brighton and Hove Albion. One player Liverpool couldn't land was Charlie Nicholas. Despite Dalglish's assurances that the Celtic striker would fit into the team with Kenny operating behind him and Rush, Charlie felt that Dalglish – his idol – and Rush were too important a partnership to split up, so he opted for Arsenal. 'For football reasons I should have gone to Liverpool,' Nicholas said to *The Independent* in 1993, 'but there was no guarantee I would get in their team. Ian Rush was playing well, and Kenny Dalglish was still there, so I thought it would be difficult for me to break through.'

Fagan's first competitive match in charge would be the Charity Shield against Manchester United at Wembley. 'I am glad Ron Atkinson is there,' Fagan said, tongue in cheek. 'He can show me the way round the place.'

Dalglish played behind the front two of Rush and Robinson, but it was United's day, Bryan Robson's double giving them the win.

Nicholas had the chance to take on Kenny and Liverpool when the Reds came to Highbury on 10 September. Nicholas didn't like being compared to Dalglish as he said he had a lot still to learn.

His former manager at Celtic and Dalglish's former team-mate, Billy McNeill, said Charlie had had it much tougher coming through at Celtic as Kenny came in to a successful team and could develop at his own pace, while the side wasn't as strong and much was expected from Nicholas when he broke through at Parkhead.

With the game goalless, Nicholas cracked a shot off the crossbar. That was as close as he would come to scoring. Craig Johnston put Liverpool in front after 17 minutes. Kenny made it 2-0 on 67 minutes with a goal David Lacey in *The Guardian* suggested may end up being his best of the season. A lovely passing move brought about the chance. Sammy Lee feinted to disguise a pass into Dalglish with his back to goal at the D. Kenny played the ball back to Lee, who knocked it on to Robinson, who chased the ball inside the penalty box. Knowing Dalglish was behind him, he backheeled it; Dalglish let it run across him, which sent Graham Rix skidding past. Kenny took a touch with his left foot, then curled it left-footed around the head of David O'Leary and into the net off the crossbar, before spinning around arms aloft to greet Lee. 'There's no team better in

Britain, and maybe in Europe in passing the ball,' said John Motson on *Match of the Day*.

Speaking with the *Sunday Mirror*, Robinson, who scored 23 times in the league for Brighton the previous season, confessed he was slowly settling into the Liverpool team. He realised he was playing with great players. He called Kenny 'the best forward in the world', and Graeme Souness, 'the most accomplished all-round player I've ever seen'.

Liverpool received an approach for Dalglish shortly after the Arsenal game. Peter Robinson, Liverpool's financial director, confirmed that Celtic had made an enquiry to take Kenny back to Celtic Park. 'That is as far as they got,' Robinson told the press, 'and it is as far as any other club will get. We told Celtic exactly what we told other clubs who have tried to sign him – that he is ours for at least the next 12 months.'

'Our approach did not get past first base,' Celtic's new manager and Kenny's former team-mate, Davie Hay, said.

At the end of September, Dalglish became Britain's record goalscorer in the European Cup with his second goal in Liverpool's 5-0 win over Odense. His tally of 15 was one better than his hero Denis Law's haul for Manchester United.[7]

Luton Town visited Anfield in the league in October. Only a point behind their hosts, they were the victims of a sensational Liverpool performance. Ian Rush scored five times, with Kenny netting the other in a 6-0 win.

In the *Daily Express*, Norman Wynne wrote, 'Liverpool were breathtakingly brilliant and if Rush was the ultimate destroyer, Dalglish was the mastermind behind everything they did.'

---

7 As of May 2025 Harry Kane is now the record British goalscorer in Europe's premier club competition with 40. He does though have the advantage of playing in an era when qualifying has been expanded to clubs who don't win their league and there are significantly more matches than in the time Dalglish played.

Rush had his first goal in the second minute and netted his second after only five minutes. His hat-trick arrived in the 36th minute with Kenny hitting a 20-yard shot two minutes later that Hatters keeper Les Sealey let squirm through his hands and across the line. Ten minutes into the second half, Rush had his fourth. The fifth came two minutes from time.

The last Liverpool player to score five in a match had been John Evans, in a 5-3 Second Division win over Bristol Rovers on 15 September 1954. Rush was the fourth Liverpool player to achieve the feat. John Miller from Dumbarton was first in a 7-0 win against Fleetwood Rangers on 3 December 1892, then ten years later, Andy McGuigan scored five in a 7-0 win over a Stoke team who lost their goalkeeper and two outfielders to food poisoning.

In October 1993, 18-year-old Robbie Fowler became the fifth Liverpool player to score five in a game when they beat Fulham 5-0 in a League Cup match. It was only his fourth senior game.

Remarkably, Rush wasn't the only player in the First Division to score five the day Liverpool beat Luton, with Arsenal's Tony Woodcock also achieving the feat in a 6-2 win over Aston Villa.

Dalglish's goal against Luton meant he was now on 99 league goals in English football.

Ahead of the match against Ipswich, in his column for *Shoot!* Kenny highlighted John Wark as Ipswich's dangerman. Ten days earlier, they had played together in the Scotland team that lost 2-1 to East Germany in Halle. He wrote that for a midfielder, Wark was a great goalscorer, who was able to time his attacking runs to perfection.

Dalglish's 100th league goal in England came in the 62nd minute of the match. Sammy Lee played a corner on the right short to Dalglish. Kenny dipped his shoulder and cut inside Trevor Putney's challenge. Ipswich keeper Paul

Cooper was perfectly placed to intercept the anticipated cross. Suddenly, Kenny curled the ball left-footed. It sailed over all the heads in the six-yard box and nestled in the top corner of Cooper's net.

Wark suggested to Kenny that it was meant as a cross, but Dalglish assured him it was intended as a shot.

'Age doesn't matter with him,' Joe Fagan said, 'he can still deliver the goods. When he got the ball, there was no danger. Then it's in the net. That's Kenny.'

Dalglish was the fifth[8] player to score 100 league goals in both Scotland[9] and England.

David McLean played professionally from 1906 to 1931. He played for Forfar Athletic, Celtic, Third Lanark, Rangers and Dundee in Scotland, scoring 233 league goals. In English league football, he scored 162 times for Preston North End, The Wednesday and Bradford Park Avenue.

Davie Brown's career lasted from 1910 to 1923. He began with Dundee, scoring 79 league goals before hitting 14 for Rangers, 11 more for Dundee, and in a brief spell with Kilmarnock, a further four. In England, he scored 126 league goals in 221 games for Stoke, Notts County, Darlington, Crewe Alexandra and Barrow.

The third player to achieve this feat was the legendary Joe Baker. From 1955 to 1960, Baker scored over 100 league goals in his first spell with Hibernian. In England, Baker scored 146 for Arsenal, Nottingham Forest and Sunderland. In the 1970s, he added another 56 back in Scotland with Hibs and Raith Rovers.

Neil Martin scored 113 goals for Alloa, Queen of the South and Hibernian in Scotland, while south of the border,

---

8 Some sources suggest that Dalglish was sixth and Jimmy McConnell who scored 124 league goals for Carlisle in the 1920s and 30s had also achieved this feat, but there is no indication he scored anything close to 100 league goals in Scotland.

9 It is, however, generally acknowledged that records for some Scottish clubs in the era before the Second World War could be patchy.

he hit 115 goals for Sunderland, Coventry, Nottingham Forest, Brighton and Crystal Palace.

Dalglish was the first player to achieve the feat with only one club on each side of the border. 'The thing to remember is that I have always been with the top club in each country,' Kenny said. 'Every goalscorer needs people to create chances, and I have been fortunate to play in great teams alongside great players. Celtic and Liverpool have been the biggest clubs in the two countries when I have been playing for them. That's been a happy coincidence for me.'

At the end of December Dalglish was runner-up in the European Footballer of the Year jointly with Allan Simonsen of Vejle BK and Denmark, both scoring 26 points. French international Michael Platini of Juventus won with 110 points.

Juventus had finished runners-up in Serie A and had lost in the 1983 European Cup Final to Hamburg. The *Manchester Evening News* suggested that, 'Platini's golden boy image seems to have influenced voters more than anything else.' They suggested that Dalglish was at least as deserving of the award as Platini.

In the 2 January match against Manchester United, Dalglish suffered a broken cheekbone after a challenge from Kevin Moran. 'Brucie had fired a ball in head height and he [Dalglish] tried to flick it on, and Kevin Moran had come leading with his elbow and caught him,' Graeme Souness said at the premiere of the documentary *Kenny* in 2017. 'He went down and I was first to him, and by that time he was up on one knee and I said "Are you okay?" and he said "Yeah I'm fine, I'm fine" and I pulled his hand away and said "No, you're not fine, stay there." There was a hole, one side of his face was concave, it was in. I went to see him in hospital later that night and they'd put a metre of packing into his jaw.'

When Mark Lawrenson visited Kenny in hospital that night, he was so shocked that nurses had to take him into a side room to give him a cup of tea.

Joe Fagan went out to the pitch-side to calm his outraged players down. He was particularly concerned about how Souness might react as he and Dalglish roomed together on away trips and Graeme thought the world of Kenny.

Moran had been wearing a support brace on his wrist, and it had caught Kenny in the face. The injury put him out of the game for eight weeks. 'There are no bad feelings,' Dalglish said to the *Daily Star* in March when he had recovered. 'I didn't know what happened, how it happened or even who or what hit me. I don't know why I was trying to head the ball in the first place.'

Dalglish said his last bad injury had happened when he had split the instep of his foot when he was 18. He was never worried that he wouldn't return to playing.

When Dalglish took over as manager of Blackburn Rovers in October 1991, Moran was the club captain. The pair got on well, Moran scoring the winning goal in the 1991/92 play-off semi-final against Derby County. 'It wasn't malicious,' Dalglish said years later. 'Kevin isn't a malicious guy.'

Liverpool: Grobbelaar, Neal, A. Kennedy, Lawrenson, Nicol, Hansen, Dalglish, Lee, Rush, Whelan, Souness (c)

Scorer: Dalglish (62)

Ipswich Town: Cooper, Burley, McCall, Putney, Steggles, Butcher, Wark, Brennan [D'Avray], Mariner, Gates, O'Callaghan

Scorer: Wark (60)

Attendance: 23,826

42

Liverpool 6-0 West Ham United

7 April 1984, First Division, Anfield

DALGLISH MADE his return to Liverpool's starting line-up in the 3-1 league win over Tottenham Hotspur on 10 March, scoring Liverpool's first goal. Dalglish acclaimed Michael Robinson for helping him through his first full match back. 'He did my running for me in the second half.' Robinson had come in for press criticism for being merely an industrious grafter rather than a cultured artist like those around him. 'It's unfair to compare me with men such as Kenny Dalglish, who is, after all, a genius,' Robinson said.

March 1984 saw Liverpool qualify for the European Cup semi-final by beating Benfica and win the League Cup by defeating Everton after a replay. Going into the match with West Ham, the Reds were leading the table on 66 points, two ahead of Manchester United. West Ham were fourth on 55 points.

Liverpool's new signing John Wark had made a scoring debut the previous week in a 2-0 win over Watford. Having played alongside Kenny for Scotland, he was glad he now didn't have to play against him in the league. 'You could never get too close to him because he'd use his backside to turn you and either score himself or play someone else in,' he recalled for the *Sunday Mail* in 2023. 'That dressing room at Liverpool was pretty special. You had Graeme Souness, Alan Hansen, Ian Rush and Mark Lawrenson in there but Kenny was the one everybody looked up to – we were in awe of him.'

In 2020, Wark described Dalglish to twtd.co.uk as, 'the best player I've ever played with. Scored goals, created goals, could link up play, could run channels, strong as an ox.'

West Ham had last won at Anfield in September 1963 when goals from Martin Peters and Geoff Hurst beat Roger Hunt's strike for Liverpool.[10] World Cup winner Hurst, who played his last league game for West Bromwich Albion in 1975, was an admirer of Dalglish's and saw parallels in the way they played. At the end of his career Hurst saw his own talents as holding up the ball and drawing his team-mates into play. 'Kenny Dalglish was perhaps the best proponent of this art,' Hurst wrote in his 2001 autobiography. 'His all-round play was such that, even when he wasn't scoring, his value was beyond price.'

Liverpool were in front after only six minutes. Sammy Lee played a ball out to Dalglish on the right. Kenny put a low centre in for Ian Rush, who dived to head the ball inside the post.

A reverse pass from Dalglish put Wark in a minute later, but the new boy's shot lacked sufficient power.

It was two after 12 minutes. Ray Stewart had his Scotland colleague Dalglish marked tightly – or so he thought – at a corner. Lee played the ball into Kenny, who, with his back to goal, juggled it and then turned to face Parkes. Graeme Souness showed for a square pass, the logical move. However, Kenny threaded a low bouncing shot through a ruck of players and into the net. It was his 150th goal for Liverpool.

Six minutes later, Dalglish played a great through-ball for Rush to run on to, and although the Welshman seemed to go too far to his left, he fired a powerful left-foot shot past Phil Parkes.

Liverpool were supremely dominant. In the *Liverpool Echo*, Ian Hargraves wrote, 'Some of Liverpool's football

---

10 It would be August 2015 before West Ham won at Anfield again in a 3-0 win over Brendan Rodgers's side.

was almost unbelievable. They seemed to have twice as many players as West Ham.'

Ronnie Whelan made it four before half an hour was played when Sammy Lee played an inch-perfect pass into him, so all the Irishman had to do was connect with the ball to net.

Only seconds later, West Ham had a great chance to get back into the game when Steve Whitton was straight through. Mark Lawrenson, though, stepped in and coolly took the ball away from him.

Rush had two chances to complete his hat-trick, and Geoff Pike had a shot saved by Bruce Grobbelaar. At half-time, the teams came off to a standing ovation.

The second half opened with Rush squandering two more chances and Dalglish sending a shot wide when he was in one-on-one with Parkes. Whelan then hit over the bar when, in the best sense of the cliché, it looked easier to score.

Liverpool made it five with just over an hour gone. Dalglish went on a run down the left and put a cross into the box. Sammy Lee missed it, and the ball went out to Rush, who cut the ball back for the in-rushing Graeme Souness, who smashed it into the net.

Souness made it six when Rush took a ball from Wark and slipped it into his captain, who once again hammered the ball home.

Hargraves, in the *Echo*, described the match as an exhibition that no other English side of the previous decade could have produced.

In the *Liverpool Daily Post*, Ian Ross wrote that the performance reminded him of Leeds United's 7-0 demolition of Southampton in 1972, a match heralded as one of the greatest one-sided games in English league history. He said that much as it was a high point for Liverpool as a team, 'it was also a personal triumph for Kenny Dalglish. The canny

Scot for whom the phrase "the complete footballer" was coined, scored one and had a hand in four others.'

The level of detail in match statistics available in the modern game wasn't around in the 1980s, but match reports suggest that Liverpool had at least a dozen other goalscoring opportunities that they passed up.

The game was West Ham legend Trevor Brooking's last at Anfield as he brought his career to a close at the end of the season. Brooking was a great admirer of Dalglish and wrote in his 2014 autobiography, 'A model professional. His strike rate never faltered. A superb all-round creator and finisher, his only weakness was probably a lack of genuine pace. I rate him among the truly great players of that era. What particularly impressed me was his speed of thought. He always seemed a second or two ahead of everyone else. That compensated for any lack of pace. He was two-footed, shielded the ball well and was always aware of the runners around him. He had the knack of picking the right pass at the right time.'

The great Scottish sports writer Hugh McIlvanney said in 2008, 'Kenny Dalglish is one of the great players without pace, he's one of the great slow players – slow being a comparative term of course.'

Ken Jones of the *Sunday Mirror* asked Jock Stein about Kenny's lack of pace. 'When did Ferenc Puskas run past anyone?' was Stein's reply.

Ian Rush hit four goals in the 5-0 win over Coventry City, giving him 46 for the season, eclipsing Roger Hunt's 42 for Liverpool in the 1961/62 Second Division season. It also brought him to 31 league goals, the first to the 30-goal mark since Everton's Bob Latchford in 1977/78.

Liverpool had been top of the league since 6 November, and their 15th title was confirmed with a 0-0 draw with Notts County at Meadow Lane on 12 May. Rush added another to his season's total with a goal in the 1-1 draw with

Norwich on the last day of the season, two weeks ahead of the European Cup Final.

Liverpool: Grobbelaar, Neal, A. Kennedy, Lawrenson, Whelan, Hansen, Dalglish, Lee, Rush, Wark, Souness (c)

Scorers: Rush (6, 18), Dalglish (12), Whelan (28), Souness (62, 70)

West Ham United: Parkes, Stewart, Walford, Bonds, Martin, Orr, Allen, Cottee, Whitton, Brooking, Pike

Attendance: 38,359

43

Liverpool 1-1 Roma (aet, Liverpool win 4-2 on penalties)

30 May 1984, European Cup Final,
Stadio Olimpico

THE 1984 European Cup Final could have been very different, with Liverpool facing Dundee United instead of Roma.

In June 1986, UEFA's disciplinary committee banned Roma's president, Dino Viola, from all official UEFA activities for four years. The committee had investigated claims that Viola had attempted to bribe referee Michel Vautrot ahead of Roma's semi-final second leg match against Dundee United two years earlier. They found the allegations proven. Viola admitted handing over £40,000 to two other men. Roma were banned from taking part in the European Cup Winners' Cup for 1986/87, but that ban would be overturned on appeal in favour of a 200,000 Swiss francs fine. It was accepted that Viola acted on his own, and there was no indication that Vautrot was receptive.

Liverpool started their campaign against Odense Boldklub of Denmark. Kenny got the game's only goal after 14 minutes. In the Anfield second leg, Dalglish netted twice, and coupled with a brace from Michael Robinson and an own goal, it gave Liverpool a 5-0 win.

'Kenneth has a heart the size of a lion,' Robinson said to author Simon Hughes in 2014. 'He was the first person when I arrived to invite me to his house. He was adorable.

King Kenny – I can't argue with that. I found him a lovely man.'

Spanish champions Athletic Bilbao were the test in the second round. The first leg was at Anfield, and the Basque side defended superbly to take home a 0-0 draw. In the 80s, it was felt that if you didn't travel to the second leg holding an advantage, your chance of progression to the next round was almost gone. The press talked about Liverpool having 'a mountain to climb' and facing 'a distinct possibility of failing to reach the European Cup quarter-finals'.

At the San Mamés Stadium, two weeks later, Ian Rush scored the only goal of the match with a rare header to see Liverpool progress to the last eight.

In the quarter-final, it was Benfica, with Anfield the location for the first leg. Ian Rush got the only goal in the 67th minute. In Lisbon's second leg Ronnie Whelan got the first goal after nine minutes. Dalglish then set up three for Craig Johnston, Sammy Lee and a second for Whelan, as the Reds won 4-1.

The first leg of the semi-final was again at Anfield; the visitors this time were Dinamo Bucharest. It was a physical encounter, with the Bucharest players accusing Souness of breaking the jaw of their captain Lică Movilă, although as the referee saw nothing, Souness escaped censure. 'I heard it,' Alan Kennedy said to Tony Evans of *The Independent* in 2020. 'A thud. I just saw a red blur and heard a boom.'

'It was the best punch I delivered in my life,' Souness told Evans. It was a niggly game and Movilă had a few digs throughout the night. 'He kicked everything that moved and three times caught me with punches off the ball. I'd had enough,' Souness said.

'Movilă was warned,' Kenny Dalglish said. 'Graeme told him that if he pulled his shirt again he'd get it. He got it.'

Liverpool came away with a 1-0 win. Dundee United beat Roma 2-0 at Tannadice on the same night.

In the first match after the European win Liverpool lost 2-0 to Stoke City at the Victoria Ground. Kenny was booked for dissent and substituted after 74 minutes for Craig Johnston. Joe Fagan said it was the worst game Kenny had played for Liverpool.

Two goals from Ian Rush gave Liverpool a 2-1 win in a second leg where the Romanian players tried to get their own back on the Liverpool captain, but Souness was too good for them.

'He rode everything they threw at him,' Dalglish recalled. 'Lesser men would have folded.'

In Rome Dundee United fell by 3-0.

Liverpool warmed up for the final by playing in Kevin Keegan's testimonial at Newcastle, which they drew 2-2. In an unusual move ahead of such an important game, they then travelled to play the Israeli national team. The idea was to play in the weather they might experience in Rome, and to give the players a chance to all be together ahead of the final. 'The players will be able to relax well away from hordes of well-wishers,' chief executive Peter Robinson said, 'and get themselves thoroughly acclimatised.' In temperatures above 80°F, Liverpool won 4-1.

While football remained the priority, Dalglish's growing celebrity was evident in other spheres. Between the intense match preparations, he found time to make an appearance in the Channel Four drama series *Scully*, written by Alan Bleasdale. The title character, played by Kirkby actor Andrew Schofield, was a Liverpool-daft teenager who dreamed of playing for the Reds. The character was a Liverpool institution, originally appearing on BBC Radio Merseyside in 1971, and then spending four years as *The Franny Scully* show on Liverpool's independent radio station Radio City between 1975 and 1979.

'I'm very fond of footballers,' Bleasdale told the *Daily Express*. 'I hope my series gives lie to the idea that all footballers are selfish, arrogant, jockstrap-swinging mindless idiots. Kenny Dalglish and Bruce Grobbelaar both happily appear in the series and they were terrific.'

Actress Gilly Coman told the *Daily Post* about Kenny's first day on the set. 'When he walked in he went bright red through shyness. I felt like grabbing him and telling him not to worry. He's a real doll and took to acting like a duck to water.'

'Kenny is in every episode with a big scene at the end,' Bleasdale said. 'As the series progresses the comedy gets blacker and Kenny has to work hard.'

With the European Cup Final set to be played at Roma's home ground, many felt that it would be to Liverpool's disadvantage. In his *Shoot!* column Kenny attempted to play that theory down. Liverpool had been in a tougher situation. The second leg of the semi-final in the 23 August Stadium, Bucharest, was as rough a night as any side could have wished to play on and Dalglish said Liverpool had reached a stage where they found more room to play away from home, as the host teams tried to pressure them.

With both clubs playing in red, the kit clash was settled amicably with Roma offering to wear their change strip of all white. Liverpool offered to toss a coin, but Roma's president said there was no need.

Roma had finished their domestic season in second place to Juventus, meaning they would play in 1984/85's UEFA Cup unless they won the final.

The former Watford striker Luther Blissett, who was playing in Serie A with AC Milan, gave his assessment of how the game would go. 'Rush has frightened everybody in Italy,' Blissett said. 'He is on every television programme and is talked about in every newspaper and magazine. All the Italian clubs would like to get their hands on him, and you can be sure Roma are going to mark him very tightly indeed. If they do it will give Kenny Dalglish the sort of time and space he rarely gets – and that man is different class. He can win games on his own.'

Blissett noted that Roma didn't play a typical Italian game. 'They do not operate with a sweeper, and play more in the English style with lots of movement on the ball.' He also suggested that the atmosphere in the ground could be beneficial to Roma, but said, 'The Roman crowds are emotional and hysterical and if things go wrong they could turn against their own team.'

As the Liverpool players walked along the corridor towards the pitch's entrance they broke into a song. They sang, 'I Don't Know What It Is But I Love It', a Chris Rea song, which was technically a hit single in March of 1984, spending four weeks in the charts and peaking at number 65. David Hodgson began singing the chorus. Soon Sammy Lee and Craig Johnston had joined in. 'Typical footballers, we only knew the chorus,' Mark Lawrenson told the *Irish Independent* in 2018. The singing continued as they passed the Roma dressing room and their players began to line up to enter the pitch. 'We just kept singing it over and over and they looked at us and absolutely shat themselves. They didn't know what was going on. It was like some sort of battle cry. It was brilliant.'

'It was just one of those spontaneous moments,' Hodgson said. 'I start singing when I get nervous, though I'm a terrible singer, so while I was just standing there in the queue to go out, I started singing that song. Gradually everyone started joining in. So you had all the greats, Dalglish, Souey, Lawro, all singing at the top of their voices.'

Craig Johnston had been playing the album the song came from, *Wired to the Moon*, for months. Johnston and Hodgson, along with Souness were all former Middlesbrough players, which was Rea's hometown.

'It must have had a big impact,' Rush told *The Guardian* in 2018. 'When I went to Juventus the first thing Antonio

Cabrini said to me was: "What was that singing all about?" I told him we did it all the time!'

'We can't have been singing for more than a minute,' Dalglish recalled in his book *My Liverpool Home*, 'but it is a moment that has gone down in football history.' Coincidentally Chris Rea and Kenny Dalglish were born on the same day.

The game couldn't be classed as a classic. Liverpool took the lead after 14 minutes. Graeme Souness played the ball down the right and it ended up at the feet of Craig Johnston. He whipped it to the far post for Ronnie Whelan. Things got a little bit chaotic from this point. Goalkeeper Franco Tancredi jumped backwards, colliding with Whelan, the ball squirmed free, falling at the feet of Rush, Bonetti got in the way but his attempted clearance was blocked. His second attempt clattered into the back of his goalkeeper, who was lying on the ground. The ball broke across the face of goal. 'If you're going to join the attack, stay with it until it breaks down,' Phil Neal remembered Joe Fagan telling him. Neal, who had scored a penalty in the 1977 European Cup Final, had joined the attack and he stepped outside two defenders and smacked the ball home from six yards.

Neal's goal made him only the second British player to score in two different European Cup finals, after Tommy Gemmell, who scored for Celtic in 1967 and 1970.[11]

Two minutes later Souness thought he had scored but the offside flag was raised. Tancredi saved well from Rush on 38 minutes.

But with only two minutes to go before half-time Roma equalised, when a pass from Conti came back off Lawrenson and Pruzzo met the subsequent cross with his head, sending the ball beyond Grobbelaar and in under the bar.

---

11 Gareth Bale has since achieved this distinction, scoring in the 2014 and 2018 finals for Real Madrid.

Roma began the second half with renewed confidence and Lawrenson had to be alert to prevent Nela getting in on goal, while Grobbelaar made a save from Falcao.

Steve Nicol came on to replace Johnston after 72 minutes. Almost immediately, he forced Tancredi into an excellent save. Five minutes into extra time Kenny came off to be replaced by Michael Robinson.

There was nothing much to report until the end of extra time when the match became the first European Cup Final to go to penalties.

Steve Nicol was first to step up. He had been signed from Ayr United for £300,000 in October 1981. A part-timer at Somerset Park, he was seen as the eventual replacement at right-back for Phil Neal, but in 1983/84 he made his breakthrough in the first team playing in right midfield. He perhaps wasn't the obvious choice to be the first penalty-taker. Nicol fired his kick high and wide. 'I know he missed it but I think it was a tremendous attitude for a young player to show,' captain Souness said afterwards, 'and it just illustrated what tremendous spirit there is in this side.'

The stadium erupted. It was advantage Roma. Agostino Di Bartolomei took their first kick and scored. Phil Neal, the regular taker, was next. Neal had decided earlier in the season not to take every Liverpool penalty in a match, as he thought goalkeepers were becoming familiar with him. He made no mistake with his kick.

Bruno Conti was next for Roma. As Grobbelaar left the team talk to take his place for the shoot-out, Fagan had shouted after him, 'Make sure you try to put them off.' Grobbelaar indulged in some antics, putting his hands across his knees like a move from the Jazz Age dance Black Bottom. Conti sent his kick over the bar. Souness made it 2-1. Urbaldo Righetti levelled it at 2-2. Ian Rush was next.

Rush recalled stepping up when speaking to *The Guardian* in 2018. 'That walk from the halfway line to the penalty spot, with 60,000 people booing me, was the most nervous walk of my life. It was such a relief to score.'

Souness would later note that the photographers behind the goal utilised the flashes on their cameras when Liverpool were kicking but didn't do so when Roma players stepped up.

Francesco Graziani approached to take Roma's fourth kick. There then followed one of the most famous moments in a European Cup Final as Grobbelaar did his famous wobbly legs routine. 'I knew from the moment he struck the ball that I did not even need to dive,' Grobbelaar wrote in his autobiography. Graziani's kick struck the crossbar.

It would be Alan Kennedy who walked up to take the kick to win it for Liverpool. While many people couldn't watch, Kennedy was cool and sent Tancredi the wrong way for Liverpool to win 4-2.

Although Kennedy's penalty shoot-out goal doesn't statistically count as a goal in a European Cup Final it did mean that he had now scored the winner in two such games. In March 2025, ahead of the Carabao Cup Final between Liverpool and another of his former clubs Newcastle United, Kennedy was asked by the *Daily Mirror* who he thought would light up the match. He picked out Mo Salah, saying he wasn't too far behind Dalglish in his list of favourite players. 'I love the way he plays his football, but I have to say Kenny will always be my No.1.'

The cover of *La Gazzetta dello Sport* read: 'Goodbye Champions Cup. What a mockery Roma! They give in to Liverpool after 120 minutes and penalties. Conti and Graziani's errors from the spot make the great European dream of the Giallorossi vanish.'

Kenny had idolised the Lisbon Lions who won Britain's first European Cup in 1967, but couldn't find the same success in the hoops. Now with Liverpool he had won the coveted trophy three times. No Scot has more European Cup winners' medals than Dalglish and his team-mates Alan Hansen and Graeme Souness.

Roma: Tancredi, Nappi, Righetti, Bonetti, Nela, Cerezo [Strukelj], Falcao, Di Bartolomei, Conti, Pruzzo [Chierico], Graziani

Scorer: Pruzzo (44)

Liverpool: Grobbelaar, Neal, A. Kennedy, Lawrenson, Whelan, Hansen, Dalglish [Robinson], Lee, Rush, Johnston [Nicol], Souness (c)

Scorer: Neal (14)

Attendance: 69,693

Kenny playing for Scotland in a friendly against Spain in 1982.

In the Milk Cup Final of March 1983, Kenny is surrounded by Manchester United's Arthur Albiston, Ray Wilkins and Gordon McQueen.

Kenny playing for Scotland in a friendly against Uruguay in September 1983.

Dalglish under pressure from Roma's Dario Bonetti (#3), Falcão (#5) and captain Agostino Di Bartolomei in the 1984 European Cup Final at the Stadio Olimpico, Rome.

A pensive Dalglish alongside Steve Nicol ahead of the 1985 European Cup Final at the Heysel Stadium in Brussels.

Newcastle United's David McCreery and Paul Gascoigne watch on as Dalglish drives forward at St James' Park, August 1985.

Now Liverpool's player/manager, Kenny sits on the bench during a match with Manchester United in October 1985.

SFA president David Will and the legendary West German international Franz Beckenbauer stand on the podium as Kenny displays his special 100th cap in March 1986.

Kenny celebrates scoring the goal that wins the league against Chelsea at Stamford Bridge in May 1986.

Kenny speaks to the media at Stamford Bridge after the league championship is secured, May 1986.

Kenny and Ian Rush wait to kick off in the FA Cup Final, May 1986.

Kenny loved an open-topped bus tour, and here he is enjoying a tour of Liverpool after the double win of 1986.

Aged 39 Kenny plays his last ever game for Liverpool, coming on as a substitute against Derby County in May 1990.

Kenny enjoys celebrating the 1990 league championship win with Ronnie Moran and Roy Evans, May 1990.

44

Scotland 3-1 Spain

*14 November 1984, World Cup
qualifier, Hampden Park*

'HOW CAN you leave out the best in the country?' Jock
Stein would regularly respond whenever anyone suggested
that Kenny Dalglish should be left out of the Scotland squad.

Denis Law told the *Daily Record* Dalglish was the
best player in Europe. 'If Scotland played Dalglish as a
target man, the way Liverpool do, there would be no
problem.'

Throughout his career, Dalglish came under constant
criticism that his performances for Scotland were never
as good as those for Liverpool, the best club in Europe
for practically all of Kenny's playing career there. His
international team-mate Willie Miller had a theory about
why, despite being one of the few world-class players
Scotland produced, Kenny regularly came in for this type
of disparagement. Unlike other players, Miller suggested,
Kenny never went missing on the pitch. 'No matter how he
was playing, he was always in the thick of the action, trying
to contribute to the team effort,' Miller wrote in his 1989
autobiography. 'Consequently, when it did not come off for
him, his failure was all the more noticeable.'

Dalglish was asked by the Scotland match programme
in 1980 what playing for Scotland meant to him. 'For me it
means everything,' he replied. 'It's all about passion and pride.
It's an experience which never fails to make you feel proud to
be a Scot. Some cynics say money plays a paramount part in

it. Don't believe that – there's a marvellous feeling when you pull a Scotland jersey over your head.'

Kenny had missed the international against England at Hampden in May, but that was always the case when he had a European Cup Final to prepare for. Archibald and Mo Johnston were the strike pairing for the June friendly with France.

Paul Walsh had signed for Liverpool from Luton Town in time for the start of the 1984/85 season. Midfielder Jan Mølby arrived for £200,000 from Ajax. He would be the natural replacement for Graeme Souness, who had left for Sampdoria in Serie A.

Souness joined up with Kenny in the Scotland squad for September's Hampden friendly versus Yugoslavia. Steve Nicol would make his international debut in the match, while John Wark would also play.

It was a rare match where Scotland gave the opposition a hammering. It was Yugoslavia though who took the lead on 11 minutes through Fadil Vokrri. Davie Cooper equalised a minute later. Souness made it 2-1 on 18 minutes. Dalglish made it three in 31 minutes when Cooper set him up. Kenny hit the ball with the side of his foot into the keeper's far corner. Sturrock, Johnston and Charlie Nicholas completed the scoring to make it 6-1.

Kenny was back in the Scotland team for the World Cup qualifier against Iceland at Hampden in October, just days after being dropped from the Liverpool team for the first time for the 1-0 defeat to Tottenham. The night belonged to a new Scottish star, the 19-year-old Celtic midfielder Paul McStay playing in his eighth international.

McStay grabbed the first goal after a short corner from Dalglish was picked up by Cooper, who whipped a ball to the far post. McStay sent a downward header bouncing high into the net. McStay's second came from a 30-yard shot just before half-time.

In the second half Kenny was replaced by Charlie Nicholas, 'Not a popular decision with the crowd,' Don McQuarry wrote in the *Belfast Newsletter*. 'Kenny Dalglish directed most of the attacks for an hour,' wrote Mike Aitken in *The Scotsman*. Nicholas turned the crowd round by scoring the final goal in the 3-0 win.

'The crowd didn't understand the full story,' Stein said, explaining the substitution. 'It's much better for Kenny to be brilliant for an hour and give us the start we need than for him to finish jaded after 90 minutes.'

In the *Liverpool Echo* Ian Hargraves wrote Dalglish had shown he was far from finished at international level and expected him to be back in the Liverpool side the following weekend.

Stein was delighted with McStay's performance. 'Paul's a splendid player,' Stein said afterwards, 'but he's lucky to play alongside Kenny Dalglish and Graeme Souness. He will learn from them.'

Souness told the *Liverpool Echo* he felt Kenny had been out to prove a point in that game, and Dalglish said, 'I keep hearing stories that I'm finished. One day one of them will be right.'

At club level Liverpool's season had not begun well. They lost the Charity Shield to Everton thanks to a Grobbelaar own goal. A run of five league games without a win led to Fagan dropping Dalglish for that Tottenham game. 'The only parts of the job I disliked were press conferences and dropping players,' Fagan said after he retired. 'But I dropped them just the same. Even Kenny Dalglish. What a daft devil I was.'

Kenny came back in for the Merseyside derby on 20 October. Everton won 1-0 with Graeme Sharp scoring what would end up being *Match of the Day*'s Goal of the Season.

The result left Liverpool in the bottom three of the First Division, the first time they had been in such a position for 20 years.

After Liverpool's 2-0 win against Nottingham Forest on 28 October, when Kenny set up both goals, Tommy Docherty, now manager of Wolves, suggested to the *Daily Record* that Dalglish should be appointed player-coach of Scotland's Under-21 team, because he would be a huge influence as an over-age player among the youngsters. 'For the kids to be in the same side would be a fantastic boost. Kenny is the complete pro. Players such as Dalglish and Souness mustn't be discarded ... They have too much to contribute.'

The Scotland team was unchanged since the Iceland game. Spain had been runners-up in the European Championship a few months before, and came full of confidence. Their plan was to mark the Scotland attackers out of the game and hit on the break.

Jim Bett and Davie Cooper both hit the post before the first goal was scored. Bett's chance came when Dalglish dummied to make space at the edge of the box and slid a pass through for Bett to shoot, while Cooper's came when Souness passed to Bett, who chipped the ball in for Cooper to head. Goalkeeper Luis Arconada touched it on to the post.

The opener came when Cooper dribbled and crossed, and Maceda headed out for a corner. Dalglish took it, McLeish headed the ball down for Nicol, who hit a delightful volley. Arconada saved but couldn't hold the ball. As it came out, Johnston, who had recently signed for Celtic from Watford, dived to meet the ball as it bounced up and headed into the net.

Craig Brown, who would go on to manage Scotland from 1993 to 2001 once asked McLeish, who played 77 times in defence for Scotland and didn't score a goal, why he kept going up for corners. 'I acted as a decoy for Kenny Dalglish,' was McLeish's reply.

The second goal came just before half-time when Bett, who was outstanding, picked up a pass from Willie Miller, and made space down the right wing. He crossed into the six-yard box where Johnston, despite being flanked by two Spanish defenders headed in his second.

At the start of the second half Emilio Butragueño came on as a substitute in place of Rincon. Talking to the *Liverpool Echo* in 2017, Butragueño, who had become a legend at Real Madrid, expressed his admiration for the Liverpool team of the 80s, and the great players that they had.

'Dalglish was the one I loved though,' Butragueño said. 'I can remember playing against Scotland for the national team at Hampden Park. It was the only time I came up against him, he scored a beautiful goal and we lost 3-1. Rush was the main goalscorer, but Dalglish was very intelligent.'

Spain got a goal back, something that shocked the sell-out 74,000 crowd. Mo Johnston gave away a free kick in a dangerous position. Camacho sent the ball into the box and Goikoetxea headed down into the ground but the ball bounced over the head of Jim Leighton, who had hesitated over coming out or staying on his line and in the end did neither.

Then in the 73rd minute came Dalglish's moment of magic. Steve Nicol went on a run into the box. When Maceda cleared the ball away Kenny allowed it to run out for a throw-in. Nicol took it, with Dalglish going square to him. Nicol hurled the ball over Kenny's head, and the heads of the two defenders marking him. Kenny quickly got on the turn. The ball fell to Davie Cooper, who laid it off into Kenny's path. With the two defenders trailing, Kenny took a touch and ran across the face of goal. He skipped round another defender and from around 15 yards out he looked up to check the position of goalkeeper Luis Arconada and curled the ball home.

'The goal was vintage Kenny Dalglish,' said commentator Jock Brown on *Scotsport*.

Dalglish told the *Daily Record* in 2020 it was his most treasured goal. 'When I turned to run to the stand [after scoring] my old man was sitting there in the front row. The look on his face was the same as mine, overjoyed.'

Sitting on the bench waiting to get on the pitch Gordon Strachan said he predicted Kenny would score, telling the other subs, when he received the ball from Cooper, he would curl it into the top corner.

The goal put Kenny level with Denis Law as Scotland's top goalscorer with 30. When Kenny spoke with the Official Scotland Podcast he said, 'To share it with somebody that you've grown up with, who you idolised, it's quite humbling really.' No one has come close to the record set by Law in May 1972 and equalled by Dalglish. The only player currently active, at the time of writing, with a chance of approaching the record is John McGinn, who, as of May 2025, sits on 20 goals.

Davie Cooper, credited with the assist, enjoyed playing with Dalglish. 'When you're playing alongside players like Graeme Souness and Kenny Dalglish if they say pass the ball, you pass the ball,' Cooper wrote in his 1987 autobiography.

Real Madrid's Jose Camacho was tight to Dalglish all night. He had several fouls allowed to go unpunished before referee Adolph Prokop of East Germany eventually took his name.

'Every one of us was at the top of his form,' Cooper wrote about the match. 'It really was a privilege to be in the side. Kenny Dalglish was an absolute joy to play alongside. They don't come along like Kenny too often and I'm glad I can say I played in the same team as him a few times.'

Before Scotland's win against Spain at Hampden in 2023, manager Steve Clarke used Dalglish's goal in his team talk to inspire his players.

Stein revealed to the *Daily Record* that Dalglish was struggling with his knee in the days before the match and it was doubtful that he would be fit. However, he was able to play and Stein didn't even see the need to substitute him after his brilliant goal.

'He had everything,' Alex McLeish told *The Herald* in 2018 about Dalglish: 'I am always asked who the best I played with was and it's Kenny. Of course. His technical ability, his brilliant goals, the will to win makes him Scotland's best.'

Alex Ferguson was assistant to Jock Stein at the time. In his 1999 autobiography, he described Dalglish's performance that night as 'vintage'. 'Looking at Dalglish in training and in the games, there was one quality that struck me even more forcefully than his technical excellence. It was his enthusiasm. He just loved playing.' Ferguson also highlighted that unique aspect of his play, calling Dalglish 'the best bum player in the game'. 'If he got that broad backside into opponents in or around the penalty area they were dead.'

'If [Kenny Dalglish] had a flaw in his playing make-up, it never revealed itself to me,' goalkeeper Jim Leighton wrote in his 2000 autobiography. 'He was the complete footballer – strong, quick and immensely talented. His brain worked overtime to keep him at least one move ahead of the less perceptive. Kenny scored all kinds of goals, from wonder shots to simple tap-ins, and created more than his fair share of chances for others. He was great fun to be with as a player. I've seen him take over the whole dining room on Scotland trips and have us in stitches.'

'He had it all,' Willie Miller wrote of Dalglish, 'balance, poise, elegance and an ability to score wonderful goals.'

Scotland: Leighton (Aberdeen), Nicol (Liverpool), Albiston (Manchester United), Souness (Sampdoria) (c), McLeish (Aberdeen), Miller (Aberdeen), Dalglish (Liverpool), McStay (Celtic), Johnston (Celtic), Bett (SK Lokeren), Cooper (Rangers)

Scorers: Johnston (32, 42), Dalglish (73)

Spain: Arconada (Real Sociedad) (c), Urquiaga (Athletic Bilbao), Goikoetxea (Athletic Bilbao), Maceda (Sporting Gijon), Camacho (Real Madrid), Munoz (Barcelona),

Urtubi (Athletic Bilbao) [Carrasco (Barcelona)], Senor (Real Zaragoza), Gordillo (Real Betis), Santillana (Real Madrid), Rincon (Real Betis) [Butragueño (Real Madrid)]

Scorer: Goikoetxea (67)

Attendance: 74,299

45

Liverpool 4-0 Norwich City

19 January 1985, First Division,
Anfield

IN NOVEMBER 1984, Dalglish had been sent off for the first time in his career, during a 1-0 defeat to Benfica in the European Cup. Portuguese defender Minervino Pietra went in late on him, only for Kenny to retaliate. Both players were sent off. 'I have never seen Kenny raise his fists to anyone,' manager Joe Fagan said. 'We have learned to accept referees' decisions, but I think he was a little unfortunate.' Liverpool had won 3-0 at Anfield in the first leg.

December saw Liverpool have another crack at the World Club Championship, played again in Tokyo. This time the opposition were Independiente from Argentina. The match was live on ITV at 3am on Sunday, 9 December. Ticket prices went up to £16 and the programme cost £3.50. Thanks to some dubious refereeing decisions Liverpool lost 1-0. 'I thought the goal was offside,' Fagan said. 'It has always been our position not to criticise officials and I'm not going to start now.'

The suspension due to that red card meant Dalglish was missing when Liverpool played Juventus in Turin for the European Super Cup on 16 January. More than 12 inches of snow was moved off the pitch in order for the match to be played on a day when practically everything else in the region had come to a standstill. Two goals from Zbigniew Boniek gave Juventus a 2-0 win.

Norwich also played in midweek, beating Grimsby Town in the quarter-final of the Milk Cup.

By this stage in the season, Liverpool had recovered slightly to sit tenth in the table, but they had now lost six games, three of them at home. Everton, sitting at the top of the league, had lost five, with Arsenal in fifth having lost eight.

Paul Walsh, who had filled in for Kenny at the Stadio Comunale, was on the bench as Dalglish came back into the side for the Norwich game. Liverpool's £65,000 undersoil heating system allowed the match to go ahead.

The sides had met at Carrow Road on the opening day of the league season in August. An entertaining encounter that included three penalties, two scored and one missed, ended in a 3-3 draw. Steve Bruce put Liverpool ahead with an own goal after fellow debutant Jan Mølby's long ball put him in two minds, resulting in him heading past his own keeper. Paul Walsh played Dalglish in to make it 2-0. Norwich fought back with Peter Mendham pulling a goal back after Grobbelaar came too far out of his goal in an attempt to claim a crossed ball. The goalkeeper brought down John Deehan just before half-time, but the Norwich striker put the resultant penalty over the bar. Keith Bertschin scrambled an equaliser four minutes into the second half. Phil Neal made it 3-2 with a penalty after Paul Walsh had been pulled down in the box. The game's third penalty came when Mick Channon went down heavily under a Mark Lawrenson challenge. The England international converted the kick to make the final score 3-3.

Manchester United's manager, Ron Atkinson, believed that Neal was the key to the Liverpool side. He felt that Neal was their central playmaker, suggesting that if you watch many of their goals, Neal was the man who would regularly start the move, 'often because he had nobody directly against him'.

Neal liked to move the ball on swiftly. This was a philosophy based on Liverpool's training routines at

Melwood, playing one-touch five-a-side games. Neal knew that the more time he spent on the ball, the more time opposing defenders had to close down Dalglish, McDermott, Rush or any other of Liverpool's dangermen, and the less time they would have on the ball to work their magic.

Before the January match, Fagan was keen to stress that there were a lot of points still to play for, and although Liverpool were 14 points behind Everton, the gap wasn't insurmountable. Their four-year hold on the League (Milk) Cup had been broken by Tottenham, who won with a Clive Allen goal at White Hart Lane in the third round. That scoreline was reversed at Anfield in the fourth round of the FA Cup.

Around 500 Norwich fans made their way up to Liverpool to witness the most one-sided of encounters, where their side failed to make any significant chances.

Liverpool took the lead in the 36th minute. Grobbelaar sent a long clearance down the pitch where Dalglish headed it on to John Wark. The Scottish international hit a first-time shot past Chris Woods.

It looked like Liverpool were huffing and puffing their way to a single-goal victory until the last ten minutes of the match. Ian Rush, who had gone close on a few occasions, made it 2-0 in the 80th minute when he headed in a Steve Nicol cross.

Six minutes later, Kenny netted just his third of the season, and his first in 22 games, when he got his head to a free kick. Rush notched his second with a minute left to play after Dalglish played him in.

The win left Liverpool in sixth position, 11 points behind leaders Everton. By 6 April, Liverpool were up to fourth but now 12 points behind their Merseyside rivals, having played a game more.

The month of April saw Liverpool in the semi-finals of two competitions. In the FA Cup they lost 2-1 to Manchester

United in a replay after a 2-2 draw. They had better luck in the European Cup. Panathinaikos, the 1971 runners-up, were defeated 4-0 in the first leg at Anfield, and 1-0 in Athens. Liverpool were now in their fifth European Cup Final.

Everton secured the title on 6 May with a 2-0 win over Queens Park Rangers, while Liverpool finished as runners-up, 13 points behind.

Liverpool's league season ended at Goodison on 23 May, where they lost to the new champions by a goal to nil. It was the first time Everton had done the double over Liverpool for 20 years. There was a protest by Everton fans in the crowd over their club's decision to change the strip for the first time in two years, calling the decision 'a disgrace'.

On 15 May the blue half of Merseyside had lifted the European Cup Winners' Cup with a 3-1 win over Rapid Vienna. It was now the red half's turn to attempt to bring home the European Cup.

Liverpool: Grobbelaar, Neal (c), A. Kennedy, Gillespie, Nicol, Hansen, Dalglish, Whelan, Rush, MacDonald, Wark

Scorers: Wark (36), Rush (80, 89), Dalglish (86)

Norwich City: Woods, Haylock, Downs, Bruce, Mendham, Van Wijk, Barham, Channon, Deehan, Hartford, Donowa

Attendance: 30,627

46

Liverpool 0-1 Juventus

29 May 1985, European Cup Final,
Heysel Stadium

AS THE players arrived at the ground, a children's game was being played on the pitch. The atmosphere was warm, and there seemed to be no sign that things would soon go awry.

When the players went out to look at the pitch, Alan Hansen found a half-brick lying at pitchside. He wondered who would bring an object like that with them into the stadium. The answer was that it was part of the ground. Heysel as a stadium, which was built in 1930, was crumbling.

It hadn't been fit for purpose when Arsenal played there in the European Cup Winners' Cup Final against Valencia in 1980, and it hadn't gotten any better five years later. Liverpool chief executive Peter Robinson said, 'There is no way this stadium would get a general safety certificate in Britain.'

Chicken wire fencing had been put up only that morning to act as a divider between supporters. The ground opened at 4.30pm, three hours before kick-off. Outside the ground, touts freely offered tickets for sale.

In the run-up to the final, Peter Robinson had sent a series of telex messages to UEFA, the Football Association, the Belgian Football Association and the Belgian government, stressing his concerns over ticket distribution, segregation and security. His messages were received but ignored.

'I asked for a joint meeting between the police and two clubs,' Robinson told the *Liverpool Echo* years later. He said that when he went to Belgium before the final, to collect the club's allocation of tickets for the game, he realised that an area for neutral spectators was situated in the middle of Liverpool's allocation of 14,500 tickets. He expressed his concern that if any of those tickets were bought by Juventus supporters, there would be problems.

Liverpool asked why they couldn't have a complete end. UEFA said this was the only way it could be. The year previously, Liverpool and Roma had had input into ticketing, but not so this time. When Robinson was left with tickets he couldn't sell for the final in 1984 he held on to them rather than send them back to Rome, in case Roma fans bought them.

Robinson couldn't understand why UEFA didn't want to listen to a club who had been in four previous European Cup finals.

Dalglish recalled that Liverpool complained publicly about the state of the stadium in the run-up to the match. Looking back on it decades later, he felt they did everything they could to warn about the possibility of crowd trouble, only to be blamed when the worst happened.

Liverpool supporters were in blocks X and Y, while section Z, which was a neutral area, was primarily made up of Italians from the immigrant population in Belgium. Before the match started, so-called Liverpool supporters in block X charged at the fans in block Z, and this caused a wall to collapse, resulting in the deaths of 39 fans.

As Dalglish and the Liverpool players prepared inside the dressing room, word began to filter back that there had been some kind of trouble on the terracing. The kick-off time was delayed and the players were told to relax and return to their pre-match routine. While some players played cards, Kenny went for a sleep.

Some Juventus players, including Sergio Brio and Antonio Cabrini, went out in their kits among the Juventus fans to appeal for calm. Liverpool captain Phil Neal and manager Joe Fagan were asked to do likewise over the public address system. 'This is my last match as Liverpool manager,' Fagan said into the mic. 'Please remember the good name of the club, please think about your team.'

Heysel was the culmination of an epidemic of football hooliganism and disasters that had blighted the English game throughout the first half of the 80s.

Over TV pictures of fans fighting, BBC commentator Barry Davies reached to find the words to sum up what he was witnessing. 'One cannot but feel the time has come – indeed if I can express a personal opinion – the time has long since passed when we have to consider the majority, and if that means that we have to take some steps to prevent the minority coming abroad to drag the name of our country into the gutter then we have to do it. Because it seems that nothing less than that will solve this problem. At least let's try to sort out the problem at home and not have to explain it to those abroad.'

Former manager Bob Paisley found his seat in the stand taken by Italian fans. He opted to leave with the chaos unfolding. He returned to his room in the Holiday Inn by the airport and watched what happened on television.

Marina Dalglish sat with the other wives and girlfriends of Liverpool players. In 2005, she spoke to John Keith, who had covered the match for the *Daily Express*. 'We were all scared stiff, holding each other's hands,' she said. 'It was just terrible, sitting there watching. It was the first time I hoped Kenny wouldn't score a goal because I dread to think what more could have happened.'

As he spoke over the unfolding scenes, Davies called it 'a sickening and bewildering sight'.

Phil Neal already had four European Cup winners' medals, the most at that time of any British player (although Gareth Bale has since won five). This time, though, was to be different. Neal was the captain in the final for the first time and approaching the match he was anticipating raising the cup. But very quickly he realised the night was unfolding in a different manner.

'Heysel was the worst thing imaginable,' Neal told *The Guardian* in 2010. 'It felt as if Liverpool had let English football down, when for 20 years they had been its finest ambassador. That's what really turned our stomachs.'

'Nealy claimed in his book that Liverpool players knew there had been fatalities. I didn't,' Dalglish wrote in his 2010 book *My Liverpool Home*.

UEFA decided that the match should go ahead at 9.40pm local time, 70 minutes after the intended kick-off. Robinson was unhappy about it, but UEFA said the decision was made 'for safety and security reasons'.

Phil Scraton, who wrote the definitive book on the Hillsborough tragedy, is quoted in Jason Cowley's book *The Last Game: Love, Death and Football*, providing an outline of the tragedy. 'The explanation is this: Heysel was caused by a group of Liverpool supporters who had probably had too much to drink and wanted to give a group of Juventus supporters a hard time. But the real scandal is that the Heysel stadium was falling apart, the ticketing arrangements were appalling and the policing was terrible. So you had the combination of bad policing, bad ground, tickets being bought on the black market, and the panic caused by Liverpool fans.'

The factors Scraton cites though, merely exacerbated the actions of the Liverpool fans who attacked the Italians. It was their behaviour that day that caused the tragedy.

In *The Guardian* in 2015 Ed Vulliamy, a researcher with the TV documentary series *World In Action* at the time of the game, wrote about what he saw that night. 'We watched Liverpool fans crash through the fence feebly separating them from the Juventus fans, across the terracing into fleeing Italians, with disbelief.'

'It's certainly true that the Heysel tragedy owed much to the failure of proper segregation, allied to the frailties of an old stadium,' Barry Davies wrote in his 2008 autobiography. 'But its true cause was of human making.'

'The game was an insignificance,' Kenny said in the documentary *Kenny*. 'You're not oblivious to what's going on round about [you], although you don't know the facts.'

'Because the start was delayed for so long, we knew it was something serious, and there were rumours going round about fatalities,' Jim Beglin, who played at left-back for Liverpool that night, said to the *Sunday Tribune* in 2005.

'I didn't need the editor's instruction not to get excited commentating on the match,' Barry Davies wrote. 'After what had happened it was hard to concentrate on two teams kicking a football about.'

The game began and the two sets of players had to find a focus on the 90 minutes ahead, however hard that proved to be. 'I saw a Liverpool side striving to win,' Beglin told *The Independent* in 2005. 'We didn't know any other way to play.'

Mark Lawrenson aggravated a shoulder injury after only three minutes to be replaced by Gary Gillespie.

The only real incident of note in the game was the penalty kick that led to the only goal. Juventus goalkeeper Stefano Tacconi sent a long ball up the field which Zbigniew Boniek and Gillespie began a foot race for. The Polish forward was always ahead, although the likelihood of him bringing the ball down and controlling it was low. Gillespie clipped his heels around three yards before he got into the penalty area. Boniek fell, rolled into the penalty box and got on to his knees, pleading for a spot kick. The referee had no hesitation in pointing to the spot.

In any other final, the outrageous decision to award a penalty for what was clearly a trip a good distance outside the box would have been a major talking point. As it was, everyone from Britain collectively shrugged their shoulders.

'It wasn't a penalty, it was outside the area, but who cares?' Beglin said.

Michel Platini stepped up and fired the kick to Grobbelaar's right as the keeper dived to his left.

At the end of the match the BBC immediately ended coverage, not waiting to broadcast the trophy presentation.

'If we had refused to play that night we would have sounded the death knell for soccer at the highest level,' Platini said to Francois de Montvalon of *France Football* a few months after the match. 'In agreeing to play the match, I think you can say that in a certain sense we saved our own sport.'

When he retired at 31, Platini gave the reason as Heysel. 'Something inside me died that night,' he said. 'For days afterwards I felt a sense of shame.'

Juventus's first European Cup win made the Turin side the first club to win all three European trophies.

'I think we may have seen the last English club to play in Europe for a long, long time Jim,' Graeme Souness said to Jimmy Hill on BBC's coverage of the game. Bobby Charlton too, co-commentating with Davies, acknowledged that English clubs – not just Liverpool – would be in for significant – and deserved – punishment.

It would be Joe Fagan's last game as manager, although it wasn't a direct result of the tragedy. Fagan had intimated to the Liverpool board earlier in the season his intention to finish up after the season's end. His decision was leaked on the morning of the game, surprising many. Graeme Souness said that he thought Fagan would have given it another year.

The strong rumour was that Dalglish would be offered the job. That Kenny would be Fagan's successor didn't surprise Souness, but he said on the BBC's European Cup Final coverage, 'I think it's a bit early for Kenny to be doing it himself.'

Terry Venables, the manager of Barcelona, said on the same show that he didn't think Kenny would be up to the task. 'It's too difficult at the very top end of the game. If you're going to make mistakes I think you should make them a little lower down where it's not too expensive. I think that you've got to learn your trade in anything you do in life and I think football management is no exception.'

While still coming to terms with the tragedy, the following day Kenny was asked to become Liverpool's player-manager. Dalglish hadn't given much consideration to going into management before he was asked. Kenny loved playing and wanted to play for as long as possible. He still had three years left on his playing contract and Fagan had been allowing him time off when he needed it.

Kenny asked why he had been chosen, but no one gave him a reason. He felt it was a huge compliment to be asked but he didn't want to let anyone connected with Liverpool down.

'While the newspapers speculated that Phil Neal was favourite for the job,' Ian Rush wrote, 'the players guessed that Kenny Dalglish would get the nod before Neal.'

Despite not considering a career in management at this relatively young age it was Liverpool, so it was hard if not impossible to turn down, so he accepted the job. Kenny knew that to take the job of manager meant the end of his playing career would get closer. He knew that he would have support from Ronnie Moran and Roy Evans. Bob Paisley would be around too, along with Tom Saunders. Saunders, a former schoolmaster, never played the game professionally but was in charge of the Liverpool and England Schoolboy teams during the 1960s and had joined Liverpool's staff on a full-time basis as youth development officer in 1970.

It was a challenge Kenny wanted to step up to, and like his playing career he would work hard at being the best in the business at it.

Of course what Kenny would first have to deal with as Liverpool's manager was the aftermath of Heysel. Two days after the disaster Kenny laid a wreath for the dead during a service at Liverpool's Catholic cathedral.

He wouldn't be able to take Liverpool into Europe, however, as the punishment for Heysel came with an indefinite ban for English clubs, with Liverpool initially being subject to an additional three-year ban, although that would end up being cut to one year.

'We have to remember because we can't afford to forget,' Ian Rush said in 2005.

Liverpool: Grobbelaar, Neal (c), Beglin, Lawrenson [Gillespie], Nicol, Hansen, Dalglish, Whelan, Rush, Walsh [Johnston], Wark

Juventus: Tacconi, Favero, Brio, Scirea, Cabrini, Bonini, Platini, Tardelli, Briaschi [Prandelli], Rossi [Vignola], Boniek

Scorer: Platini (56, pen)

Attendance: 50,000

47

Everton 2-3 Liverpool

*21 September 1985, First Division,
Goodison Park*

PLAYERS STILL called their new boss Kenny, and
Dalglish didn't object. However, Ronnie Moran and Roy
Evans spoke with the squad and reminded them that things
had changed. On the pitch, he was still Kenny, but off the
field he was Boss or Gaffer.

Mark Lawrenson told the Sacked in the Morning podcast
that Kenny imposed a divide straight away. 'There was him,
me, Ronnie Whelan, occasionally Gary Gillespie. We all
travelled in together and straight away there was none of
that.' The players in that carpool, and their new boss, all lived
in the Birkdale area of Southport and soon the playing staff
realised that whenever they went out, word would travel back
to Kenny. 'Everybody was telling him, "Oh, I saw him. He
was in the bar last week on Thursday night. He's supposed
to be at home with his feet up."'

Ian Rush recalled that despite being the boss Dalglish
accepted any stick or moaning coming his way on the pitch
from his team-mates. 'Dalglish may be the greatest player I
have ever played with, but he's no bighead. In fact, he shuns
the limelight. And that attitude from the top reflects on the
whole team. There was not a single player in those days who
could ever be accused of conceit.'

Kenny's first game in charge was a friendly at Turf Moor
against Fourth Division Burnley in July. Dalglish kept himself
on the bench as an Ian Rush hat-trick helped the Reds to a

5-1 win. The European ban even applied to friendly fixtures. Liverpool couldn't go abroad on a tour in the summer of 1985. All their pre-season games were in England.

While new signings weren't brought in, other changes were quickly made. Phil Neal had only taken over the captaincy a year earlier after Graeme Souness left. Kenny took the armband off him and handed it to Alan Hansen. 'We were playing Brighton in a pre-season friendly,' Hansen said in an LFCTV documentary, *Liverpool The Double 1986.* 'I'm sitting beside him [Dalglish] and we had a ball, and he goes, "You take the ball." And I never, ever took a ball out. I was superstitious. I said, "No, no." He said, "Are you stupid? You take the ball. You're captain." I went, "Oh."'

The rest of the players thought the appointment was the right one. They knew Hansen was close to Dalglish and he would be the perfect bridge between players and management.

Phil Neal, who Dalglish had to take aside when he maintained calling his boss 'Kenny', would start only 11 league games that season, while Alan Kennedy would only play in eight. They would both leave before 1985 was out. Kennedy joined Sunderland while Neal signed for Bolton Wanderers.

Liverpool had finished in the top two for all but one of the last 16 years. Only in 1981 had they finished outside that, in fifth. Dalglish didn't set any targets for the season ahead, simply it was to do the best they could.

The league season opened with Kenny in the number 7 shirt as Liverpool took on Arsenal at Anfield. Steve Nicol set up Ronnie Whelan for Liverpool's first after 33 minutes while the player-manager assisted Nicol for the second on 61 minutes as Liverpool won 2-0.

One of the changes for the players under Kenny's management was that the team wasn't announced until an hour before kick-off. Paisley and Fagan had both announced their team on a Friday morning. Kenny didn't want anyone to relax, and for everyone to act professionally on the Friday night.

With Dalglish injured, Craig Johnston wore the number 7 shirt when Ipswich came to Anfield at the end of August. Johnston had been at the club since 1981, but he didn't feel like he was truly a Liverpool player. In 1984/85, he had only played in 11 league games. 'I think Kenny Dalglish appreciated my frustration,' Johnston said in that LFCTV documentary. 'Kenny has got a way of motivating without motivating. He didn't put an arm around me, and he didn't encourage me as such. He challenged me, and he said, "If you really think you're good enough to get in this team, well then prove it."' The Australian set up two and scored another in a 5-0 win. Johnston played in 41 of the 42 league games that season.

David Miller of *The Times* visited Kenny at his office in Anfield in September 1985 to ask him how he was adapting to life as a manager and if Liverpool was too high profile a club at which to learn his trade. 'The administration and finance of the club is so well organised that I have no worries there, only to produce a team that's decent on the pitch,' Dalglish replied. 'Ronnie Moran and Roy Evans look after the training, and discipline's already inbred in the players. Tom Saunders, our chief scout, who also assesses opposing teams, and Bob Paisley, are there for me to ask advice. What club in the third or fourth division can provide you with a background like that?'

Dalglish wasn't embarrassed about asking for help. 'It's a compliment to Bob that almost every decision I have to make I'll discuss with him. It's only right that I should listen. Ronnie and Roy can see some things on the pitch which maybe I can't, but I'll see things they don't.'

Dalglish's first Merseyside derby as manager took place at Goodison on 21 September. Everton went into the match seeking their fifth win in a row over Liverpool. Gary Lineker had been signed from Leicester City in the close season and was playing in his first Merseyside derby. In Liverpool's midfield was Steve McMahon, who had signed earlier that month from Aston Villa. McMahon had played for Everton in seven previous Merseyside derbies.

Everton's Kevin Sheedy had spent four years at Liverpool from 1978 to 1982, but only played five first-team matches, playing alongside Dalglish in all of them. 'I played and trained with the likes of Kenny Dalglish and Graeme Souness, fantastic players in very different ways,' Sheedy wrote in his 2014 autobiography. 'Observing their good habits was a great learning curve for me.' Sheedy was impressed by the pass-and-move philosophy he saw on the training field at Melwood, and it helped to shape him into the outstanding player he became with Everton.

The BBC and ITV were warring with the English League over TV rights and so there was a blackout on football highlights at the start of the 1985/86 season. The Thames Television cameras were in attendance at Goodison, but the coverage was for foreign markets only.

'Kenny Dalglish is the first manager I can recall who hasn't joined me for a drink and a chat before an Everton home match,' Everton's boss, Howard Kendall, wrote in his newspaper column. 'He declined my offer … because he was playing in the game of course.'

The game sparked into life immediately. Everton kicked off and played the ball long into the corner. Alan Hansen prevented it from going out for a throw-in and headed back to Grobbelaar. The keeper passed short to Nicol who played a long ball down the right to Rush, who knocked the ball back to Dalglish, around 20-odd yards away from the Everton goal. The shot he unleashed was so powerful, and pinpoint accurate, that it left keeper Neville Southall stranded. He could only watch as it flew into the roof of the net. Only 21 seconds of the game had passed.

Kenny employed a sweeper, with Lawrenson sitting in behind Hansen and Mølby, but Liverpool were all-out attack, and with just 16 minutes gone, they were two up. Ronnie Whelan played a ball forward, Gary Stevens hesitated and Rush nipped in to score.

There were three minutes left before half-time when it was 3-0. Dalglish set up McMahon to belt the ball in from 25 yards.

Everton obviously had a rocket from manager Howard Kendall at half-time. Adrian Heath came on for defender Ian Marshall as they went three up front. 'It was too easy and we stopped a little bit,' Lawrenson said to LFCTV. 'And I just remember they went route one, and we were under all sorts of pressure.'

Seven minutes into the second half, Graeme Sharp volleyed the Toffees back into the game. Lineker then hit the bar.

Dalglish was clean through twice, with time to pick his spot. The first time he sent the ball over the bar, and on the second occasion he fired wide of the post. In *The Sunday Times*, Brian Glanville wrote that Dalglish, 'struck one extraordinary goal than missed two sitters'.

With eight minutes remaining, Heath crossed for Lineker to claim his eighth goal for Everton. There was a minute remaining when Hansen made a last-ditch challenge to prevent Lineker equalising.

Dalglish said afterwards he would return to his sweeper system whenever Liverpool visited potentially awkward opponents.

'You've got to have the players available to work the system, which isn't easy to do, and the players have got to believe in it. They quite enjoyed playing it.'

'You cannot see football like that in any other country in the world,' the England manager Bobby Robson said as he left the match.

'I've still got a headache from the noise,' Lineker said post-match. 'I've never played in anything like that before. It was magic.'

Talking with the PFA for their YouTube channel in 2024, Lineker enthused about Dalglish. 'He's one of the reasons Rushie scored so many goals. Kenny was unbelievable. Him and Gareth Bale, for me, are probably the two best British players in my lifetime. Dalglish was incredible.'

Kendall wrote of Dalglish in his column, 'He showed that at 34 he remains the most complete forward in English football.' Kendall noted that as Dalglish was now playing in a deeper role behind the strikers, his key attributes on display were now his 'football intelligence and astute distribution'. Kendall said that although it was disappointing to have lost, it had been a pleasure to witness Dalglish in top form, showing all his class.

Over the course of their time on the pitch together, Dalglish made 39 assists for Ian Rush, while Rush made ten for Dalglish. Only Ian St John and Roger Hunt had more goal combinations for Liverpool.

'He was easy to set up,' Dalglish said to author Tony Evans. 'He took up good positions. He sat on the last defender's shoulder and went into the space behind him. No one could catch him.'

'It was a beautiful partnership and I would have to say that he made things very easy for me on that pitch, something to this day he knows I will always remind him of,' Ian Rush told PA Media in 2021. 'I have so much respect and admiration for Kenny not just because of the insatiable instinct he had to deliver on the pitch, but the style in which he did it, such passion and pride.'

Everton: Southall, Stevens, Van den Hauwe, Ratcliffe, Marshall [Heath], Harper, Steven, Lineker, Sharp, Bracewell, Sheedy

Scorers: Sharp (51), Lineker (84)

Liverpool: Grobbelaar, Nicol [Neal], Beglin, Lawrenson, Whelan, Hansen (c), Dalglish, Johnston, Rush, Mølby, McMahon

Scorers: Dalglish (21 secs), Rush (16), McMahon (42)

Attendance: 51,509

48

Scotland 3-0 Romania

*26 March 1986, Friendly, Hampden
Park*

DALGLISH NEVER took playing for his country for
granted. He felt it was an honour and he was very proud to
play every game. Scotland was proud of him too, and two
days before this match – his 100th cap – Kenny received
the Freedom of the City of Glasgow at a reception at the
City Chambers. The honour allowed him to graze his cattle
on Glasgow's grass and to hang out his washing in George
Square. 'When I was a boy living in a council high-rise we
couldn't even hang our washing out on the verandah,' Kenny
quipped.

He had previously made it clear that if and when he
reached 99 caps, he did not want to receive the 100th out
of sentiment. He wanted to be selected on merit every time.
There was no doubt that he was.

In the night's match programme Kenny's long-time
friend, team-mate and opponent Sandy Jardine spoke to
Rodger Baillie about Kenny's talents. 'Without a doubt
he's the best Scotland player during my time in the game.
I think Kenny himself would admit he was never a flying
machine. But he more than made up for it. Quite simply he's
the quickest thinker in football. He's always had tremendous
vision and the great ability to use his body so well to shield
the ball. As an opponent I know how hard that makes it for
a defender to take the ball off him. When you played with
him one of his greatest assets was his ability to help take the

pressure off the defence. If the ball was cleared to Kenny you knew it wouldn't come right back again before you had time to blink. He always manages to hold it to let the rest of the team regroup.'

Kenny's contemporaries had a lot of respect and admiration for him, but by the 1980s young players coming through had watched Kenny and hoped to achieve similar things in the game. He was idolised by most of the young strikers coming into the Scotland team, who played alongside him and then were eventually expected to take over from him.

Of his debut against Australia in November 1985, Frank McAvennie said on his podcast in 2025, 'I got my instructions from Kenny that night. I was just to do the running and let Kenny take the punishment. I could look after myself, but nobody could look after themselves like Kenny Dalglish on a football park. It was incredible. He used to back in with that big backside of his, and get free kicks. He'd somehow manage to stand on the guy's toe and the guy would be rolling about, but we'd get the free kick. He was very good.'

To commemorate Kenny Dalglish's achievement of winning 100 caps for Scotland the SFA arranged for him to receive a special gold and silver cap. Franz Beckenbauer, then the manager of West Germany, came out on to the pitch alongside David Will of the SFA to make the presentation. Beckenbauer certainly knew how to get himself noticed, dressed as he was in a brown leather trench coat. Lining up to welcome Kenny were his team-mates from his first international in 1971. Sandy Jardine was the last to give him a warm handshake and a smile as Kenny went up on the platform to receive his honour from the German World Cup winner. Kenny then went on a lap of honour around the ground.

In the Romanian team was Lică Movilă, the Dinamo Bucharest defender who had been on the receiving end of that punch from Graeme Souness in 1984.

Dalglish combined well with Graeme Sharp early on, the Everton striker's shot being turned behind for a corner. Kenny had a great chance himself soon afterwards when he went through on goal. He went round the goalkeeper, but finding himself too far wide, had to check back inside. He got the shot off, but Silviu Lung got back to make the save at the near post.

The opening goal came in the 18th minute when the Romanian defence cleared away an attack led by Dalglish. As the ball left the penalty box, Gordon Strachan ran up to it and calmly sent a chip high over Lung's head and in for his third Scottish goal.

Strachan wrote in 1993, 'From what I have seen in British football, Kenny Dalglish was the best of the lot. I don't go as far back as the likes of Stanley Matthews or Tom Finney, but as far as I am concerned, Kenny had everything.'

Sharp sent a shot from the six-yard line over the bar under pressure from the defence after Kenny had crossed in to him from the right.

The Scotland fans played their part on the night, singing 'Kenny, Kenny, Kenny, Kenny,' throughout the 90 minutes.

It was 2-0 to Scotland with 27 minutes gone. Dalglish's header was sent out of the box by the defence. Strachan was there to meet it again, but this time he slid a pass to his right for Richard Gough, who thumped a shot home.

Craig Brown, later to manage Scotland, was part of the coaching staff, and wasn't satisfied with the 2-0 lead. 'At half-time against Romania I gave him [Dalglish] a rollicking on the night he won his 100th cap,' Brown told the *Daily Mail* in 2011. 'Those were the days when I was younger and a bit more fiery. We had been poor so when we got the players back to the dressing room I told him straight: "That was not acceptable."

'I said their No 8 was running the show and he hadn't been able to get near him. Kenny looked at me and said:

"Sorry." He went back out there to put things right and we went on to win 3-0. At the end when the boys came back in I told them it had been a lot better. Then Kenny looked at me and said: "Thank you." So this was one of my first internationals with Kenny and he said three words to me the whole time.'

Pat Nevin came on for his debut after an hour when he replaced Strachan. 'I was fortunate enough to play with Kenny,' Nevin told Radio Scotland in 2013. 'My first games with Scotland were his last games with Scotland ... I had pictures of Kenny on my wall when I was a kid and there I was suddenly playing with him! He's probably the best player this country's ever produced. He became better and better as he got older but he was more exciting when he was at Celtic. I loved all the different stuff that he did.'

Graeme Sharp went off to be replaced by Charlie Nicholas, who also got a great reception from the Scotland fans.

With eight minutes remaining, a cross came over from the left from Eamonn Bannon. Gough put a cushioned header back across the penalty box, Roy Aitken hit it sweetly on the half-volley and the ball fired into the bottom corner for 3-0.

Gough headed against the crossbar in the final minutes. Try as he might, Dalglish couldn't get the goal that would have given him the international scoring record on his own.

'Kenny was the best player on the field,' Graeme Souness said afterwards. 'I am his greatest fan.'

Although selected in Ferguson's Scotland squad for the 1986 World Cup in Mexico, Dalglish would pull out in May. A specialist told him that his knee ligament injury, which he picked up three weeks before the season's end and aggravated in the FA Cup Final, meant he shouldn't risk going. He was advised to rest for three weeks. 'You've got a certain responsibility to your club, haven't you?' Kenny said in 2024. 'I mean, I was player-manager, so there's just no way I could have gone.'

Rumours persisted that Dalglish was unhappy that Alan Hansen hadn't been selected for the squad. In his 1996 autobiography, Kenny emphasised strongly that Hansen's exclusion had nothing to do with his decision. When Alex Ferguson called Kenny to let him know he was in the squad, he also told him he wouldn't be taking Hansen. Kenny queried Ferguson's selection but, of course, acknowledged that Ferguson was the boss and that it was his decision.

While Ferguson and Dalglish would have an occasionally volatile relationship when both were managers in England's top flight, there was no denying that Ferguson was a great admirer of Kenny's. In his 1999 autobiography, he reflected on Kenny's withdrawal from the squad. 'Dalglish was a massive loss to us,' he wrote. 'He blossomed magnificently in his early 30s and was fit company for the very best players in the world … Kenny was physically and mentally tough and he had an aura around him that would have been priceless in the Scotland camp.'

The press thought that was the end of his Scotland career, but it was not. After Scotland's World Cup exit at the group stage on goal difference, Ferguson stood down. Andy Roxburgh came in as full-time boss and put Dalglish on the bench for his first game in charge against Bulgaria in September 1986. Kenny came on for Charlie Nicholas in the 53rd minute of the 0-0 draw.

Kenny's final cap came in November 1986 at Hampden, in a 3-0 win over Luxembourg. In that game, Brian McClair made his debut, and Ally McCoist won his second cap. Dalglish's 102nd cap came 15 years and three days after his first. As of April 2025, this is the sixth-longest career span of any Scottish international.

Roxburgh had hoped to include Kenny in the Scotland squad for the February 1987 game against the Republic of Ireland. However, an injury on Boxing Day 1986 kept Dalglish out of the Liverpool team until Valentine's Day. He would make only seven more appearances that season.

Dalglish never actually announced his retirement from international football. 'It's always strange when you hear of players retiring from international football,' Dalglish said in 2016. 'I thought you had to be selected before you could retire. I don't understand that one.' When Roxburgh failed to select him for the May games against England and Brazil, the press surmised that Dalglish had won his last cap. 'A number of players have been left out for personal or club reasons,' Roxburgh told the press. 'We must acknowledge that some of them are getting too old now.'

In a 2024 interview with the Official Scotland Podcast, Kenny reflected on the profound importance of representing his country. He expressed that words couldn't adequately convey the significance of playing for Scotland, emphasising his deep pride in both his Scottish and Glaswegian roots.

He acknowledged that his success hadn't been achieved alone, but was made possible through the sacrifices and support of numerous people throughout his journey from aspiring footballer to international player. 'A lot of people have helped me to be fortunate enough to play for [my] country once, and to do it 102 times is beyond all expectation. So it's not just about me playing, it's about the contribution other people have made to that.'

Scotland: Goram (Oldham Athletic), Gough (Dundee United), Malpas (Dundee United), Souness (Sampdoria), Narey (Dundee United), Miller (Aberdeen), [Hansen (Liverpool)], Dalglish (Liverpool) (c), Strachan (Manchester United) [(Nevin (Chelsea)], Sharp (Everton), [Nicholas (Arsenal)], Aitken (Celtic), Bannon (Dundee United)

Scorers: Strachan (18), Gough (27), Aitken (82)

Romania: Lung (Universitatea Craiova), Rednic (Dinamo

Bucharest), Movilă (Dinamo Bucharest), Ungureanu
(Universitatea Craiova), Andone (Dinamo Bucharest) [Cireasa
(Chimia Ramnicu Valcea)], Iorgulescu (Sportul Studentesc)
(c), [Nicolae (Dinamo Bucharest)], Coras (Sportul Studentesc),
[Gabor (Corvinul Hunedoara)], Klein (Corvinul Hunedoara),
Camataru (Universitatea Craiova), Mateut (Corvinul
Hunedoara), Hagi (Sportul Studentesc)

Attendance: 48,927

49

Chelsea 0-1 Liverpool

3 May 1986, First Division,
Stamford Bridge

ON 22 February, Liverpool lost 2-0 to Everton in the league. Bruce Grobbelaar allowed a weak 25-yard strike from Kevin Ratcliffe to squirm under his body for the first, with Lineker scoring in the 77th minute to seal victory.

It would be the last fixture Liverpool lost that season. It left them in third, eight points behind Everton at the top of the table. Manchester United were in second, five points ahead of Liverpool and with a game in hand. United had won their first ten games in a row, and the press had started to talk them up for the title. They had still been top in January, but defeats to Nottingham Forest and West Ham allowed Everton to overtake them.

Tottenham were defeated 2-0, then Queens Park Rangers came to Anfield. 'There is nothing finer than watching a master craftsman at work,' Ian Ross wrote in the *Daily Post*. 'The veteran Scot single-handedly destroyed Queens Park Rangers.'

Dalglish, operating in midfield, set up goals for Rush and Wark as Liverpool won 4-1. QPR had beaten Liverpool – without Kenny – in the Milk Cup only a few days earlier. Michael Robinson was now wearing number 7 for QPR. 'Dalglish made them a super team again,' he said to the *Daily Mirror*. 'It was like meeting a different side from last week.'

Kenny's name was in the headlines again when Milk Cup finalists Oxford United were the Anfield opposition on 22

March. The scoring got underway inside a minute. There was only 45 seconds played when at the end of a five-man move Kenny set up Rush for the first. Russell Thomas in *The Guardian* wondered why Kenny ever employed a sweeper system when Mølby was orchestrating the midfield and Dalglish and Rush were operating so well in attack.

It was two when Lawrenson got on the end of Dalglish's deft pass with 18 minutes gone. It was Rush's turn to assist when he set up Whelan in 39 minutes.

Shotton pulled down Rush for a penalty, which Mølby converted. Mølby put Rush in for the fifth on 71 minutes, and Dalglish set up Mølby with two minutes remaining.

In the *Daily Post*, John Osborne wondered who could replace Kenny on the pitch when he finally decided to retire. His answer was no one. He also expressed the view that Dalglish should pick himself more often. 'With all due respect to the likes of Paul Walsh, who would command a regular first-team spot at any other club, Liverpool just don't tick half as smoothly without the man's magic.'

'It amazes me that he's not playing more,' Oxford boss Maurice Evans said to the *Sunday Mirror*. 'He's still got enough to compete at the highest level.'

The result got even better when news came through that Everton had lost away at Luton, leaving both clubs tied on 66 points at the top of the league. 'I'm happy that we're spreading the goals around,' Kenny said. 'If others want to contribute to our success by losing I'll accept it.'

At White Hart Lane in April, Liverpool needed extra time to beat Southampton in the FA Cup semi-final with Rush netting twice. Everton beat Sheffield Wednesday 2-1 in the other semi-final.

In the league Ronnie Whelan hit a hat-trick as Coventry were beaten 5-0. It was the same scoreline against Birmingham City on 26 April; this time the hat-trick hero was Gary Gillespie. 'If anyone asks me who the best player

I played against was, I always say Kenny Dalglish,' Gillespie said to lfchistory.net. 'He was outstanding, he could make goals, score goals, and was always a handful.'

A 2-0 win over Leicester City at Filbert Street on 30 April, coupled with Everton's 1-0 defeat to Oxford, left Liverpool knowing that three points, perhaps even one from their last league game at Chelsea, would seal the title. Everton's game had kicked off 15 minutes earlier than Liverpool's, giving the fans a chance to enjoy the moment.

West Ham had beaten Ipswich 2-1 on the same evening to go one point ahead of Everton, and with a game in hand could capitalise if Liverpool lost in their final league match.

To get some perspective on Dalglish's talents, *The Guardian* spoke with Malcolm Macdonald, the former Newcastle and Arsenal striker, who, despite being only a year older than Dalglish, had by 1986 been eight years retired. 'Dalglish is one player I could watch every day of the week,' the 14-times-capped England international said. 'He has brought a new dimension to the art of turning the centre-half, and is a brilliant striker of the ball.' He praised his youthful enthusiasm and deft touch, neither of which had been dulled by age, and said his joy when he scored 'radiates from the pitch to the terraces'.

Going into the match, Liverpool's recent record at Stamford Bridge wasn't great. They had won 2-1 in an FA Cup match on their last visit in January, only four months earlier. However, their last win in the league had been in August 1974, although Chelsea had spent seven seasons out of the top flight in between.

Lawrenson was employed as a sweeper behind Hansen and Gillespie, giving Liverpool five at the back. They struggled to get out of their own half for the early exchanges of the match.

Kevin MacDonald had the game's first real chance with a shot from the edge of the box that was well saved by Godden.

Jim Beglin had a shot cleared off the line by Keith Jones and out for a throw-in. Importantly, Beglin stayed in attack and from the throw, the ball went into the Chelsea penalty area. The defence swept the ball out. It landed about 25 yards out at the feet of Ronnie Whelan. The Irish international attempted to launch it back into the box, but Darren Wood charged down his long ball. It spun in the air. Whelan got up and nodded the ball forward, where it was knocked on left-footed by Beglin. Dalglish was on the edge of the box, and he began to move for the ball, with John Millar trailing behind. Kenny chested the ball down, now in front of the defenders and bearing in on Godden. As the ball dropped, he stuck out his right boot and placed it beyond Godden's despairing dive and into the far left-hand corner.

'Yes!' cried John Motson. 'The player-manager scores the goal that may edge Liverpool nearer to their 16th championship.' The goal is one of the enduring television images of Dalglish's career; so too is the shot of Dalglish's smiling face with arms outstretched in celebration.

There was dejection in the West Ham dressing room at the Hawthorns after they had beaten West Bromwich Albion 3-2 when they discovered the Liverpool result. 'How hard was it for me when I heard who'd scored?' Frank McAvennie told author Tony Evans. 'Kenny was my hero. It was one of the greatest moments of my career when I played with him. I was delighted for him but sick for myself.'

In an interview with David Davies on the BBC, while he was still dripping with sweat, Kenny was quick to acknowledge 'the work of a lot of other people', and deflect the glory away from himself. Davies asked him if he had sympathy for Everton and West Ham, who would finish second and third. 'I don't think they'd have any sympathy for us,' Kenny said with a smile on his face.

Davies then turned to the upcoming FA Cup Final, pointing out that 'the Double' was something 'Bob Paisley didn't achieve, Bill Shankly didn't achieve, Joe Fagan didn't achieve.' Kenny quickly shot back, 'If we achieve anything next Saturday, Bob Paisley will be part of that, and Bob Paisley is very much involved, and he's been a great help to me along with everyone else.'

'Bob never told me what to do,' Dalglish told Tony Evans. 'But every now and again you'd see him round and about more than usual. I'd say, "Bob, you want to tell me something?" He'd mumble in that Northumbrian accent and say, "No, son, it's fine but I was just thinking ..." and then he'd suggest something. He never made me feel he was telling me what to do but it was the best advice a young manager could get.'

Dalglish had played in exactly half of the 42 league fixtures. Without Dalglish, Liverpool lost seven of their 21 games and dropped 26 points. With Kenny in the team, they won 16, including the last seven in a row, collecting 51 points and the title. Jan Mølby, who was missing from the side due to a stomach complaint, said, 'He got the side right in the end. He played in our last 14 games and we didn't lose.'

The press were keen to highlight Kenny's achievement, but the man himself was typically modest, always emphasising how much help he had received from Paisley, Ronnie Moran, Roy Evans and Tom Saunders. He told the *Daily Post*, 'I don't think it is right to single out any one person or player. We worked together to succeed.'

Mark Lawrenson told the Sacked in the Morning podcast how he felt about Kenny's successful transition from player to player-manager. 'I've got so much respect for that – to go from being a key player in the dressing room and having all the friendships [with other players], to be able to distance himself and get results as well. Also the other thing about being a player-manager, is that for me, it's well-nigh impossible. Like, there's not been very many successes when it comes to player-managers. He's probably the one that's held up as the best example of it, because he must have so much discipline to be able to switch on and off from what he was like prior to getting the job.'

Chairman John Smith said, 'Kenny Dalglish is the best player we have signed this century and ... one of the best decisions this club ever made was to appoint him player-manager. He has so much pride in his profession. He is a perfectionist but he is still modest and sets a very high example to everyone at the club and in the game. I have the greatest admiration for him.'

The following day, Dalglish was at Hampden Park playing in his testimonial, where an Alex Ferguson XI took on a Tommy Docherty XI. Kenny scored for both sides, and Docherty's team ran out 5-2 winners. Ferguson had played against Kenny for Rangers reserves. He had even given the young Kenny a lift in his car on occasion. 'Kenny Dalglish was one of the best players ever,' Ferguson wrote in 1995. 'He embraced every concept of one's imagination as a footballer.'

Before the FA Cup Final, there was the semi-final second leg of the Screen Sport Super Cup, which was a competition the English League installed for the clubs who had missed out on Europe due to the ban. Liverpool beat Norwich 4-2 on aggregate, but the final against Everton would be held over until the following season.

Two years after the first all-Merseyside cup final at Wembley, in the Milk Cup, there was now the first ever all-Merseyside FA Cup Final.

Everton were in control in the first half. A long ball from Peter Reid through for Gary Lineker led to the first goal. Lineker did Hansen for pace, and even though Grobbelaar saved his shot, Lineker followed up and put in the rebound. 'Hansen the pundit would have slaughtered Hansen the player,' Alan Hansen said to LFCTV. 'When Reidy chips it through, the golden rule is you either push up and let him [Lineker] run and go offside or as soon as he's gone and I'm reading he's going to hit it, just turn and run. But I'm caught between the two of them.'

'When you kicked Kenny Dalglish when the ball was played into his feet, which I did more than once,' Peter Reid wrote in his 2017 autobiography, 'he was as hard as nails. He wasn't looking to go down and win cheap free kicks. He wanted to hold you off and use his tricks and ability to get the better of you.'

In midfield Craig Johnston thought the game had passed him by. 'It was half-time and I hadn't had a kick.'

'Craig was his own worst enemy,' Dalglish said to Tony Evans. 'He just didn't believe in his footballing abilities. When his form deserted him, Craig became depressed.'

Ronnie Moran and Roy Evans paced the dressing room and encouraged the players. There was no ranting and raving, they just let the players know they needed to improve.

Grobbelaar and Beglin got into an argument over a miscommunication in defence, but it let everyone know that the players were passionate.

The equaliser came in the 57th minute. Ronnie Whelan read Gary Stevens's intended pass and intercepted the ball, then got an attack going. He played the ball to Mølby, who passed through Derek Mountfield's legs for Rush, who ran on to the ball, went round goalkeeper Bobby Mimms and slotted the ball in.

It took only six minutes for Liverpool to go in front. Johnston ran into the penalty area, seeing Mølby with the ball down the left. Johnston's only thought was to get to the far post. When the ball arrived, he put it in from the six-yard line.

After that, Mølby passed to Whelan on the left. Whelan swung a ball with his right foot over Kevin Ratcliffe's head. It fell to Ian Rush's feet, and Rush slammed the ball home. It was 3-1 and Liverpool were only the third team in that century, after Tottenham and Arsenal, to win the Double.

Liverpool: Grobbelaar, Gillespie, Beglin, Nicol, Whelan, Hansen (c), Dalglish, Johnston, Rush, Lawrenson, MacDonald

Scorer: Dalglish (23)

Chelsea: Godden, Wood, Millar, Rougvie, McLaughlin, Jones, Nevin, Spackman, Dixon, Speedie, Canoville

Attendance: 43,900

50

West Ham United 2-5 Liverpool

6 September 1986, First Division,
Boleyn Ground

IN 2024, the journalist and football historian Jonathan Wilson summed up Dalglish's contribution to Liverpool and English football. 'From joining Liverpool in '77 for the next decade, he is consistently one of the best players in the league,' Wilson said. '[He had a] great partnership with Ian Rush. [Dalglish] played in a position that was a little bit unusual at the time. He played off the front man, somewhere between midfield and Rush as a centre-forward.

'A great creator, scored goals himself, incredibly intelligent player, technically very good. But the thing that set him apart was his spatial awareness. His ability to work out where passes had to be played and his ability to weight passes.

'He really was the absolute key to Liverpool's success because he was the one who created goals persistently. No matter how deep teams sat against [Liverpool], no matter how massed their defence, he was the one who found space. I don't think there's anybody really close in that period as a rival to him as the best British player.'

Rangers legend John Greig was asked by *Shoot!* in 1987 to pick the six most outstanding players from his career in Scotland. Despite Old Firm rivalry, Dalglish was one of his selections, with Greig saying he was 'arguably the greatest player ever to come out of Scotland'. 'As a teenager [he] had the lot. I'm not the least bit surprised he's gone on to become a truly world-class player. What I admire most ... is the way he's carried his success and stardom.'

In terms of strengthening the squad for the 1986/87 season, in the summer Kenny brought in Barry Venison from Sunderland and Steve Staunton from Dundalk, while Sammy Lee, who made 26 appearances the previous season, left to join Queens Park Rangers.

Liverpool were allowed to play abroad in pre-season, and embarked on a small tour of Denmark and Sweden. They also played in testimonials at Hamburg and Real Sociedad before the Charity Shield match with Everton, who had finished as runners-up in both league and cup.

Kenny came off the bench at Wembley and set up Ian Rush for the equaliser in the 1-1 draw, which meant that the sides shared the Shield.

Arsenal were the opposition in Liverpool's third league game of the season, Kenny selecting himself in the number 7 shirt. Jan Molby put Liverpool ahead with a penalty after 19 minutes, only for Tony Adams, with his first goal for Arsenal, to level the score.

'What I also remember about that day was Kenny Dalglish winding me early on with an arm across the solar plexus,' Adams wrote in his 1999 autobiography. 'It was the sort of professional stroke older strikers used to pull. Also, you give the defender a push to spring off him and send him backwards and all of a sudden you've got ten yards of space instead of five. That was another useful learning experience, although I didn't feel it at the time. I only weighed about 12 stone and Dalglish put me out of the game for about five minutes.'

Ian Rush netted the winner after 57 minutes. 'I owed Kenny at least half my goals at Liverpool,' Rush said in 1997. 'He was a master at making space in the penalty area and then laying the ball off. His finishing was clinical and he always seemed to have so much time to do things on and off the ball.'

According to Mark Lawrenson, who spoke to the Sacked in the Morning podcast in 2024, Dalglish's success as a player was partly due to his disciplined routine. Lawrenson revealed that Kenny would consistently go to bed every afternoon after training, a habit supported by his wife Marina, whom Lawrenson described as 'absolutely fantastic' for her role in helping Kenny maintain this routine.

Dalglish rarely drank alcohol during his playing days, though Lawrenson noted that he has 'made up for that now'. On the pitch, Dalglish was known for being incredibly fierce and uncompromising: 'fearsome' as Lawrenson put it.

Despite his brilliance at holding up the ball and his exceptional awareness, 'eyes in the back of his head', Dalglish had a demanding on-field personality. Lawrenson recalled that he and Alan Hansen would regularly have heated arguments with Dalglish during matches, especially when passes to him weren't perfect. Even after successfully receiving the ball, Dalglish would often berate his team-mates with expletives if the pass wasn't exactly to his liking.

However, Lawrenson emphasised that these conflicts never lasted. After matches, particularly following victories, Dalglish would approach his team-mates, shake their hands, and say 'Well done boys, another win,' immediately putting any on-field disagreements behind them.

Liverpool lost their first game since February when Leicester beat them 2-1 at Filbert Street on 3 September. Kenny came on for the last half-hour, pulling a goal back but being unable to secure the draw.

Three days later, for the match with West Ham United, Kenny picked himself again to wear the number 12 shirt.

West Ham's Frank McAvennie had ripped up the English First Division in his first season, 1985/86. He had made his full Scotland debut up front alongside Dalglish against Australia in a World Cup play-off match in November 1985. 'I hope some of Kenny's magic rubs off on me,' he said before the game. 'It is a great thrill to play along with him as I reckon Kenny is the best player ever to pull on a jersey for Scotland. There will probably never be another like him.'

McAvennie scored the opening goal in the 2-0 win. He credited his performance that night to Dalglish's influence. 'He created so much space for me by attracting three and sometimes four markers that I more or less had a free hand. Even then, he would manage to shrug them off and lay the ball to me. He goes out with the view that the more players trying to pull him out the game the merrier. For a small man, he is exceptionally strong and is very difficult to put down.'

In an interview with the *Liverpool Echo* in May 1986, McAvennie revealed that he was one of the thousands of Celtic fans who were gobsmacked by Kenny's move to Anfield in 1977 but, despite holding a grudge against him for some time, he was effusive in his praise for his Scotland colleague and the way he brought out the best in the other players. 'I believe his total love and dedication to the game makes him stand head and shoulders above most others.'

Against West Ham, Dalglish had opted for another sweeper system. It was a tactic the home side were used to, with four of their five opponents so far this season playing it.

West Ham had a penalty with eight minutes gone when Gary Gillespie tripped Tony Cottee as the West Ham forward shielded the ball at the edge of the box. Ray Stewart, who scored 76 penalties for the Hammers, fired it high into the net.

Hansen had pulled a hamstring and had to come off after just over a quarter of an hour had gone. His injury, West Ham manager John Lyall would say, was 'one of the worst things that could happen to us'. Dalglish stepped up from the bench. There was no way it was going to be a like-for-like substitution. Kenny went up front and Liverpool, who now had to abandon the sweeper system, moved from three centre-backs to two, to play in a 4-4-2 formation. Quickly, they began to get more of the ball in the last third of West Ham's half.

The equaliser came with 24 minutes played when West Ham could only head the ball out of defence to Whelan 25 yards out. The Dubliner hammered a shot that flew past Parkes. The pressure Liverpool were putting on the Hammers meant that McAvennie was now spending much of his time tracking back to help his defence.

Craig Johnston intercepted a pass inside West Ham's penalty area and slid the ball home for 2-1.

West Ham were awarded an indirect free kick inside the box for a high boot from Johnston. When the kick was played out to Stewart, his shot was deflected high into the air. Mike Hooper, making only his sixth appearance in goal for Liverpool, opted to rush out to punch when he was better leaving the ball to his defence. He didn't make clean contact, and it fell for Cottee, who spun and forced the ball over the line to equalise.

Dalglish picked up a booking for something he said to the referee.

Jim Beglin spotted Kenny making a run in behind the West Ham defensive line and slipped the ball through. Dalglish latched on to it and clipped his shot past the outstretched leg of Alvin Martin and over Parkes to make it 3-2.

A wayward high ball back into his defence from Mark Ward led to Liverpool regaining the ball, where MacDonald knocked it on to Rush, who took a touch, then fired it in from the edge of the penalty area.

Kenny picked up the ball at the edge of the box, dropped a shoulder, found space and cut a shot that was deflected into the net, as the match finished 5-2.

In the *Sunday Mirror*, Richard Keys wrote, '[Dalglish] was the only man on the field with class enough to create time for himself in a harum-scarum atmosphere.'

The result left Liverpool second in the table after five matches.

In the League Cup second round first leg, Fulham were hammered 10-0. Everton were beaten 7-2 on aggregate in the final of the Screen Sport Super Cup. It would be the only silverware Liverpool collected that season.

In December, Dalglish would finish third in the BBC's Sports Personality of the Year award.

Liverpool's FA Cup defence ended on Luton Town's plastic pitch at Kenilworth Road in the third round second replay with a 3-0 defeat. Kenny had bought John Aldridge as a replacement for Ian Rush, who would be leaving to join Juventus at the end of the season.

In April, Charlie Nicholas was to play his most memorable game for Arsenal when he scored twice to defeat Liverpool in the League Cup, now known as the Littlewoods Cup. It was the first match that Liverpool had lost in which Ian Rush had scored. 'It felt like the end of an era,' Rush said years later to *The Guardian*. 'The following week we went to Norwich and lost 2-1 and I scored then too.'

Liverpool beat Everton 3-1 in the league in April to go three points behind them in second, albeit having played a game more. Although Everton could only draw with Manchester City the following week, Liverpool's defeat to Coventry left them with an impossible task in terms of catching their rivals.

The title was settled on Monday, 4 May, as Everton beat Norwich at Carrow Road. Over at Anfield, Ian Rush played in his last home game for Liverpool before his transfer, scoring the only goal of the game. It would also be the last time Dalglish named himself in the starting line-up.

Dalglish made 18 appearances in the league during that season, and 25 in total. It was the last season he would play consistently for Liverpool. He would only play another five times for the club as he focused more closely on his managerial position.

As a manager, Dalglish was now passing on his skills and wisdom to the strikers under his charge. In 1987, he signed 26-year-old Peter Beardsley from Newcastle United. Talking on The Rest is Football podcast, Beardsley said Dalglish taught him something he had never known: how to use shadows on the ground to know where the defenders were. Beardsley explained, 'He said, "The shadows will always be there. It'll be a sunny day or there'll be floodlights." It was incredible. It was life-changing for me. To be able to work out where the pressure was and then to turn the opposite way. It really couldn't have helped me any more.' On the same show, Alan Shearer confirmed that Kenny taught him the same trick when he played under Dalglish at Blackburn Rovers.

In *The Athletic* in 2020, Shearer wrote, 'As a fellow forward, his advice was golden, little tips about where to move, where to run, how to back into defenders; there was nobody better at that skill than him … Once, he said to me, "Instead of making contact with the defender when the ball is coming to you, why not look at where his shadow is?" I still don't know whether that was another piss-take. What happens if it's not sunny?'

Dalglish's final competitive game was a late substitute appearance against Derby County on 1 May 1990, on the night Liverpool were presented with their 18th league championship trophy. The 39-year-old Dalglish asked the stadium announcer to jokingly say the substitute was 'a trialist' as he came on. The next day, the back page of the *Daily Mirror* had a full colour picture of Kenny's 14-year-old son Paul, spotted on the terracing in a Juventus shirt with a Liverpool scarf held proudly above his head.

In 1997, the legendary journalist Brian Glanville compiled his 100 Greatest Footballers of All Time for *The Times*. Dalglish was placed at number 97. Glanville wrote,

'One of the finest Scottish players since the war. Tactically and technically an outstanding outside-right.' Brazil's Ronaldo was at number 100.

The true measure of greatness in football often reveals itself in what's absent – the 'what ifs', 'if onlys' and 'might have beens' that haunt lesser careers. In pubs across Britain, countless debates have centred on talented players who 'never lived up to their potential'.

It's clearly not something you could level at Kenny Dalglish, who blended natural ability with hard work to achieve his tremendous success on the pitch.

The arc of his career stands as a lesson in sustained excellence – a 22-year testament to consistency that defied conventional wisdom about athletic decline. He scored prolifically and created generously. Dalglish's adaptability transformed him from Celtic's attacking spearhead to Liverpool's midfield orchestrator without diminishing his influence. He inspired team-mates through example rather than exhortation, maintained remarkable discipline when lesser players would have retaliated, and somehow avoided the serious injuries that curtailed so many careers of his era.

Most tellingly, from his first full season at Celtic in 1971 until his gradual transition to management in 1986, Dalglish competed for major honours every single year – a record of sustained relevance unmatched by any British contemporary.

No hyperbole is necessary for the final assessment: Kenny Dalglish was the greatest British footballer of his generation.

West Ham United: Parkes, Stewart, Parris, Gale, Martin, Pike [Keen], Ward, McAvennie, Dickens, Cottee, Orr

Scorers: Stewart (9 pen), Cottee (60)

Liverpool: Hooper, Venison, Beglin, Gillespie, Whelan, Hansen (c) [Dalglish], MacDonald, Johnston, Rush, Lawrenson, McMahon

Scorers: Whelan (24), Johnston (51), Dalglish (66, 90), Rush (70)

Attendance: 29,807

Bibliography

Books

Adams, Tony; Ridley, Ian. *Addicted* (London: CollinsWillow, 1999)

Ardiles, Osvaldo; Langley, Mike. *Ossie: My Life in Football* (London: Sidgwick & Jackson, 1983)

Atkinson, Ron, *The Manager* (London: DeCoubertin Books, 2017)

Baillie, Rodger, ed. *Playing for Celtic No. 6* (London: Paul, 1974)

Brooking, Trevor; Hart, Michael. *My Life in Football* (London: Simon & Schuster, 2014)

Brown, Craig. *The Game of My Life* (London: Blake, 2001)

Campbell, Tom. *Jock Stein: The Celtic Years* (Edinburgh: Mainstream, 1999)

Case, Jimmy; Smart, Andrew. *Jimmy Case: My Autobiography* (London: John Blake, 2015)

Connolly, Kevin; MacWilliam, Rab. *Fields of Glory Paths of Gold: The History of European Football* (Edinburgh: Mainstream Publishing, 2005)

Cooper, Davie; Clark, Graham. *True Blue: The Davie Cooper Story* (Edinburgh: Mainstream, 1987)

Corr, Matt. *Harry Hood: Twice as Good* (Place of publication not identified: The Celtic Star, 2021)

Cowley, Jason. *The Last Game: Love, Death and Football* (London: Simon & Schuster, 2009)

Dalglish, Kenny; Gallacher, Ken. *King Kenny: An Autobiography* (London: Stanley Paul, 1982)

Dalglish, Kenny; Winter, Henry. *My Liverpool Home* (London: Hodder & Stoughton, 2011)

Dalglish, Kenny; Winter, Henry. *Dalglish: My Autobiography* (London: Hodder & Stoughton, 1996)

Dalglish, Kenny. *My Life* (Liverpool: Trinity Mirror Sports Media, 2013)

Davies, Barry. *Interesting, Very Interesting: The Autobiography* (London: Headline, 2008)

Davies, Dai; Roberts, Iorwerth (trans.); *Never Say Dai* (Mold: Siop y Siswrn, 1986)

Deans, Dixie; McNab, Ken. *There's Only One Dixie Deans: The Autobiography* (Edinburgh: Birlinn, 2011)

Docherty, Tommy. *The Doc: My Story: Hallowed be thy Game* (London: Headline, 2006)

Dougan, Derek; Murphy, Patrick. *Matches of the Day 1958-83: A Footballing History* (London: Dent, 1984)

Dunkin, Neil. *Anfield of Dreams: A Kopite's Odyssey* (Studley: Know the Score!, 2008)

Evans, Tony. *I Don't Know What It Is But I Love It: Liverpool's Unforgettable 1983-84 Season* (London: Viking, 2014)

Evans, Tony. *Two Tribes: Liverpool, Everton and a City on the Brink* (London: Bantam Press, 2018)

Fagan, Andrew. *Joe Fagan: The Authorised Biography* (London: Aurum, 2010)

Ferguson, Alex; Ball, Peter. *A Year in the Life: The Manager's Diary* (London: Virgin, 1995)

Ferguson, Alex; McIlvanney, Hugh. *Managing my Life: The Autobiography* (London: Hodder & Stoughton, 1999)

Ferguson, Alex. *A Light in the North: Seven Years with Aberdeen* (Edinburgh: Mainstream, 1985)

Gemmell, Tommy; McColl, Graham. *Tommy Gemmell: Lion Heart* (London: Virgin, 2012)

Gray, Andy; Drewett, Jim. *Flat Back Four: The Tactical Game* (London: Boxtree, 1999)

Greaves, Jimmy; Giller, Norman. *Goals: A Unique A to Z Collection* (Chambers Harrap Publishers Ltd, 1981)

Grobbelaar, Bruce; Harris, Bob. *Bruce Grobbelaar: An Autobiography* (Sevenoaks: Coronet, 1988)

Hansen, Alan; Tomas, Jason. *A Matter of Opinion* (London: Partridge, 1999)

Hay, Davie; Gordon, Alex. *The Quiet Assassin: The Davie Hay Story* (Edinburgh: Black & White, 2009)

Holmes, Bob (ed.). *The Match of My Life* (London: Kingswood, 1991)

Holmes, Bob (ed.). *Fifty Football Stars Describe My Greatest Game* (Edinburgh: Mainstream, 1993)

Hughes, Simon. *Red Machine: Liverpool FC in the 1980s: The Players' Stories* (Edinburgh: Mainstream Publishing, 2014)

Hurst, Geoff; Hart, Michael. *1966 and All That: My Autobiography* (London: Headline, 2001)

Jardine, Sandy; Aitken, Michael. *Score and More: The Sandy Jardine Story* (Edinburgh: Mainstream, 1987)

Johnston, Willie; Bullimore, Tom. *Sent Off at Gunpoint: The Willie Johnston Story* (Studley: Know the Score!, 2009)

Jordan, Joe; Lawton, James. *Behind the Dream: My Autobiography* (London: Hodder & Stoughton, 2004)

Keegan, Kevin. *Kevin Keegan: My Autobiography* (London: Little, Brown, 1997)

Kelly, Stephen F. *Dalglish* (London: Headline, 1992)

Kennedy, Alan; Williams, John. *Kennedy's Way: Inside Bob Paisley's Liverpool* (Edinburgh: Mainstream, 2004)

Kennedy, Ray; Lees, Dr. Andrew. *Ray of Hope: The Ray Kennedy Story* (London: Viking Penguin, 1993)

Law, Denis; Harris, Bob. *The King* (London: Bantam, 2003)

Leighton, Jim; Robertson, Ken. *In the Firing Line: The Jim Leighton Story* (Edinburgh: Mainstream, 2000)

Lennox, Bobby; McColl, Graham. *Thirty Miles From Paradise* (London: Headline, 2007)

Macari, Lou. *Football, My Life* (London: Bantam, 2008)

MacBride, Eugene. *Talking With Celtic* (Derby: Breedon, 2001)

Macpherson, Archie. *Jock Stein: The Definitive Biography* (Newbury: Highdown, 2007)

Maddren, Willie; Allan, Dave. *Extra Time: Willie Maddren: The Official Biography* (Place of publication not identified: Willie Maddren MND Fund, 1998)

McDermott, Terry; Richardson, John. *Living for the Moment: My Autobiography* (Liverpool: Trinity Mirror Sport Media, 2017)

McFarland, Roy; Price, Will. *Roy Mac Clough's Champion* (Liverpool: Trinity Mirror Sports Media, 2014)

McGrain, Danny; Keevins, Hugh. *In Sunshine or in Shadow* (Edinburgh: John Donald, 1987)

McNeill, Billy. *Hail Cesar: The Autobiography* (London: Headline, 2004)

Miller, Willie; Macdonald, Alastair. *The Miller's Tale: An Autobiography* (Edinburgh: Mainstream, 1989)

Miller, Willie; Robertson, Rob. *The Don: The Willie Miller Story* (Edinburgh: Birlinn, 2007)

Moore, Bobby (ed.). *The Book of Soccer No. 15* (London: Stanley Paul, 1972)

Mortimer, Dennis; Sydenham, Richard. *The Full Morty* (Durrington: Pitch Publishing, 2022)

Motson, John. *Match of the Day: The Complete Record Since 1964* (London: BBC Books, 1992)

Murray, Stephen. *Kenny of the Celtic* (Scotland: CQN Books, 2016)

Neal, Phil; Schofield, Harry; Doyle, Derek. *Attack From The Back* (London: Arthur Baker Limited, 1981)

Nicol, Stephen Hamilton. *The Scout: The Bobby Dinnie Story* (Place of publication not identified: Club Books, 2014)

Nicol, Stevie; Donaldson, Mark. *Stevie Nicol: My Autobiography 5 League Titles and a Packet of Crisps* (Liverpool: Sport Media, 2016)

Okwonga, Musa. *A Cultured Left Foot: The Eleven Elements of Footballing Greatness* (London: Duckworth, 2008)

O'Leary, David; Miller, Harry. *David O'Leary: My Story* (Edinburgh: Mainstream, 1988)

Paisley, Bob. *A Lifetime in Football* (London: A. Barker, 1983)

Peel, John. *The Olivetti Chronicles: Three Decades of Life and Music* (London: Corgi, 2009)

Potter, David; Rowan, Marie. *The Celtic Football Club: 125 Years of Competitive Matches* (Great Britain, Celtic FC, 2012)

Reid, Peter; Barrett, Tony. *Cheer Up Peter Reid: My Autobiography* (Liverpool: Sport Media, 2017)

Sephton, George; Wilson, Keith. *This is Anfield Calling!: Liverpool Football Club From a Different Angle* (Birkenhead: Red Rag, 1998)

Sheedy, Kevin; Keith, John. *So Good I Did it Twice* (Liverpool: Sport Media, 2014)

Shilton, Peter. *Peter Shilton: The Autobiography* (London: Orion, 2004)

Signy, Dennis. *Golden Heroes: Fifty Seasons of Footballer of the Year* (London: Chameleon, 1997)

Strachan, Gordon; Gallacher, Ken. *Strachan Style: A Life in Football* (Edinburgh: Mainstream, 1991)

Strachan, Gordon. *Gordon Strachan's Soccer Skills: A Complete Step-by-Step Guide* (London: Hamlyn, 1993)

Sturrock, Paul; Duddy, Charlie; Rundo, Peter. *Forward Thinking: The Paul Sturrock Story* (Edinburgh: Mainstream, 1989)

Sturrock, Paul; Richards, Bill. *Luggy: The Autobiography of Paul Sturrock* (Worthing: Pitch Publishing, 2015)

Sullivan, Stephen. *Sean Fallon: Celtic's Iron Man: The Authorised Biography* (Back Page Press, 2013)

Thompson, Phil; Rogers, Ken. *Stand Up, Pinocchio: From the Kop to the Top. My Life Inside Anfield* (Liverpool: Sport Media, 2005)

Thompson, Phil. *Do That Again Son, and I'll Break Your Legs: Football's Hardmen* (London: Virgin Books, 1996)

Tomkins, Paul. *Dynasty: Fifty Years of Shankly's Liverpool* (Wigston Harcourt: GPRF, 2008)

Turnbull, Eddie; Hannan, Martin. *Eddie Turnbull: Having a Ball* (Edinburgh: Mainstream, 2006)

Villa, Ricky; Miller, Joel; Ardiles, Federico. *And Still Ricky Villa: My Autobiography* (London: VSP, 2010)

Whelan, Ronnie; Conlon, Tommy. *Walk On: My Life in Red* (London: Simon & Schuster, 2011)

Wilson, Bob. *Bob Wilson's Soccer Focus* (London: Pelham, 1980)

Withe, Peter; Goodyear, Simon. *Peter Withe: All For the Love of the Game* (G2 Entertainment, 2021)

The Herald Book of Old Firm Games (Edinburgh: Canongate, 1995)

Newspapers

Belfast Newsletter
Birmingham Daily Post
Coventry Evening Telegraph
Cumbernauld News
Daily Express
Daily Post
Daily Record
Dundee Weekly News
Evening Standard
Evening Times
Glasgow Times
Liverpool Echo
Manchester Evening News
Northern Echo
Scotland on Sunday
South Wales Argus
Sunday Mail
Sunday Mirror
Sunday People
Sunday Post
Sunday Tribune
Sunderland Daily Echo and Shipping Gazette
The Independent
The Observer
The Scotsman
The Sunday Times
The Times
Toronto Star
Weekly News
Western Daily Press

Websites

archive.org

Britishnewspaperarchive.co.uk

brucesrecordshop.weebly.com/shop-launch.html

celticfc.com

celticquicknews.co.uk

cumbernauldunited.co.uk

enfa.co.uk

englandfootballonline.com

genome.ch.bbc.co.uk

herecomesthesong.com

history.co.uk

independent.ie

killiefc.com

lfchistory.net

liverpoolfc.com

liverpoolfc.com/heysel

marca.com

morningstaronline.co.uk

museumofjerseys.com

newspapers.com

nytimes.com

officialcharts.com

olympics.com

peel.fandom.com

sportingnews.com

theathletic.com

thecelticwiki.com

therangersarchives.co.uk

thesefootballtimes.co

tribalfootball.com

twtd.co.uk

whufc.com

youtube.com
youtube.com/@castlegalleries
youtube.com/@HistoryOfFootballFM
youtube.com/@The_PFA
https://www.youtube.com/@TNTSports

Periodicals

Kenny Dalglish Soccer Annual
Match
Shoot!
The Celtic View
The Topical Times Football Book 1979

Television and Film

This Is Your Life – Kenny Dalglish, 16 February 1983
Match of the Day
Scotsport
Football's Greatest
Football's Greatest Teams
Kenny Dalglish: Portrait of a Natural Footballer (Andy Melvin, 1985)
Kenny (Stewart Sugg, 2017)
Double Winners 86: On the March with Kenny's Army (Mark Platt, 2024)

Podcasts

It Was What It Was: The Football History Podcast
Let Me Be Frank
Sacked in the Morning
Talksport – Premier League All Access – The King: A Tribute to Kenny Dalglish

The Anfield Wrap
The 7NWA Podcast
The Official Scotland Podcast
The Rest is Football

Football Programmes

Hamilton Academical vs Celtic, 25 September 1968
Wales vs Scotland, 12 October 1977
Celtic vs Liverpool, Jock Stein Testimonial, 14 August 1978
Scotland vs England, 24 May 1980
Liverpool vs West Bromwich Albion, 13 September 1980
Scotland vs Northern Ireland, 25 March 1981
Kenny Dalglish: The First 100 International Caps – Testimonial programme
Scotland vs Romania, 26 March 1986
Celtic vs Liverpool, 30 April 1989